COLLEGE WRITING TIPS AND SAMPLE PAPERS:

A STUDENT SUCCESS GUIDE
FOR THE IMPERFECT STUDENT

Josh Kresse

DEDICATION

I would like to dedicate this book to my extraordinary parents who are vessels of God and an inspiration to me. I would also like to dedicate this book to my teachers and peers who pushed me to my limits. The people with the most natural ability are the ones who need to be pushed the most in order to avoid complacency. I thank them all for helping me stay motivated by pushing me and encouraging me! This book would not have been possible without the support of my family, friends, and professors.

TABLE OF CONTENTS

ABOUT THE AUTHOR

Josh Kresse is a recent graduate of Ottawa University. He received his B.A. in Communications (with a focus on Business Communications). He earned a 3.9 GPA at Ottawa University. After writing hundreds of assignments and discussing his work with other students and professors he realized that many students are at a total loss as to how to begin an assignment. Despite the plethora of books about writing, they are still lost. He wants to put you on the path to writing success. That was the genesis of this book.

Josh is a website content consultant, newsletter writer, and business-to-business services provider. He would love to help you. You can reach him at joshkresse@gmail.com.

INTRODUCTION

I compare obtaining a college degree to climbing a mountain. At the beginning it seems impossible. As a matter of fact it is nearly impossible without people who guide, support, and assist you. Becoming a college graduate began with my love for books when I was child. My parents, grandparents, aunts, and uncles nurtured my love of learning, education, and achievement. My parents and grandparents have always nurtured my wordsmith tendencies. My grandmother and I swap stories and sayings, which really delights me. It meant everything to have the ongoing love and support that my parents gave to me. Two elementary school teachers (Peggy Oxley and Lauren Duncan) also encouraged my love for books and my creativity.

On another personal note I would like to thank Jerry Schneider. I worked for him while staying at a ranch in Wyoming. Jerry had been struck in the head by a horse's hoof and survived it. He went on to run a ranch helping troubled youth change their lives. I hate that term, but I was one of them. I, too, was expected to change myself and so were the other boys that had even worse problems than mine. Although Jerry had a million responsibilities and things on his mind he taught me to strive to be what God put me here to be. He taught me to become a leader. Another special man at the ranch was Dan Burrs. He was an athlete before he messed his back up. He is a nice man, an electrician, a dad to his children, and a father figure to all the boys who were there in the middle of nowhere in Wyoming. No, don't worry; we had beautiful scenery and a wonderful lifestyle there. I just don't want anyone to end up at a youth ranch because it is pretty. That being said, I want to continue to thank the staff there who continue to support me. They tell others about me to encourage them to change, and help other boys who have changed their lives into something remarkable.

There were many professors at Chandler-Gilbert Community College (CGCC) who played key roles for me and I thank each of them. All of my professors there were special to me. My speech teacher, Robert Doherty, was a very sensible man who had been in the military. He was funny and smart. He showed his students what dissecting speech and communication was all about. He provided my first taste of thinking quickly on my feet. I still ponder his theories and recommendations. It's funny how you can learn the most from a class after it's been over for awhile, and I already learned a lot from that class while I took it. My criminology teacher (Leon Kutzke) was fascinating as well. He had been the chief of police for a town in Illinois, and was now teaching at my little but awesome community college. I thank my philosophy professor, David Munoz, Ph. D. as well. I should have earned an A in that class, but skipping the extra credit brought my grade down. Lesson learned.

I would like to point out and thank all of my teachers at CGCC who listened to me at all times and actually valued what I said. My English teacher (Candace Komlodi) was one of those people. I hadn't built any negative stereotypes for community college professors, yet this teacher eliminated whatever was left of any false perceptions I had about teachers. She disciplined us more than any teacher I have ever seen. She was a Catholic woman who actually lived her faith. Isn't it ironic that the people who are best at putting us in our places for the right reasons never tell us they are going to "get tough"? They just do it. I admire that. I think that students in general tend to forget that teachers have families and lives just like the rest of us. Candace Komlodi's encouragement helped me produce an amazing semester project. It, too, is in this book.

Scott Crooker was my CIS teacher. CIS stands for Computer Information Systems. That class is proof that anyone can learn about computers (which can be really fun and rewarding) if they have the will to do so. Scott loved math and numbers, and under his guidance I now do. He taught me so much more than that. He taught me that I love competition and will work even harder in a competitive situation. Each week he provided a list of everyone's grades for us to see. He protected our anonymity by using codes instead of people's names. But you could still see how you were doing compared to each other. I was at the top of the class and worked doubly hard to stay there. I don't like to say that the people who did poorly in that class (seemingly on purpose) motivated me to do well, but it really did. Scott Crooker encouraged me to continue on beyond my Associate's Degree and saw my gifts.

I am thankful to the fitness teacher at CGCC. She told me that she was amazed that time seems to slow down when a person is forced to do physical work of any kind. I thought, "yeah, and it stinks". Now I think, "Wow, I get more time to not think any negative thoughts that might have been building that day". She told me in all honesty that she had never seen a person improve so much in their cardio before. The fact that she even mentioned it means I must have been outside the usual range. Taking the fitness class was a great idea that term because I had 5 other very intense classes that semester and needed to keep my mind, body, and spirit balanced.

I want to also thank my psychology professor, Scott Silberman and my history professor Jim Austin. Both of these professors were outstanding, knowledgeable and inspirational. Their love for their subjects was obvious, and the caring they showed to each student helped students learn the material even if they didn't like the subjects. I continue to see them around the community, even at my health club. Jim Austin's course completely changed my feelings about history. In grade school I had actually hated history. Jim Austin changed that. The right teacher really does make all the difference.

I thank my environmental biology professor, Tracy Blondis. I remember her saying to me what other teachers of mine had only been thinking. (OK, I wasn't that great but I was pretty "greaoooood" – that isn't a typographical error, it is a phrase I coined!) She told me I was ready to be in the next level class in that subject. Ah, the simple joy of personal gratification, just from the act of learning!

I want to thank all of my professors at Ottawa University as well: Dr. Karen Bryson, Ph. D., Karen Carr, Bryan Conner, David Cook, Dan Foxx, Dennis Lancaster, Teresa Lorenzoni, Jerry Malizia, and Nanette Winston. What an incredible group of caring and inspirational professors these people are. Each of these professors helped me develop my writing, learning, and speaking skills. Each course required an enormous amount of work, but oddly enough the requirement for an almost insurmountable amount of work is what took me to that next level.

Two of these professors, Teresa Lorenzoni (Interpersonal Communications) and Karen Carr (Business Communications) taught online. I think it must be especially difficult to be inspirational and encouraging when you are an online professor. You don't have the face-to-face give and take that you do in a classroom. I am so grateful they both found a way to make their classes come alive. They helped me to have an outstanding experience in my online courses. Their encouragement, support, and guidance helped me to succeed, learn the material, and compile fabulous presentations and write terrific papers. These two professors were among the first professors I had at Ottawa University. Their complete support and encouragement played a key role in my motivation and success in my future classes as well.

I remember when I took Intercultural and International Communication from Nanette Winston. The same week I had surgery on my toe, so did my teacher. We both had the bandages on our big toes to prove it! I would never have seen this synchronicity if she hadn't been brave enough to wear sandals. She actually worked on a reservation, and this fact added a wonderful dimension to classroom discussions about cultural sensitivity and awareness. Each person in the class came away with a new ability to build that sensitivity and awareness into our everyday dealings. This knowledge and understanding is a critical factor in a global economy. What a wonderful professor and course!

Dan Foxx and Dennis Lancaster taught the two constitution courses that I took. They made very detailed classes really come alive. They related the legalistic material to history and communications. This effectively helped me (and others) learn how constitutions affect our lives.

Jerry Malizia was both a professional man and a professor. His work experiences added so much to my understanding and knowledge. He was an incredible teacher, and I enjoyed every moment of classroom time I had in his courses. He worked hard to inspire me to think deeply and write professionally. I always looked forward to his classes to watch him interact with me and the other students as well. His persuasive communications course taught me to be quick on my feet, develop fabulous speeches, and deliver them so well I could hardly believe it was me! Never again will I be intimidated by the prospect of having to do a presentation.

Two of my other professors at Ottawa were also especially business oriented. This was very good for me, of course, since my specialization is business communication. In addition to Jerry Malizia and Karen Carr (whom I already discussed) I would include Bryan Conner (Organizational Communication) and David Cook (Capstone Course) on this list. They had true credibility in these courses as they are highly respected businessmen and consultants. These men really pushed me and worked me hard. Understand, I already was working hard; but these men saw my future and knew how hard I was going to have to continue to work in today's world. They expected me to step up to the plate and begin to perform at a new level. This was terrifying and exciting all at the same time. There were times that I did not have a clue what they wanted or expected. This was good for me as it taught me to think, analyze, and make connections in a new way. After I completed these demanding courses I had reached a new mountain top!

Last, but definitely not least of my Ottawa University professors, I wish to thank Dr. Karen Bryson, Ph. D. What a wonderful professor. She taught my two humanities seminars (Proseminar and Grad Review) and my Stress Management Course. Believe me, in the midst of completing 48 semester hours in 14 months I needed a Stress Management course! Karen Bryson's gift for teaching is apparent to everyone. The humanities seminars pull together a cross-cut of topics. This can make it especially challenging, as not everyone excels at all of the breadth areas, as Ottawa University calls them. This includes: history, civics, politics, literature, art, writing, science, math, values, ethics, and even current events. Karen Bryson masterfully taught all of these and helped me to continue to grow as a lover of learning. Her respect for her students is apparent in all of her dealings with them. I admire her greatly and loved her courses.

Many thanks go to Angela Hoy at Booklocker.com Publishing, who guided me through this process and to Richard Hoy who provided wonderful marketing advice. I extend a special thank you to Todd Engel, who designed my book cover.

Finally, I want to mention my parents once again. It made me feel so good when they admired my work ethic and the quality of my work. The more I learned throughout my college career, the more I was able to communicate with them as the adult I was becoming. At the beginning of my college education it felt almost unachievable. I didn't know how I was going to be able to actually take all of those courses! They were supportive all the way through. They provided a listening ear, a sounding board, and great advice. Finally, in today's world, faith seems to take a back burner to the rest of the hustle bustle of life. My mom and dad showed me by example how to live for God and family. I am glad I have the rest of my life to show them how thankful I am for their guidance and loving outreach.

1

WRITING ADVICE: ARE YOU STUCK ON THAT ASSIGNMENT?

When you looked at the table of contents of my book you may have felt it will only be helpful if you are taking the specific listed classes. That is not the case. As a matter of fact, the purpose of including writing samples is to show you that it is definitely possible to meet your professors' expectations. My tips and writing samples can provide you guidance no matter what course you are writing for. I am eager to help you. Having my tips and papers in hand can help you get "unstuck".

When given a writing assignment it sometimes is difficult to know where or how to begin. Many of my classmates have shared their anxieties and frustrations over the years with me regarding their difficulties with writing assignments. I know you have been given countless lectures and maybe even read countless books on the topic of writing effectively. Many say the same things: pre-write, create an outline, organize your thoughts, and other similar advice. However, after reading these supposedly excellent resources, you still are baffled. You may say to yourself, "how do I know what to write for this paper for this class"? Or you may think, "What should the paper look like"?

Am I right? That is why I wrote this book. I wanted to tell you what I did, and show you the results of what I did. What is often forgotten in the instruction process of college writing is that there are different learning styles. Some people need to be told in general or even step-by-step what to do. That would include instructions such as: brainstorm; create an outline; write a rough draft; edit; and write a final draft. As I have said, there are literally hundreds of books that explain this process. But maybe you are still stuck.

Other people have a learning style that needs to understand the concept and feeling of what writing is. Furthermore, they need to see multiple examples and samples of what the result of writing for various requirements actually looks like in a final product. They cannot visualize their own process unless they see an example of what the professor (or a boss) could mean. An example of this would be if the professor says "write a reading summary for chapter 3". Some students are simply frozen because they haven't any idea what that really means. That learning style needs wonderful examples. Welcome to my world of wonderful (not perfect, but wonderful) examples!

I used to get stuck and frozen on writing assignments, too. However, once I understood what good, solid essays, research papers, and analysis papers actually looked like, I was far less fearful. I really did have to physically see them. I realized that I had been expecting my final draft to just flow out of me as soon as I first sat down to begin writing an assignment. I assumed that is how it worked for everyone. That isn't how the process works. Here is what I do now. When given an assignment I will just sit down and write anything that comes into my mind. Sometimes it has absolutely nothing to do with the actual assignment. That doesn't matter at all, as it turns out. Why? The thoughts that run through your mind can end up leading you to connections between the assigned topic and other related topics. On the surface it may seem that what you are writing down isn't related at all. Write it down anyway, because more thoughts will continue to flow to you. Even if you don't use what you have written down for this assignment, keep the writings. You may be able to use the writing for another project!

Furthermore, it is important for you to remember that each student is unique. Thus, what you think of while writing all of your thoughts down can end up being some very unusual and highly unique connection between two topics that on the surface are completely unrelated. This uniqueness is what will raise your writing from the mundane to the extraordinary. I always have a couple of notebooks and pens close at hand. That way I can write down whatever comes to mind. As a matter of fact some truly great authors, such as Pat Conroy, keep all of their notebooks and writings. Remember, what you write down won't be your final draft. What it will be is content that will ultimately go into a writing project, whether for this assignment or another assignment.

I find such pleasure in the actual process of holding the pen and writing the ideas down. It is helpful to have a pen that is a pleasure to use, and paper that has a nice feel to it. For me, it is important to use pen and paper for everything but the unedited final draft. This keeps my mind aware that I am far from finished, and tells my mind to keep pumping out the ideas. It was important that I learn to love the actual process of writing. The reason for that is related to the type of learner that I am. Once I realized that I will stay focused and work hard toward something I love, I knew the key. Every time I write I think more clearly. I'm glad I didn't wait until I was 30 to start writing for mere pleasure. It is always going to feel right to be the age you are, but you must keep it in perspective and examine how much time has passed and how much time will continue to pass.

The key is to love the process of learning. This is possible even if you are taking a subject or reading a book that completely bores you or frustrates you. Use your writing to link things you love to the assigned topic that bores you. For instance, let's say you hate your physics class but love playing basketball or reading novels. You can relate physics concepts to each of these hobbies. Just try to imagine how to do that!

If you feel blocked whenever you pick up a pen and start writing (or sit at a keyboard and start typing) all is not lost. You do have options! You can ask a friend to write or type as you talk. Tell the friend not to worry if what you say makes any sense or is repetitive. Another option is to record what you say and try to write or type it up later. Having a recorder handy helps me a great deal because I can get my thoughts out and write them down later. Yet another option is to get Dragon speech recognition software. Just the same, there is something helpful about you being the one to write it down. Why? It creates new pathways from your hand to your mind. An important writing tip is to take adequate breaks from writing. The more you write down or record your thoughts, the more you will discover that your brain never stops working in the background (even during breaks) if you have trained it right.

Professors aren't trying to torture you through writing assignments. Writing gives you a voice. Professors can be a great help to you. I think many of us forget that we can just go up to our teachers and talk to them. To be blunt, I had a few teachers when I was young that should have turned me off to the whole share your feelings thing, but nope. I'm better than that. It's a good thing, too. As my grandma says, and my mom reminds me; a person is blessed to have had just one awesome teacher in their life. I have had so many great teachers. They have helped me become a lover of learning and writing.

I have a problem with peers who have said and think that they don't (or shouldn't) have to do any work to get good grades. If they don't have to then they can't really compare themselves to kids who have to work harder than they do. Yes, I use the words kids for college age, but I prefer calling people younger than that children. Kids are actually goats, right? Anyway, these kids say that the work just comes naturally. Since when does work come naturally for anyone? Remember, if one knew everything about a certain subject then why would they take the class? If they are doing it just for the credit, then they should be down on their knees everyday thanking God that they get to earn college credit. The teacher's job includes ensuring the students aren't turned off to the subject. This doesn't mean all the students will love the subject. Even if they do, they may find other avenues to explore. That is what all great writers do, too.

The point of school isn't to fry your brain; of course, it does that very well. The point is to expose a person to a wide selection of subjects. This helps to both learn about those subjects and determine where your interests lie. Hard work and big demands help students to develop high standards within themselves. Lesson plans and requirements change as you go through college. This is to be expected. Education is earned, it is not automatic. If everyone could get a decent job and have a great life simply by choosing "the right school" don't you think people would have all flocked there by now? I am grateful for the professors that I had; they taught me more than the subject matter. If you look carefully at what your professors require, you will find the path they want you to try. Most people that truly try (by committing themselves to the task) do succeed. However, there are some people that haven't discovered how to reach their potential. The trick is to be reliant on others for the right reasons. Don't expect others to do the work for you.

I remember watching a kid walk in to class one day. I was studying outside the classroom. He asked me if I was ready. I don't remember what I said to him, but I do know that he was not ready. He was late to class frequently and was obnoxious. The burden of being an adult is viewing people as obnoxious if they just aren't charming. Well anyway, small talk is just small talk. The point is he always expected others to do his work for him. When I was a young boy, I spoke with a cashier in New Jersey. She said to me, "Oh you like school now, but wait until you get older". Again, the implication was there is something wrong with being expected to work hard. Perhaps she was just in the negative frame of mind regarding school and education. Your frame of mind has a lot to do with what kind of student you become and what you will achieve. With me, there is no gray area. I either like all of school or dislike all of it. It's real simple and it works great because I would imagine there is something that everyone can like about school. Believing you can succeed helps you succeed. Case closed. Don't waste your time hating your assignments. It keeps you from progressing. Remember, the pursuit of your degree is like climbing a mountain. You cannot reach the top while sitting in the path complaining that the path is steep.

We each come into this world with negative cash flow so to speak. We don't start out contributing to society. Hopefully you do know you must contribute to society. Why not become a writer? Writers are very special. They say if you can't write for yourself you shouldn't write for anyone. Your assignments give you the chance to write for yourself, not just your professors. My mom has gotten me interested in finding excellent quotations. I now think in terms of book titles and poetic lines. My writing has helped me become interested in marketing. Marketing (and writing) is a process of persuading or informing people.

Writing will help you beyond your school assignments of course. In the "real world" excellent writing skills are essential. No one will hire you if you aren't even at the level where you would hire yourself. Writing effectively will help you make the world a better place. Remember, it isn't just what the story (or report) is. It is how it is told. Make sure your writing pulls the reader's interest along. Read through what you wrote with an objective, critical eye. If you were to read your paper to your class, would they follow your writing and logic? Will it inform and persuade them? You do not want your writing to be like the local news. So often, all they have is hype and no depth in the topic. This satisfies no one.

Effective writing means analyzing the topic thoroughly. Most people are good philosophers but are unaware they are. In other words, they may wonder about both sides of an issue. Just because the majority of society believes that information means one thing doesn't mean they should avoid exploring the opposite side of the issue. A terrific example of this is the topic of global warming. Many people and scientists have come to believe that global warming and climate change are caused by people and carbon emissions. An exceptional paper about the topic would include scientific data and other research from both sides of the issue. This can result in a much more satisfying paper. Remember that theories are powerful and keeping an open mind is essential.

As a student who has experienced great success I will tell you that time is even more valuable to me now. A great stress reducer is to begin your writing assignments as soon as they are assigned. This strategy gives you ample time to write down everything that occurs to you so you can comb through your writings and choose which parts to retain for this assignment. Beyond this, taking advantage of free time (and building it into your schedule) is great if you use this time to get ready for the next battle of school work. Live, work, and write without regrets. You don't want to be saying in a few years "gosh, what kind of success could I have had if I had really worked hard the whole time"? Why not just go ahead and work your hardest now? You only have the one chance at it, so make the best of it! Ultimately, the question in life is, "would you do it again"? If you answered yes, then would you do it all over again before you were even done? Now that's philosophy. Each time you need to write, get your thoughts on paper or tape. Then refine and search for the best way to communicate what you are trying to say. Work hard, write hard, but do it joyfully. As the boxers say, "leave it all on the mat". Through this book I will show you the ropes. But you still will have to do the climbing. Please believe me; the struggle to the top is definitely worth it.

School generally won't help you become your own employer. However I don't go as far as Rich Dad Poor Dad by saying that it completely doesn't help a person. Of course, if there was time to learn everything then people would teach everything. So many fields are advancing every day. Let me encourage you to stay current on social trends. Seize the day. You wouldn't be reading this if (a) you didn't buy this book and (b) if you weren't interested in any enjoyable topic imaginable. That is the first step to being a good student and writer. Interconnectedness is the key. Connecting the dots and looking for clues to your success story. The future is ours. Hopefully we all get to the point where we exceed our teacher's expectations. The reason I love reading and selecting books to buy and learn from is you never know how it will change your life. Often times we buy something just because of a specific element in the material we really loved. Later we learn that all of the knowledge was meaningful. I recommend that you read and re-read not only my book but your own writings as well.

Remember to have fun and enjoy what you have written. I hope you get excited when something clicks and you think of something new and fresh you can add to your assignments or work. This also applies to your career and life. Always try out your ideas, writings, and skills on a new audience. You will be surprised at who will listen and who needs to hear your message. If you think this book can't help you in a huge way, then think again. We all have to learn to communicate. It's important. Trust me. I believe you will never know how much you are capable of until you try. Always try and find complex answers to life's persistent questions. Most people surf the web to get their questions answered, yet I often come away from browsing the web with more questions than answers. This is a good thing for a writer.

If you have seen the movie Anger Management you might remember when Jack Nicholson asks Adam Sandler who he is. Adam Sandler keeps telling him what he does and not who he is. Comedy ensues, but the point is that it tends to be easier for people to write about what they think others want to hear. Hopefully you will, or already have, taken some writing or psychology classes to get in touch with your inner self. It's ironic that some of us have inflated egos, but when those individuals are asked to write about themselves it becomes difficult. That is because it takes a certain amount of courage mixed with humility to share how one feels about themselves. Basically what Jack Nicholson wanted Adam Sandler to do was to admit to himself that he had lost touch with his inner self. My philosophy is that if you set out to succeed but fail you never really had a plan to succeed in the first place. Sometimes you can do more than change the world just by thinking the right way. Perception is everything. Hard work pays off. If no one got paid for doing work, do you think that people would just sit around all day? No. There will always be an open free flowing market for new possibility combined with the human element. I wrote this book to show people that saving and revisiting your work is important. Writing is all about confidence. I hope this book provides all that you need so that you realize that you had the confidence and capability all along. This book will help you develop the skills. Please pass this confidence along to others. Writing skills begin long before you put pen to paper. Ask yourself, "Would I read and enjoy what I wrote if I was a consumer who bought the book or content that I wrote?"

Let's be honest. You wouldn't have found this book (or it wouldn't have found you) unless you were supposed to have it. I actually experienced many of my school buddies needing help with their assignments. They always came to me because I was organized, thorough, and tough. Now you can help your peers, family, and classmates with just this one book. You are probably a good student. You just might lack some simple writing skills. Hey, what did you want me to say? You lack complex writing skills? Is it possible for me to make you enjoy writing even more than you do already? You tell me; but only after you have finished my book from front to back. Ignore this instruction if you are a psychic guru. If you are that is pretty stinking cool! (My psychic skills just told me you aren't chuckling at my cleverness). Learn to love your brain again. But if that sounds too stressful I suppose you could hate your brain instead. (The latter is not recommended and I am not liable for your brain. If you bought his book your brain will love you back). Learn to channel your thoughts to increase productivity. Become a powerhouse of wisdom. This book is a slice of my entire life until now. It was custom designed with you in mind. Please tell your friends and associates about it. Train yourself to never be bored again. This book is the real deal. Everything in this book can be used the day you buy it. Please pass what you learn on to everyone who needs it. (All I ask is that you always learn before you teach). You can't buy the knowledge that is owed to you. In school you are not paying for what you learn, you are paying for the skills that your knowledge will gain for you! This book provides you an excellent resource as a starting point. Many people don't finish high school, let alone college. The national average for people who graduate from college is 25%. My book can help you be in that 25%! You can become a successful writer in your college courses. A final note: learn to reuse your content and writing material. Remember; don't be afraid to put pen or pencil to paper. Paper is cheap. Your ideas are not. So let's begin! Success is just around the corner. Your playbook is finally here in your hands.

2

ENGLISH 101: ENGLISH COMPOSITION

ADVERTISEMENT ANALYSIS

This analysis is about a real estate agency's advertisement. Specifically, it is an ad that describes the real estate agents and how they are able to give good deals to homeowners and non-homeowners alike. The team of realtors is called The Ryan Team, which is named after the owner, Bill Ryan. The ad contains a quote from Bill that makes the ad interesting. Also included is a statement that declares that "We charge just as much as the amateurs do, but we are experts." This is beneath the pictures and house specifications. At the top of the ad are pictures of the team players and their smiling faces.

The use of the colors red, white, and blue are used very subliminally to create a patriotic feel. In the post 9/11 era this strategy is used often by many companies. In a state as Republican as Arizona, it is a strategy that many people both seek and respond to in a favorable way. As you look over this ad, the urgency to read it is strong. The sense of urgency comes from the colors and sizes of the letters. It also comes from the unique slogan that says, "Celebrating 30 years of excellence." The use of the digits for 30 rather than the word 30 is significant. The numbers are given a unique shape which grabs the attention of the reader.

In the title "Celebrating 30 years of excellence in the Chandler Real Estate Market", the phrase is depicted in small letters to symbolize maybe it's no big deal to say they are in real estate because they are experts, and it is just normal to them to be selling houses. It is the reverse of what would normally be in big letters. They want you to focus more on celebrating thirty years of excellence, and not pay as much attention to the prices. This is a typical strategy used to keep customers' attention diverted from the price.

In the ad, Bill Ryan's people look very happy, but not ecstatic. The visual message creates the impression that they are professionally enthusiastic about what they do. The colors of their clothes are ordered so that they look like one team. The team's appearance, in turn, creates the idea in the reader's mind that the entire team would be working for the potential seller or buyer. However, the clothes are not exactly alike. For example, the blue on one side is lighter that the other side of the group. The same strategy is used with the red clothes. One is an off-pink while the other is darker. Varying the clothing color draws your eye to all of them at once and creates harmony in the brain. The colors of their shirts correspond to the shades of grass, houses, and sky in the photographs of the houses located below.

The third aspect of the ad makes the pictures and people on the page look more realistic. Even though you know it's just a picture of a house on a flat page, it looks as though the photo is right there because of the shadowing in the ad which makes the pictures look like a scrapbook page. The phone numbers and email addresses on the page grab the reader's attention because of the great use of white space. Appropriate balance is kept throughout the ad between providing information, showing pictures, and having sufficient white space.

The other point of significance is that this ad doesn't really look like a typical real estate advertisement. Some people will say, "Wow, it's about houses, but doesn't have the same old, same old marketing strategies. Maybe Ryan and his team really are above the rest." For many people that will be buying and/or selling a house, this element of caring is crucial since it is easier to justify paying a commission if you know they care about you and have treated you like royalty!

Making the reader of the ad feel good is definitely a goal here. Leaving the prices off the houses lets the reader focus on the sizes of the houses. Ryan's quote, "Buy any of these homes from my team and I will buy yours for cash!" is a real attention-getter these days because it is hard for sellers to sell their homes. This eliminates a barrier for people wanting to sell their house and trade up to a more expensive one. Removing barriers is one of the most basic strategies used in marketing.

In conclusion, I believe that the goal of the ad is to tell the potential customer to relax because the team at the top is trustworthy and professional while building excitement about using the Ryan Team. The ad's goal is to build confidence about making the decision to use the team. Each person in the picture is a Caucasian; this will grab many white people's attention. The message of the ad depicted through the pictures is that "we are elite and we know it." It shows elitism in this aspect, in order to further convince the reader that the Ryan Team is the best. Despite what people may say in casual conversation, elitism is often a big part of many major financial decisions such as home buying.

Since there are so many people in the ad, the odds are very good that each potential customer will see a picture of a realtor that they believe they can trust. The overall purpose of the ad is to inform people about the agency and convey the message that the agency is a team that will work for you if you use them. It is my belief that this ad accomplishes that goal for these reasons; the emphasis on teamwork and professionalism, and the unique selling proposition that the team will buy your house. This ad will definitely influence potential buyers and sellers to consider using this team to buy and/or sell properties for them.

ANALYSIS OF THE POEM "IF" BY RUDYARD KIPLING

IF…..by Rudyard Kipling

If you can keep your head when all about you
Are losing theirs and blaming it on you,
If you can trust yourself when all men doubt you,
But make allowance for their doubting too;
If you can wait and be tired by waiting'
Or being lied about, don't deal in lies,
Or being hated, don't give way to hating,
And yet don't look too good, nor talk too wise:
If you can dream – and not make dreams your master;
If you can think – and not make thoughts your aim;
If you can meet with Triumph and Disaster
And treat those two impostors just the same;
If you can bear to hear the truth you've spoken
Twisted by knaves to make a trap for fools
Or watch the things you gave your life to, broken,
And stoop and build 'em up with worn-out tools:
If you can make one heap of all your winnings
And risk it on one turn of pitch-and-toss,
And lose, and start again at your beginnings
And never breathe a word about your loss;
If you can force your heart and nerve and sinew
To serve your turn long after they are gone,
And so hold on when there is nothing in you
Except the Will which says to them: 'Hold on!'
If you can talk with crowds and keep your virtue
'Or walk with kings – nor lose the common touch,
if neither foes nor loving friends can hurt you,
If all men count with you, but none too much;
If you can fill the unforgiving minute
With sixty seconds' worth of distance run,
Yours is the Earth and everything that's in it,
And – which is more – you'll be a Man, my son!

The theme of this poem is that each of us really is like the person telling the poem to the son-like figure, and the son-like figure who needs to become a man. Only if we try to *become men* will it start to happen. Kipling says all of these things in a way to suggest that it is very hard but yet so rewarding to be a man. The symbolism in this poem says to me in a way that we are all striving to be and to do what is right. Only if we do this will it count for anything. For example, people don't want to remember evil men. They remember honest men. Thus, in order to be remembered, you must be different than the group or the ignorant crowd. The whole poem symbolizes remembering that all of one's actions and struggles impact what one becomes. The final verse states, "If you can walk with crowds of virtue and keep your virtue, or walk with kings nor lose the common touch". This is talking about the difficulty of remembering to become virtuous. Another theme that I picked up on was the fact that if you are none of these good things the poem is talking about, you will still be accepted by some people. That is what makes it truly hard to do the things it takes to become a man.

What is ironic is that we never really are a true man in the Holy One's sight because we all need to continue to change and improve, no matter how perfect we are. The list of positive aspects is very long, and most of us don't even think these are qualities of being a man. This is ironic, especially in today's society. Irony is a difficult thing to talk about. In the end of the poem when he says if you can fill 60 seconds worth of effort basically in every day you will not get fame or popularity or happiness even, but glory in the kingdom to come. We all fall short and overlook it. This is the mental, or interior, part of life which can be more difficult than even the physical because our lives are not balanced. The point of view is that of true wisdom and owning up to one's deeds. Rudyard Kipling also tells it in such a way as to not offend anyone who might read it, but inspire them instead. I like it because he puts what is truly right on the table but doesn't force anyone to eat. He wrote this poem in a way that is memorable. We might not give a second thought to the fact that we don't live up to these standards and make excuses for falling short. This is why the only way to get people to choose well is not to force it into people's heads.

At the same time, I also see him speak of kings and masters. He might be speaking of an old point of view. At least I think that is the imagery Kipling wanted to create in the reader's mind. I also think he was speaking to all fathers and sons. The poem inspires the reader to focus on what is important in life.

DESCRIPTIVE ESSAY: MY MEMORIES OF THE NEW JERSEY SHORE

Everyone has a place that is near and dear to their heart. For me, that place is in New Jersey. Specifically, that place is on L.B.I., which stands for Long Beach Island. Some people think that L.B.I. is a place in New York, but that is Long Island (without the B). Long Beach Island is a beautiful beach on the Jersey shore. As a kid of roughly 2 to 8 years old, with lots of friendliness and freckles, I enjoyed the beach. The times I spent at the beach are special and important to me.

L.B.I. is the place that is so special and memorable for me that I can visit it in my mind. It is a barrier island on the Atlantic Ocean. L.B.I. was about an hour from where I used to live in the southern part of New Jersey, so we went there often. The summertime temperature is relatively mild, especially compared to Phoenix. The waves are very large and the beach is relatively flat, long, and wide. The sand is powdery and rough at the same time. As far as sharks are concerned, in all those years I only saw two sharks in the water a long way out, and one sand shark that washed up on the shore. Since the waves are very big at L.B.I., the island didn't attract many tourists or sunbathers, and really only a few surfers. The sand was nice and warm, and since the beach was not crowded, there were some people who searched for money or valuables beneath the sand and shells. By comparison, in the more crowded beach towns in other parts of the Jersey shore, there wasn't space for the people to search!

When my mom and I would arrive at L.B.I., we would walk up through a path created by dune grass that was beside an old red slatted wooden fence held together at the top and bottom by some wire. Up over the hill was the beach and ocean. As soon as we got out of the car we could hear the ocean and seagulls, but we couldn't see anything until we reached the little hill's summit. Lifeguards sat in their lifeguard chairs which were evenly spaced across wide distances across the beach. Usually upon arriving, my mom would get her tan beach bag and reach inside for a ball to play "step-back catch". We invented this game, I think, but we don't have a patent for it. Accuracy is the key to the game, and practice makes perfect. We start out toe-to-toe facing each other and throw the ball back and forth. We each take a step backwards with each successfully completed round. If either of us misses, we start over, toe-to-toe again.

Most of the time I would play in the ocean and either swim or ride my boogie board. If we were all worn out or wanted to dry out from playing in the water, my mom and I would walk over to the wet shoreline near some shells of all sizes and placements in the sand. We would start out by skipping the little shells into the ocean. Back then my hands were smaller, so to me even the small shells felt big and rough. There were always lots and lots of shells, and we would skip them for a long time. I could launch them far and usually beat my mom in this game of shell skipping by having my shells skip more times. I didn't get bored very often. Even when I did, I'd just watch people to pass the time.

Occasionally we would go to the lighthouse on the far north end of the island, which was about five miles north of the beach we usually visited. Especially memorable to me is the first time we went to the lighthouse, but each time we went the experience was the same. I could see the lighthouse from our beach most days, unless it was foggy. When we arrived at the lighthouse, I saw huge rocks covered with green algae and barnacles. The bright sun and waves made the lighthouse look like it was on a moving craft in the water.

Upon entering the lighthouse we had taken only a couple of steps when we quickly realized we could not see a thing! Our eyes were not yet used to the peace and darkness that this strange circular edifice enticed us with. Then our eyes adjusted. After climbing many flights of stairs and hearing our shoes sticking and clicking on the yellow painted metal stairwell we reached the top. Looking out onto the ocean was amazing, but feeling the gusty wind and smelling the salty air was incredible. Walking around the top of the lighthouse was a rush because, other than a railing, there wasn't anything to stop my family from falling off the lighthouse! The lighthouse was probably a little more than 200 feet high, but not very wide. I raced from one side to the other and looked through my binoculars to watch people parasailing in the air almost as high as we were now. We decided that parasailing would be a fun activity for another day.

The very next day my mom and I went up on a parasail and the boat took us over near the lighthouse. As my dad is afraid of heights, he was more than happy to watch us from the boat and be the one to take the photos. We were as excited as children on Christmas morning when they unclipped us from the boat which was going about 40 miles per hour. The wind pulled us up and we were sailing high in the air behind the boat. The winds were calm and quiet while we parasailed, unlike the gustiness at the top of the lighthouse. My mom and I had a wonderful view of the boaters, seagulls, and all kinds of things. It was thrilling.

At our beach there was one very memorable day. As my mom and I were comfortably swimming in the ocean one afternoon a storm approached to the north from the south. It started out slow at first and as water and wind speed picked up, the lifeguards became edgy. At that point there was nothing serious happening, though. My mom moved our blankets back further from the water, just in case the water rose up the beach to our level. There was a girl who was swimming near us; she was splashing and having a good time. She kept diving out further and further, and going under the water, just like I like to do. I looked down the shoreline and saw fishermen with long poles extended far out into the water. They were near the rocks that cut into the water at some spots along the shoreline.

The afternoon sky was darkening, making afternoon look like night. Slowly yet truly the storm had arrived. I was under the water so much that I rarely knew the weather above the surface, but this time I could even *feel* the shift in weather. As I poked my head out of the salty, clear water, I saw the happy little girl who had been swimming and diving under the water all day come roaring past my legs. An undertow had just gone out to the ocean, and a huge wave came in. She was caught in the grasp of the ocean. There was a sea wall that is used to slow erosion on the rest of the beach from waves. She hit that sea wall very hard and went back under. At this point I was thinking, "That's it! It's time for me to go!" I went up to my mom and saw the girl standing there as if it was just a normal day. She was fine. I was amazed, but I saw the power of the waves and saw her when she was dragged 100 yards up the beach. These events along with the nearby fishermen told my brain to always know my surroundings even if I happened to swim on a clear day at the ocean. A storm could get me just like that!

Despite the storm experience, all of these activities at the shore were fun. The feeling I get at Long Beach Island is like no other. It is a happy, sunny place. We always stay at the part of the beach that isn't crowded or touristy. Each visit is heartwarming. It clears my mind to visit Long Beach Island because it is not very crowded. Being at the shore takes me away from it all and I like that. It makes me feel new and refreshed.

ENGLISH 102: COMPOSITIONS AND RESEARCH REPORTS

ENGLISH 102 SEMESTER PROJECT

The second semester English Composition course consisted of a semester-long project that included researching a topic, analyzing the information and putting together a portfolio. This was a very involved and engrossing project. We learned skills that can later be applied in any business setting. I chose to do my project on the benefits of sustainable homes. It is surprising how much information you can find when doing a thorough research project!

RESEARCH PAPER: SUSTAINABLE HOMES WILL BENEFIT EVERYONE

Introduction

The house a person chooses to live in is a reflection of what that person values. Architects and builders know that a home's architecture is where design, function and environment meet. The design and structure of the home must take into account the environment (of the people, the surroundings of the home site and the neighborhood). Sustainable homes are beneficial for society and homeowners because sustainability addresses the interconnectedness of the home with the environment.

Global Warming

Sustainable homes attempt to provide solutions to the problem of global warming. Global warming is the theory that carbon emissions are damaging the environment and causing climate change. The major contributors to carbon emissions include the use of carbon based products to produce electricity and for transportation. Proponents of the global warming concept say that the harm is measurable and go on to point out that the future impact of continued global warming could harm humans, animals, the climate, and the polar ice caps. "Every year, buildings are responsible for 39 percent of U.S. CO_2 emissions and 70 percent of U.S. electricity consumption" (Holowka 148). These facts bring attention to the need for sustainable buildings.

Many other scientists do not believe that global warming exists. The common belief that those scientists have is to not exactly deny the existence of global warming, but make the issue obsolete. They insist that "a warmer world is better for human health on average. It tends to boost agricultural productivity, which reduces hunger and the illnesses that inadequate nutrition help produce" (Avery 112).

There are numerous other scientists who believe that the so-called global warming experts have it wrong. "Does anyone think that the CO_2 pressure on soda pop is warming it" (Robinson 1). Robinson goes on to state that these scientists accept that temperatures are warmer, but argue that the warmer temperatures could not be caused by CO_2; instead, the warmer temperatures cause the CO_2 levels to increase. Although there is disagreement about the existence of global warming, it still is beneficial to take better care of the environment. The scientists that do not believe in global warming provide no evidence on chemical reactions caused by CO_2, thus leaving CO_2 guilty of the charges that it at least contributes to the global warming and climate change problem.

Nuclear Energy

The use of nuclear energy would greatly reduce carbon emissions in the production of electricity. Noted scientist Alan S. Brown points out that "leading greens like the fact that nuclear plants do not release greenhouse emissions" (Brown 16). Using nuclear energy to power a home would make it more sustainable. The builder and the homeowner cannot directly install nuclear power at the homeowner or neighborhood level. Converting to nuclear power requires governmental approval and action. The decision about building new nuclear power plants in this country will eventually be made. In the meantime, builders and homeowners can impact carbon emissions through the installation and use of solar power.

Those who are opposed to nuclear power have very specific concerns. Their concerns are the operational safety of nuclear plants, the disposal of nuclear waste, and the potential for nuclear byproducts to fall into the hands of terrorists. They do not feel the added risk is worth the many benefits that could occur from nuclear power.

The concerns expressed by opponents are certainly valid concerns, but these opponents are short-sighted. European countries re-use their nuclear waste, and as a result do not have a nuclear waste problem. This fact may lead to the re-use of nuclear waste in this country. Governmental monitoring can help ensure operational safety and safety from terrorists.

Solar Power

Solar power is especially useful in a sunny climate like Phoenix. There are two main categories of solar power; passive and active. Passive solar power means situating the home so that the windows and structure capture (or avoid) the sun, the building's heating requirement. Active solar power involves the installation of photovoltaic panels to capture the sun's rays, which then disperse power to the home to provide power to the home and heat the water. In order for solar power to be widely available, companies that produce the solar panels will need to grow exponentially. "Solar power currently accounts for 0.1% of the electricity in the United States, but by all accounts, the solar power industry is the fastest growing industry in the world" (Perry 16).

A major argument against solar power is that it is an expensive source of energy, especially compared to nuclear power. According to Alan Brown, noted scientist, in most places solar power costs about 20 cents per kilowatt hour. This is five times the cost of nuclear power. Besides the ongoing kilowatt cost, the panels themselves are very expensive, although they are beginning to come down in price (Brown).

The pro-solar side correctly argues that there are currently multiple tax and power company incentives provided to offset some of the expense of solar power. The credits are good until 2016. "The typical system costs $42,600. Federal tax credits are $12,780. Utility and state incentives in Arizona are $19,900 (Taylor D1). These credits and incentives go a long way toward making the switch to solar more affordable.

As a result of converting the home to solar, there will be less usage of electricity generated by the power company, which in turn reduces carbon emissions. If individuals can look beyond the price of the solar system, the market will flourish. Homeowners and builders will begin to look at the addition of solar panels as a way to reduce both future energy costs and carbon emissions. Solar power will then be thought of as a mandatory commodity for people.

Every institution and business relies on the other. There is an inherent interconnectedness that society has forgotten about. Americans need to rely on each other a bit more during this economic struggle. It starts with education. America needs to get re-addicted to education, so that once people of the Baby Boomer generation are gone, strong leaders with entrepreneurial minds will take control. Governmental involvement in addressing energy resources and global warming can help. People need to give up the old ways for long term goals of improvement and change to be met. If the government continues to give tax incentives for installing solar and for using other sustainable building methods, it can also stimulate the economy. If mortgage lenders give special discounts to homebuyers that build sustainable, the stock market would benefit from building green.

Urban Planning

The other aspect of sustainable building includes planning neighborhoods, developments, and cities so that it minimizes transportation requirements because businesses are close by. The urban planning focus that is in keeping with the sustainable building movement is called new urbanism. This involves building green homes (or retrofitting existing homes) that are close to the cities, instead of in the distant suburbs. Rather than creating suburban Mc Mansions, architect Marianne Cusato states the importance of learning to live in tight spaces and designing homes that suit needs rather than mere wants. "Returning to traditional, compact, mixed use community design will solve a host of economic ills" (Stinson 50). Author Sonya Stinson further adds that architect Marianne Cusato is the designer of the Katrina cottage, which is now also used in other communities for smaller, yet just as beautiful homes.

The moral imperative

There is a moral imperative facing society. This facet is the driving force that truly adds strength to the sustainable home argument. Every action and decision affects the environment. The imperative to focus on sustainability is clear. Architect Buckminster Fuller challenged, "Never change things by fighting the existing reality. To change something, build a new model that makes the existing model obsolete". Sustainable architecture is that new model.

There are some who buy green products but are not making the lifestyle changes that really help the environment. Sustainable building is how society can improve life. "Architects McDonough and Braungart take it further, and state that building materials should be geared toward the concept that 'waste equals food'. Ensuring that all building materials can eventually be either re-used or composted" (Lacayo 92).

Separating a house from the environment is as illogical as ignoring the interdependence between government, individuals, and society. The home must fit with the local environment. Society is now beginning to realize that materialism does not bring happiness. The current problems in the economy may cause materialism to come to an end and bring forth renewed commitment to real solutions.

The Architecture and Structure of a Sustainable Home

Good design is connected with nature and history. There is more to building a sustainable home than simply equipping it with solar panels. This includes the use of more sustainable products for the exterior and skeleton of the house. The focus should be what best fits the environment the home is being built in, and in reducing the overall size of homes. It is not easy being green, but to help, the United States Green Building

Council (USGBC) established a certification organization called the Leadership in Energy Efficiency and Design (LEED) to provide specific standards that must be met to have certified buildings. The certification for sustainable buildings has been for commercial buildings and schools. LEED has now developed certification standards for sustainable homes as well. These standards are in keeping with the five areas that the United Nations defined for sustainable architecture: "ensuring a healthy interior environment, efficient use of all resources, use of ecologically benign materials in construction, the use of measures to protect the environment of the site, and good design that is beautiful, efficient, and durable" (Howard).

Many sustainable homes are traditional in style, but are built with sustainable materials. The structure itself ends up looking traditional, but the materials used in the construction are all renewable and non-toxic. "The sustainable home must be set on the building lot so as to take advantage of the pattern of the sun, and the landform. One of the LEED requirements is that the lot be at least three quarters of an acre" (Holowka 148). This reduces the number of homes a builder can put in a development, but homeowners graciously accept the larger home site. Stewardship requirements for the land itself include minimal topsoil disturbance and erosion control. Instead of just xeriscaping, homeowners can also plant other native plants that work with the weather cycles. Taryn Holowka also specifies that LEED does require that 25% to 75% of the bordering perimeters of green certified communities be touching developed communities. This is to help make sure that transportation needs are minimized.

There are many green options in the building materials category. The roofing material should work in conjunction with the solar panels. Some homeowners have gone to the extent of planting gardens on the roof. In any case, the gutter system should include a method of water recapture to allow for the storage and re-use of rainwater.

Sustainability should be the focus in selecting insulation material, windows, roofing material, the type of material selected for building the studs of the house, and the drywall material. Every single category of home construction material is available in non-toxic sustainable form. Instead of using fiberglass insulation, there are insulation products made of recycled blue jeans, which insulate even better than the fiberglass insulation. There are non-toxic versions of drywall. The woods used in the walls of the house should be a renewable wood, such as bamboo. The use of these products will help to reduce the likelihood of sick house syndrome. Sick house syndrome is a category of respiratory and other illnesses that is linked to toxic products in the home, inadequate ventilation, or both.

Opponents argue that green materials are often more expensive. However, as more people choose these types of building materials, more companies will begin to manufacture the products. The competition between these companies will bring the prices down. It is estimated that energy efficiency will increase from 35% to 65% through the use of green building materials, all while improving health by the elimination of toxic chemicals.

Current construction materials have a lot of waste. Homebuyers and builders did not realize the impact of the traditional materials on the environment. "Every year the average American generates 10 to 20 metric tons of CO_2 through day-to-day activities through home energy use and transportation" (Weeks 4). The use of alternate materials, according to the Office of Technology Assessment, could take 6.5 tons of waste each year and make it reusable.

Interior Design

The interior design of a sustainable home must be both green and beautiful. The aesthetics should bring a good feeling to the people that live in the home. "The home should preserve the natural environment in the home, and the health of the occupants" (Robertson 25). This helps make the homeowner happy to live there. Non-toxic homes provide health benefits to the homeowner as well. The need for simplicity in interior design is best explained by noted architect Marianne Cusato. "The overuse of ornamentation is a symptom of the infection called design by checklist" (Stinson 50).

The flooring should be tile, concrete, stained concrete, or a renewable wood such as bamboo. These products are both beautiful and renewable. In addition, they do not contain the toxic chemicals that are found in carpets. Trim and cabinetry should also be constructed out of renewable woods such as bamboo. Countertops can be made from renewable products such as concrete, bamboo, or products made from recycled paper.

There are specific household appliances that reduce overall energy usage. They should be included in every sustainable home. Energy Star appliances should be the starting point. Energy Star appliances are those that meet government standards for energy efficiency. These appliances include refrigerators, dishwashers, washers, dryers, furnaces, air conditioners, hot water heaters, electronics, and other small appliances. "The EPA estimates that over 2 billion Energy Star products were sold in 2006, saving enough electricity to power more than 15 million average American households for a year" (Weeks 9). There are other items that are easy conversions for households to make. Incandescent light bulbs should be replaced with compact fluorescent light bulbs (CFLs). Another strategy is to install low water usage toilets and faucets. These save thousands of gallons of water per year, an important consideration in Phoenix.

The Argument against Sustainable Homes

The opposition states that builders and architects should continue on the same path of traditional home building. The advantage is that the building materials are mass produced, and the homes can be built in any style regardless of the environment and location. This often makes the homes cheaper to build and buy. Changing to new methods is risky. Builders and homeowners may not want to risk changing their ways and then are unable to sell the homes.

Those who do not want to change to sustainable building methods are quick to point out that some of the green homes are not beautiful, and do not necessarily save energy or money. "What bugs me most about the fad for green architecture is the notion that virtue makes for better design. I suppose an ugly green build is better than an ugly non-green building, but it's still ugly" (Mcguigan and Stone 77). This shows that the ideas and functionality of green architecture cannot be refuted by non-green homebuilders.

Opponents to the sustainable home movement believe that focusing on the home instead of building power plants and investing in drilling for geothermal energy is short-sighted, and will not really solve the energy problem or global warming. They lastly point out that the disposal of solar panels and of CFLs could be a future pollution problem.

The answer to the points that sustainable building opponents make is that the more the focus is placed on sustainable buildings, the better job builders, architects, and designers will do in making the homes beautiful and affordable. Investing in solar energy and sustainable homes does not have to mean that the nation ignores the need for nuclear energy and geothermal exploration. This is a nation capable of multi-tasking the efforts that it makes.

Conclusion

Sustainable homes are beneficial to the homeowner and society, and building them should be the strategy for the future. There is a moral imperative for each person to take care of the planet. Sustainable building makes excellent use of limited resources. Homebuilders now recognize the need to build sustainable homes. In a recent Business Week article, it was noted that "today there are about 40,000 solar homes in the U.S., but that number is set to spike" (Aston 88). This should encourage each person to have a sustainable home, which will lead to a more sustainable planet. Without building new homes as sustainable architecture, the human carbon footprint could well become a carbon footpath.

References

Aston, Adam. "A Warming Trend for Solar Homes". Business Week. 3 Nov. 2008:88. Master File Premier. EBSCOhost. Chandler-Gilbert Community College Library, Chandler, AZ. 6 Nov 2008.

Avery, Dennis. "Global Warming Benefits Life on Earth." Opposing Viewpoints: Global Warming. Ed. Cynthia A. Bily. Detroit, MI: Thomson Gale 2006. 108-112.

Brown, Alan S. "The Emerging Alternate Energy Consensus." The Bent of Tau Beta Pi. Fall 2008. 16-22.

Holowka, Taryn. "The LEED Rating System Helps Create Greener Buildings." Opposing Viewpoints: Eco-architecture. Ed. Cristina Fisanick. New York, NY: Green Haven Press, Inc., 2006. 147-153.

Howard, Bion. "The Basics of Green Homes and Communities." Opposing Viewpoints: Eco-architecture. Ed. Cynthia A. Bily. Detroit, MI: Thomson Gale 2006. 21-32.

Lacayo, Richard. "William McDonough and Michael Braungart. (Special Issue: Heroes of the Environment)(Heroes of the Environment, Moguls & Entrepreneurs)." Time International (Europe Edition). 170. 17 (Oct 29, 2007): 92. Opposing Viewpoints Resource Center. Gale. Maricopa County Community College. 29 Oct. 2008. http://find.galegroup.com/ovrc/infomark.do?&contentSet=IACDocuments&type=retrieve&tabID=T003&prodld=OVRC&docld=A170207694&source=gale&scprod=OVRC&userGroupName=mcc.

Mcguigan, Cathleen and Daniel Stone. "The Bad News about Green Architecture. (Project Green)." Newsweek. 152. 11 (Sept. 15m 2008): 77. Opposing Viewpoints Resource Center. Gale. Maricopa County Community College. 29 Oct. 2008. http://find.galegroup.com/ovrc/infomark.do?&contentSet=IAC-Documents&type=retrieve&tabID=T003&prodld=OVRC&docld=A184664427&source=gale&srcprod=OVRC&userGroupName=mcc_main&version=1.0.

Perry, Hugh. "The past, present and Future of Sustainable Housing Design: Part One of Sox." Natural Life Magazine Sept—Oct. 2008: 16-17.

Robertson, Kat. "Designing Sustainable homes: A Chat with Two Eco-Architects." Natural Life Magazine. May—June 2006: 20-25.

Robinson, Arthur B. "Correlation vs. Causality". Access to Energy. Vol. 35. Jan 2008. 1-4.

Stinson, Sonya. "Big Ideas for Small Places": Notre Dame Magazine. Autumn 2008. 50-51.

Taylor, Ed. "Solar Boost: Sunshine/Energy Economy Gets a Tax Break." The Arizona Republic. 12 Oct 2008: D1-D2.

Weeks, Jennifer: "Buying Green: Does it Really Help the Environment." The CQ Researcher Online. 29 Feb. 2008. Chandler-Gilbert Community College. 15 Oct. 2008. http://library.cqpress.com/cqresearcher/document.php

RESEARCH PAPER: SUSTAINABLE HOMES WILL NOT BENEFIT EVERYONE

Rather than entirely focus on one side of an argument, we were expected to thoroughly research the other side of the argument, and formulate a position paper for that side as well. The purpose of this is to become adept at seeing both sides and form clear arguments. This is what a truly educated person does.

Sustainable Homes Will Not Benefit Everyone

Introduction

The house a person chooses to live in is not a reflection of what that person values. Rather, it is a reflection of what the buyer can afford and whether the buyer believes that the house will retain its value or increase in value. Now is not the time to make costly changes in construction methods. Long-term goal setting is a luxury that society cannot afford at this time. Sustainable homes do not benefit society; the true benefit is from affordable houses.

Global Warming

Global warming theorists explain that the increase in carbon emissions is warming the planet, and that this is harmful to people, animals, and the environment. Increased carbon emissions means there is more carbon dioxide in the air. This is good for photosynthesis, which helps plants and crops grow. "History shows that a warmer world is better for human health on average. It tends to boost agricultural productivity, which reduces hunger" (Avery 112). In this way, improved agricultural output can help solve global hunger. Regarding carbon emissions, "buildings are responsible for 39% of U.S. CO_2 emissions and 70% of U.S. electricity consumption (Holowka 148). This does not mean that we need to build sustainable buildings. It does mean that society should seek less polluting methods of generating electricity.

Most carbon emissions actually come from transportation. It would be wrong to eliminate automobile and truck transportation. Restricting people's rights to transport themselves or their goods would harm society. Workers must be able to get to their jobs. Businesses and farmers must be able to move their products and foods so that they can be sold. In today's economy, people cannot necessarily afford to purchase hybrid cars. Solutions are not real solutions unless people can afford them.

Alternative Energy Sources

Electricity is essential to society. Environmentalists want the world to switch to solar power or wind power to generate electricity. These two methods are not realistic for society. They are both expensive methods and cannot really be widespread. Solar power cannot be stored, and neither can wind power. There are two alternative methods that can be available on a widespread basis. These alternatives are storable and economical: nuclear energy and geothermal energy. Both methods provide cheap energy through the grid. Off the grid solutions are elitist and are unacceptable for that reason.

Nuclear energy is very cheap and has zero carbon emissions. It is a form of energy that environmentalists (including Al Gore) do not like, because of the dangers that they see in it. Nuclear energy has dangers, but the dangers can be addressed while building new plants. Nuclear waste concerns will be almost eliminated if the laws are changed to permit re-burning of nuclear waste.

The safe non-polluting alternative to coal-burning electricity is geothermal energy. "A 2006 report by the National Renewable Energy Laboratory estimated that America has enough geothermal energy within two miles of the surface to supply the nation with thirty thousand years of energy at current rates of consumption" (Brown 21). This is a resource that should be used and causes no carbon emissions.

The Moral Imperative

The moral imperative that society faces is not the building of sustainable homes. The imperative is to provide affordable housing. To insist on sustainable home building is an elitist and expensive strategy. This is only beneficial to the people who can afford them. It is true that materialism does not bring happiness, but neither does an elitist building strategy. Careful and thorough urban planning is part of this moral imperative. Towns created by new home building must have services and businesses nearby. This helps to reduce global warming by reducing the need to drive. Affordability has many facets.

Exterior and Interior of the Affordable Home

Those who insist on sustainable homes rely on specific standards. Leadership in Efficiency and Design (LEED) provides specific standards that must be met to have certified buildings. "The broad nature of the 'green rating system' can serve as a trap for design professionals attempting to design to a preselected certification level. Higher sustainable levels usually require more design effort and often greater construction costs" (Musica 44). Obviously, building green is typically more expensive for the home buyer. The only real considerations for the architecture and structure of a home should be the affordability and durability factors. Traditional building materials are mass produced, widely available, and economical. Current home building designs can be re-created anywhere in the county and do not have to be specifically designed for a specific area.

Sustainable interior design is still an unusual strategy for homeowners. People have a desire to fit in, and have a sense of belonging with the people in their neighborhoods. If the interior design of their homes is green (sustainable), this will make them feel as though they do not fit in with their neighbors. It is difficult enough for people to make connections and friends in their neighborhoods without adding this impediment. It is more important for people to be connected to their communities than it is for them to have luxuries such as floors made from bamboo.

Conclusion

Houses that are affordable and durable benefit the homeowner and society. Requiring sustainable homes is far too restrictive and restricting. Architect Buckminster Fuller said "You never change things by fighting the existing reality. To change something, build a new model that makes the existing model obsolete". The position to build affordable, durable homes recognizes where the common person is at along the home buying continuum when making home buying decisions.

The old model to be made obsolete is the habit of only looking at a small piece of that continuum. The sustainable home movement places too much emphasis on the present and not enough on the progress that has already occurred. Problems serve to motivate society to develop solutions. Solutions are twice as effective when driven by the need to solve the entire problem. The current problem of home affordability can only be solved through continuing current building methods.

References

Avery, Dennis. "Global Warming Benefits Life on Earth." <u>Opposing Viewpoints: Global Warming</u>. Ed. Cynthia A. Bily. Detroit, MI: Thomson Gale 2006. 108-112.

Brown, Alan S. "The Emerging Alternate Energy Consensus." <u>The Bent of Tau Beta Pi</u>. Fall 2008. 16-22.

Holowka, Taryn. "The LEED Rating System Helps Create Greener Buildings." <u>Opposing Viewpoints: Eco-architecture</u>. Ed. Cristina Fisanick. New York, NY: Green Haven Press, Inc., 2006. 147-153.

Musica, Frank. "Eco-Architecture Can Be Risky for Business." Opposing Viewpoints: Eco-architecture. Ed. Christine Fisanick. New York, NY. Green-Haven Press, Inc. 2006. 40-45.

ORIGINAL POEM: CARBON FOOTPATH

Alternative methods are useful and practical.

Houses are curious about prices.

Economy hears the usual thing.

Environment sees the potential impact

Global climate change needs appropriate action.

Alternative methods are useful and practical.

Houses pretend to be useful in very situation.

Environments feel different no matter what people say.

Houses touch caring people.

People worry about themselves and not the environment.

Pollution cries to be sustained.

Houses pretend to be useful in every situation.

Government understands how theory is false.

Pollution says stop worrying.

People dream of a safe air to breathe.

The environment tries to save the creatures.

Al Gore hopes in a different way than most government officials.

Government understands how theory is false.

FILM ANALYSIS: THE 11TH HOUR

Part of the English Composition portfolio project included choosing a film that fit the scope of the research project, watching it and writing an analysis of the paper. This is a much more active process than simply viewing the film as a piece of entertainment.

Background Information About the Environmental Crisis

Does protecting our environment fall into the category of responsibility? It most certainly does. Does it fall into the category of morality? We can theorize that some atheists have stronger morals than some who practice religion. I'm not saying that atheists are smarter, or care where they are going after they die (perhaps because they know where they are going, the ground). The philosopher Kant would agree when I say we need to model ourselves after something greater than our expectations and values. In other words, living in the present moment is the only way to get to the future. This means we can and must fix the earth.

Let me suppose the position of a third party who is neither for global warming nor against it. Could it be possible for advocates like Al Gore to win people's hearts and change things while not intruding on America's well being and other countries' privacy? In other words, "no matter whether we look at it from the point of view of a Texas oilman or an environmentalist, something has to change" (Brown 22).

The earth needs help. It sustains us but we don't always recognize this. We are commercialized and have an ideology that is selfish. Sometimes change needs to happen. Again, a little bit of Kant's philosophy; you rationally can only be doing one or the other (in this case, in favor of helping the environment or continuing on the same path of harming the environment). I'm assuming wars were fought for the protection of family, country, and God. All not in vain, I hope. The battle for the environment is just as important.

If we changed our country's contribution to global warming (35%-40% of the world's global warming) we could eventually sway other countries to do the same thing. People have individual rights, though. There are also tax breaks for going green. This is how the federal government can effect change, in a good way, mind you. The reason it is currently more expensive to build green is because there are new products to be developed and manufactured. There is a learning curve. As of now it is still very expensive to go solar.

Helping the environment has become a moral imperative. Since global warming and dwindling natural resources are both huge considerations, homes must be built with this in mind. If you are going to mandate environmentally friendly houses, then you must make them affordable. The government must play a big role in this by continuing tax breaks for businesses and homeowners that use solar and other alternative sources of energy. Environmentally friendly homes need to be even more affordable than the non-environmentally friendly homes on the market today, in order to shift demand.

Analysis of the Film

The film that I studied is related to my topic of sustainable homes. It is entitled *The 11ᵗʰ Hour*. It was narrated and produced by Leonardo DiCaprio. The film relates to my topic because it is important to understand the motivation behind the build green movement, in order to determine whether there should be a shift in how society decides to design their homes. I want to find out how to change the direction of consumerism and at the same time make homes affordable, comfortable to live in, and still build them with sustainability as the goal. Thus, it is essential to address sustainable energy and environmental concerns. The movie addressed several global warming issues, such as pollutants that leak into the air and water, population management, and energy shortages. It supports the idea that homes and businesses can reduce their dependency on oil, power, and transportation. We will be killing two birds with one stone if we all forced government to pass laws that ensure the environmental future of our planet. Living with sustainable homes and getting our power from technology put to good use will actually make us more comfortable.

The film is presented in an informational lecture style. The movie takes the side supporting environmentalism. It was not a balanced movie with pros and cons. It was meant to ridicule anyone who did not agree with the environmentalist standpoint. It brings to light the concept that the small things we do as humans can help us accomplish great things. The creation of the Smart Car and the Prius came about partly because of the demand we put on car manufacturers as consumers.

One part of the firm directly showed the attacks the environmentalist movement receives. The film kept comparing humans to nature. The New York Times actually ridiculed this portion of the film, "even a magical-mushroom guy goes through the arguments, presents the data, and criticizes the anti-green faction" (Dargis p. 2). For example, there was a man who got high on a hallucinogenic mushroom in the rain forest. The tribes in the rain forest wanted him to see the visions of nature. The man later explained that through his experience he realized that plants as simple as grass have the same intelligence as humans, in that to do the job of photosynthesis it has to create electrical signals. The reference to this event would have us believe that plants and humans have a similar intelligence, excluding the brain. Our chemical and electrical systems respond similarly. The lesson here is that nature protects us.

This 2007 film was written and directed by Nadia Conners and Leila Conners Petersen. The way the DVD case shows an encrusted footprint on earth's surface creates a sense of urgency. The New York Times called it a "surprisingly affecting documentary about out environmental calamity" (Dargis 2). The camera angles made you want more of the gorgeous views. This was because the beautiful landscape looked significantly better after seeing the destruction done to planet earth. The lighting seemed natural. The designs for new architecture had small print for labeling. This made me want to re-read them or watch the film again. The music seemed to be dark, but also new age and peaceful when it was needed. When the various experts were given center stage to talk about their specialty, a blue or green backdrop was used to symbolize planet earth. After a topic was complete, Leonardo DiCaprio would then introduce each new topic. The sequencing helped me to focus on the film by allowing me, the viewer, to feel entertained. I was entertained in two ways. The sorrowful parts made me want a happy conclusion. The happy, informative ways we can change the planet gave me hope to be part of our finest moment.

Conclusion

The movie provides scientific research to back up its claims. It also points the consumer/viewer onto a path to easily make a global difference. "Scientists, environmentalists, authors, academics, and activists weigh in on topics that go well beyond global warming in examining the scale of the footprint humanity has made" (Crust 1). Architecture and home design must go hand in hand with environmental concerns in regard to sustainable energy and global warming. The homes must be affordable for the homeowner. "Homer thinks that home should be entangled with its environment" (Duran and Hosey 6). Would it really be hard, then, for humans to create greener houses, cars, and commercial buildings? Of course it is challenging, but it is doable.

On the flip side, freedom of choice needs to be intact in order for the majority of people to be on board. How do experts weigh in on the subject of homes, architecture, and the environment? Should the architect focus on the nature around it? "Thoreau says a house does not become a home through dramatic design, but through profound empathy between people and place" (Duran and Hosey 6). This is true even more so today than in Thoreau's time.

"Ayn Rand says that the home is a place or vessel for the self. She says the designer house has become an excuse to live out the architect's dreams, not accommodate those of the client or community" (Duran and Horsey, 7). It is obvious to me that in light of environmental concerns, and the need for sustainable energy and other sustainable home building products, that home design and home architecture need to be changed from the current ways to more responsible ways. Re-thinking what types of products are used in the design and structure of today's home is the environmentally responsible course of action.

"Connecting to natural flows allows us to rethink everything under the sun: the very concept of power plants, of energy, habitation, and transportation. It means merging ancient and new technologies for the most intelligent designs we have seen. Eco-efficiency is seen as the tool in service to a larger vision, not a goal in itself" (McDonough and Braungart 130—131).

References

Brown, Alan S. "The Emerging Alternate Energy Consensus." <u>The Bent of Tau Beta Pi</u>. Fall 2008. 16-22.

Crust, Kevin. "Movie Review – The 11th Hour." Los Angeles Times. 17 Aug. 2007:
   <u>http://www.calendarlive.com/movies/reviews/cl-et-hour17aug17,0,2830729.story</u>.

Dargis, Manohla. "Movie Review – The 11th Hour." New York Times 17 Aug. 2007:
   <u>http://www.movies.nytimes.com/2007/08/17/movies/17hour.html</u>.

Duran, Sergi Costa and Lance Hosey. <u>Green Homes: New Ideas for Sustainable Living</u>. New York: Collins
   Design, 2007.

<u>The 11th Hour</u>. Dir. Leila Conners Petersen and Nadia Conners. Nar. Leonardo DiCaprio. 2007. DVD.
   Warner Video.

McDonough, William and Michael Braungart. <u>Cradle to Cradle: Remaking the Way We Make Things</u>. New
   York: North Point Press, 2002.

LOGOS/PATHOS/ETHOS: TOPIC ANALYSIS

The purpose of this assignment was to analyze my topic from three different perspectives.

Logos

Advocates of nuclear power say that "nuclear power can provide the largest amount of electricity to the U.S. without contributing to climate change" (Weeks). Opponents argue we don't have long-term policies to manage the nuclear waste problems. Advocates of nuclear power are quick to point out that the potential nuclear waste problem in the U.S. comes from the fact that the nuclear power plants are not allowed to recycle the nuclear waste as they do in France. The Energy Information Administration (EIA) says there will be more demand in the future than actual nuclear energy available. Too many errors already exist in the plants. The EIA says the nuclear power is clean, but has a shortage for availability in the future. My assessment is that we should all be willing to defend our freedoms. Planet Earth gives us our identity.

Pathos

"Adding expensive and unnecessary subsidies to a global warming bill doesn't increase support for doing something about the issue" argues PIRG's Aurilio (Weeks 6). Although environmentalists agree with this thinking, I stand separate from them. Most churchgoers are urged by their leaders to give up many bad things. Now British bishops say to give up carbon emissions and change everything to become energy efficient. "Richard Chartes says that we all have a pivotal role to play" (Weeks 2/29/08 1).

I think for the sake of solving global warming we need to allow all countries to build nuclear power plants, not just our allies. In the area of managing nuclear power plants, taking rules from the rule-givers ensures success. Since the rule givers are at least partially involved, a line can become blurred between normal behavior and criminal behavior. Is technology exceeding the mind of man? Wars are fought over land in the interests of human domination, not the union of nature and man. Can we really stop people like terrorists from doing what they want to do? I think that's a really good question. My conclusion is that energy policy needs to supersede the politics of any particular country.

Ethos/Experts

Experts agree that nuclear power is an excellent alternative to coal burning sources of electricity so that CO_2 emissions are reduced. Enormous fines are paid at nuclear power plants. Nuclear energy critics say "the Nuclear Regulatory Commission is not aggressive enough at regulating the industry. In early 2006, the owners from Ohio's plant agreed to pay a $28 million fine to escape criminal prosecution" (Weeks 3/10/06

3). This attitude generally assumes out-of-sight out of mind. Obviously, nuclear power plants need constant oversight.

A Personal Note

Clearly this is a moral issue. It is also an ethical issue, as science has its place. The most important thing for me is our government and its relation to others, for this defines our modern morality. Our ecological economic situation has lasted this far because it has been slow and steady. Maybe our wallets are crying out for change. Even the least of us can see humans and technology have a link, just like humans and global issues. Now is the time to plug technology into the equation, but only if it seeks global change as an end.

Works Cited

Weeks, Jennifer cqexpress2/29/08 p 1

Weeks, Jennifer, cqpress 3/10/06 p.1and 3

WESTERN CIVILIZATION

ANALYSIS AND APPLICATION OF CONCEPTS

History Appraisal Assignments: These assignments consisted of answering various questions through analyzing the text and synthesizing the concepts within the course with concepts previously learned. This is the key to demonstrating knowledge and understanding of the concepts to your professor. Professors are looking for more depth than a simple restatement of the textbook and class lectures.

Contrast Napoleon Bonaparte with Adolf Hitler and explain why one dictator was a "builder of civilization" whereas the other was a "destroyer, even of his own people".

Napoleon and Hitler both came into power when their county's economy was in shambles. France was in bad shape as a result of the French Revolution and Germany as a result of World War I and the reparations. Napoleon was a dictator of a civilization and Hitler was a destroyer of one. Napoleon studied many things in his youth. He never used his power for his own evils. History and math were his best subjects in school. Hitler did not do well in math. On the other hand, Hitler was very smart. However, he never used rational thoughts for the good of his men, rather it was all for his own glory. His selfishness stemmed from his intense hatred for the Jews. He blamed the Jews for all of the troubles that Germany had.

Napoleon used his almost perfect photographic memory in forming strategies. He used his understanding of mathematics to make sure things would work. Hitler could not use or exploit this skill. At the age of 27 Napoleon had all of the French army under his control because of his intelligence. Napoleon was able to gain power and have the people in accord with his will because of the general principles he was seeking to accomplish. These principles were legal equality, religious toleration and economic freedom.

In contrast, Hitler did not seek any of these principles. Part of Hitler's philosophy was to say that no foreign person was to be given a chance to serve his country. He also decided that none of the people that serve their country would have special rights. This meant that everyone was the same in his control, but no free enterprise.

Eventually he combined his hatred for the Jews along with socialism. He used everything to create chaos. He used lies and propaganda to create fear. He divided the people and turned them against each other through fear. He used this fear to control the people and advance his cause, which was to murder all of the

Jews. Napoleon used common military strategies to make the empire greater (and larger). He persuaded his people using his intelligence, not creating fear. Plus, Napoleon didn't go haywire and try to exploit the fact that the French people might have gone through difficulties in order to get them on his side.

In this age of Enlightenment, Napoleon was defeated by nationalism and the intense guarding of Great Britain as an island. No matter how smart Napoleon and Hitler were, it was clear that they didn't get enough people on their side for total domination. In the case of Hitler, most of the world eventually fought against his armies and his cause. Even after all this time, when so many people think of Germany, they think of Hitler's atrocities. This is proof of the destruction of that civilization. In the case of Napoleon, because of his egotism, eventually the brotherhood of the French middle class along with Great Britain held down Napoleon's armies. This did not destroy their civilization, however.

Explain what conditions were ripe for the Industrial Revolution to begin in England before its spread to the rest of the world? Why did China and Russia ignore it for so long?

The main Industrial Revolution included the beginning of Great Britain's largest producers in goods and the wealthiest countries in the world at that time. The agricultural practices changed because of an ingenious idea to switch crops in rotation according to the field and soil. In addition, they could be more efficient in their farming. Thus, the society in Great Britain became less agrarian, and people began to move to the cities. This gave Great Britain more workers for factories. Great Britain was a huge importer of raw materials from other countries. These goods were turned into manufactured goods in British factories. There were many inventions developed and used to manufacture goods in the factories.

The use of capital (money) in Great Britain was known because of their banking system. This was a good idea for keeping track of money and transactions. The society was very advanced in their ability to use and invest money. Entrepreneurs were widely known in Great Britain as enjoying wealth and dreamed of being rich. The use of machines and equipment was very much a change from the old labor intensive methods to a capital system based more on money making principles.

There were many natural resources in Great Britain and many places to get them from. The short span of roads to all the major locations made it easy to get supplies. By 1780, roads, rivers and canals were linked by land and by sea. This infrastructure was necessary for the Industrial Revolution to work. Since Great Britain could make more goods than it could use, they had plenty of goods that they could sell to other countries. This brought even more wealth to powerful Great Britain. Other countries were not eager to change their ways to keep up with Great Britain and the Industrial Revolution. Granted, some countries were changing, but others held fast to the agrarian ways and controlling governments.

Russia and China's civilizations were far different from Great Britain. Their societies were still very agrarian. Furthermore both countries were very protective of keeping things the way they were. Russia in the 1800's was run by the Tsar. The people were serfs, and certainly were not moving from the farms to the cities. China was also very agrarian. In order to maintain control over the farmers, the rulers of China and Russia did not want the changes that the Industrial Revolution would bring. In contrast, in Great Britain the government was more than willing to give freedom to businesses and to protect people's property. All of these things were necessary in order for the Industrial Revolution to take hold. Neither Russia nor China was willing to try these things in the early days of the Industrial Revolution.

The period from the Era of Metternich (1815-1830) through the 1850's in Europe was categorized by the rise and development of the "Ism's". What were these "isms", and how do they continue to shape our lives in the Western World even today?

The beginning of the 1850's brought many isms. This means a system or way of doing something, a belief, or an idea. In the era of Metternich, Great Britain, Austria, Prussia and Russia stayed united to gain control after the reign of Napoleon. They met in Vienna to settle on an agreement for their ideas. Metternich was a very prideful man, in my opinion, and very conceited.

Chartism took place in 1838 from the document to demand universal male suffrage. This was payment to the members in Parliament. It was indeed payment for the government, because it created the elimination of property qualifications for members of Parliament. The British were tired of these conditions of work; many British folks signed a petition and gave it to the Parliament saying "Peaceful if we can, forcibly if we must".

Romanticism contained poetic writing and inner feelings of art and self work. Focusing on discovering one's self was common instead of discovering God. Romanticism therefore led to individualism, which carried many if not more of the same self-worth ideas. In Germany the Grimm brothers wrote fairy tales, and Hans Christian Andersen did the same in Denmark. Playwrights and poets all rubbed off on people, and people grew beards and wore outrageous clothing to reinforce their individualism.

Socialism was begun in Europe in the beginning of the 1800's. People got the idea from the Marxist way of belief. This theory basically said "If I can't have it all, no one will". Socialism meant making everyone equal under a supreme ruler, not to enjoy the democratic capitalism, or free enterprise. This socialism was the early stages of communism. The Utopian socialists were very much against free enterprise as well.

Liberalism was a system or idea that began in the 1830's. This was an idea of economics, where the government was allowed to be only in three areas; police, defense of the country, and public works too large for any public citizen to undertake. The idea of this is that if anything should happen to us as citizens, we should be able to take care of it because of the role we play in economics; being free and not controlled by the higher government. Restrictions, yes, but for goodness sakes, no wasting the money!

What was the significance of the Franco-Prussian War of 1870-1871?

The significance of the Franco-Prussian War for western civilization was the loss of power that the French had taken away with the deposed Queen Isabella II. This was in the process of being taken a step further by putting a prince in power over France that had background in the Prussian relatives. It never happened, but the Prussian leader, Bismarck, made an apology from the Prussians seem meaner than it was.

This caused the French to get angry, resulting in the Franco-Prussian War. Bismarck wanted this as an ally to France, because he knew that France was soon to turn because Germany's other allies were not France's allies. Germany then joined with Prussia to fight against France. Napoleon III's army was captured as well. The French empire collapsed. After fighting had stopped, France had to pay Germany $1 billion, and give up some of their land. Otto Von Bismarck had claimed the new French land and stood in Louis XIV's palace, when William I was proclaimed Kaiser. Unity with Prussia and Germany was made merry with both sides and a new way of doing things was brought about to the European people.

During the previous Danish War, the Austrians and Prussians formed an alliance. Bismarck realized that in order for Prussia to expand they needed to exclude Austria. Eventually, Prussia fought against the isolated Austria. Bismarck made this possible through an agreement with Italy. The Franco-Prussian War is important because of the strength that the new republic of Germany gained. They gained land, power and influence. They had new alliances, and France was weakened and vulnerable. In addition, it made the French people very insecure and weakened their country, because of the influence and land that they sought. The strengthened Germany now was in a position of strength in Europe, which later made them able to start World War I.

Describe the universal status of women and work during the 19th Century. How did World War I affect this status?

The role of women in the 19th century was largely dictated by society. Women had been expected to be at home tending to domestic duties. The industrial revolution had opened up factory jobs, but not always for women. However, in some cases, women were able to get jobs. Usually, however, they were in sweatshops. Women's jobs were not that great compared to men's jobs. The presence of women in the workplace simply didn't suit some men who were used to not having women in factories and banks. Personally, I think women should be looked at just like men when it comes to job opportunities. Without women, how could men be established or even created, for that matter?

The fact that women were not even considered for most jobs both before and after World War I was due to the fact that society was just that way. People behave and do things in the way that society is used to doing them. In most situations, hiring women just wasn't done, so it wasn't going to start. In shell factories during World War I, women were needed, because the men were off fighting the war. However, when the men came back, the women were thrown out of work. In my opinion, why hire women if you are going to throw them out later. Each gain that women made was due to things like that. In the late 19th century there was a shortage of men, so women were hired for white collar jobs, but not paid very much. Business owners hadn't hired women before, but now they do because they are desperate. Men needed to fight in the wars, so they had to take women on to fill the jobs. But after the men came home society went back to its ways of selfishness and pride. The "thanks but no thanks" attitude seems to not work too well in times of war. It was the same in the United States. Women were for the most part homemakers, teachers or nurses. Women were just expected to take care of domestic things, which kept them dependent on their fathers or their husbands. They did work in the offices and factories during the World Wars, but that was in the early 20th century.

Great Britain had economic problems, but regained this money after the Industrial Revolution. Great Britain loved money, that's why they taxed the 13 colonies. Power can be good, but God gave this to all people to be free and prosper, which is the foundation of democracy. Trying in the U.S. to keep peace without looking like our armies are trying to take over a country is hard. There is a balance that is hard to keep if a nation is run by a government that still believes in partial enslavement of women, through denying them opportunities. Certain women refused to be part of the women's suffrage movement.

In Russia, women were dealing with a Czarist form of government. Peasants and serfdom was still a part of this unconstitutional monarchy. Neither the men nor the women were doing well economically.

Suffrage became a march through St. Petersburg as we know it today. This contained about 10 thousand women who continued along with Russian soldiers who marched with them in protest.

Alexandra, the wife of the Czar Nicholas II, told him, but by this time the situation was out of control. In a week of this event which yielded International Women's day, the Tsarist regime had fallen apart. So the democrats that had some power made a working government that included some ideas on democracy, civil equality and eight-hour work days.

Describe the conditions in Czarist Russia during Nicholas II's reign and what became of the last of the Romanovs?

In the time when Nicholas II was in power as Czar or Russia, the time was after 1905. His revolution did not bring what Nicholas was looking for, so he had to keep a strong grasp on his country. Peasants were dissatisfied with hours, wages, and equality issues. Meanwhile, Alexandra, his wife, was accused of doing things with a monk named Rasputin. The government thought this man was a holy one (once a peasant), because he alone could cure Nicholas's son Alexis. Too much power was given to Rasputin and too much gossip fell on the Czar's wife. So in December of 1916, Rasputin was killed.

After the revolt against the Czar's government with women and soldiers, his power fell. A new power was created similar to democracy and the American way of government. Although there were still two powers that existed, these two were the Mensheviks and the Bolsheviks. The Mensheviks wanted a system like ours in the West. The Bolsheviks wanted Marxism to prevail because of his search for faith in something after his brother died. In 1917, just when the conflicts of other countries were at a climax, Russia received an idea from Lenin. This was the leader of the party for Socialism. They saw soldiers and workers. These were all they needed to manipulate a wrongful government.

The voting of Lenin and his communists didn't work at all, because of the voter ratio. 225 men were delegates for voting on Lenin's side and 420 were for the Socialist's revolutionary side. The anti-communist group had the upper hand because of the women suffrage revolt, but Lenin was still going to look for a loose end. Power was now in the hands of the new laws and rightful anti-socialist people. A treaty was signed by the upset Lenin for control of all what he previously owned. He said it made no difference because socialism would still prevail.

Civil war broke out in Russia, and the Czar and his wife had the problem of being taken into custody along with their beautiful five children. July 16 was when he and his family and his wife were shot by local soviet army members in Siberia. The communists wanted the Czar out of commission because Nicholas was not a communist. Nicholas II ran a monarchy, which is better than communism. The anti-communists were weak and disjointed. In 1918, the Bolsheviks occupied at least 50% or more of Russia.

At the time of the war with the White Army, the peasants were not happy with the Bolsheviks. A letter was sent to the Bolshevik leaders, addressing a clear distaste and true rage against the harm they had caused to all of mother Russia. Even the factories, heating, and bread making had stopped. People were cut off from everything during their regain of power over the Mensheviks. Another letter says how the Bolsheviks were hired by Nicholas II, but now they go against his form of government to suppress the people and have socialism be the mainstream of government.

What was the genesis of Hitler's Mein *Kampf* and who did he surround himself with to carry out its message of hate and world domination?

The genesis of Hitler's *Mein Kampf* was his intense hatred and mistrust of the Jews. He felt that the time he spent in his studies in Vienna, Austria were largely responsible for how he came to view things for the rest of his life. He was greatly influenced by Georg von Schoenerer, Karl Luger, Adolf Lanz von Liebenfels, the artist Vonotuch, and Richard Wagner. Wagner's main influence on Hitler was on the need to dominate. Obviously, Hitler heard that message!

Georg von Schoenerer is the one who influenced Hitler because of his strong views on uniting all Germans. The power that this would bring to the German people and the appeal to the nationalistic views that were becoming stronger influenced Hitler in how he carried out his plans in the early stages. Hitler could see the importance of having all German-speaking people being united as one country.

Karl Luger impressed Hitler in his ability to move and manipulate people with emotional appeals and propaganda. Obviously, it was a big piece of how Hitler influenced the German people when he became chancellor, but it also influenced Hitler's writings, and made emotionalism as a tool very appealing to Hitler. In addition, since he was a very strong mayor at the time and was popular with his people, Hitler had proof that this method would work.

Adolf von Lanz von Liebenfels is who influenced Hitler to become even more anti-Semitic. Hitler grew to hate the Jews and everyone else that he considered to be inferior. Ultimately this meant anyone who was not Aryan. This racism was the guiding force for every step Hitler took. When Hitler wrote Mein Kampf he laid out very clearly and specifically his plans for himself and the future of Germany. Even though he wrote it all out, and people read it, almost no one thought he would really do it.

He then expanded the Nazi party and brought young people, rural people, and poor people into it. This expanded the party and gave people a voice that had previously been voiceless. This made those people very devoted and loyal to Hitler. When he gained more power, he brought in Herman Goering and gave him lots of power, and he replaced the entire police force. With all of the new Nazis in charge of just about everything, Hitler could then do whatever he chose.

Why was appeasement the initial path diplomats chose to follow with Adolf Hitler? Could the same be said about Iraq?

The Treaty of Versailles had weakened and limited Germany. The rest of Europe and the United States felt that this was necessary after World War I. Germany was allowed only a relatively small army of 100,000, a small navy and an air force consisting of only gliders. Peace was of the utmost importance to Europe, and diplomatic means of solving differences was what countries preferred. There was a great tendency to avoid war at all costs, because of the huge cost in lives, money, and property brought on by World War I. Hitler knew all of this, and he felt that the Treaty of Versailles had been too severe a punishment against Germany. He also felt that he could secretly get away with not following the treaty. So he increased his army to about 500,000 men. Then Hitler announced it to the world.

Great Britain, France, and Italy condemned Germany and Hitler for doing this, but really did nothing about it. Ultimately they went along with Hitler on re-empowering his military. They signed a pact with Germany allowing them to increase the size of their navy. This was really the start of Great Britain's appeasement policy. They believed that if the satisfied Hitler and Germany, Hitler would then be content, and peace would be maintained.

Like a spoiled child, as soon as Hitler got what he wanted, he wanted more. He marched his army into the Rhineland and took it over. Again, Britain felt this was reasonable and did nothing about it. They really believed peace could still be maintained. To help himself, Hitler then made both Italy and Japan into allies. Still, Britain believed the best path was appeasement. At that point, Hitler decided that he wanted Austria. He forced Austria to put Austrian Nazis in charge, and then his troops marched in and took over Austria. Still Britain (and France) felt that they did not need to stop Hitler.

At that point he wanted to take over the Sudetenland of Czechoslovakia. Then the major powers convened in Munich and met Hitler's demands, as they believed he only wanted to reunite more Germans with their motherland. Of course, he then destroyed Czechoslovakia. Now Britain and France knew that Hitler could not be trusted. When he announced he was going to take over Poland, and then marched his troops in, Britain (and France) ended the policy of appeasement under Prime Minister Neville Chamberlain, in a very direct way. They declared war on Germany. They finally knew that you cannot appease someone who is determined to fight. Sir Winston Churchill saw Hitler for what he was – a mad man.

When considering the situation that developed in Iraq, I see similarities. Sadam Hussein was a bloodthirsty tyrant while he was in charge of Iraq. Most of the world felt that they should just stay out of the situation, and that Hussein did not want a war. The people of Iraq, however, may feel differently. The world powers felt that sanctions through the U.N. should be all that should be done. However, Iraq ignored the sanctions and did not allow weapons inspections. The U.S. went to war with Iraq because they said that Iraq was violating the agreements and accumulating weapons of mass destruction. Great Britain went along with us and went to war. France and Germany did not. It turned out there were no weapons to be found. However, the mad man Saddam was removed. World opinion (and now many Americans) says that we should not still be there, and should be handling things diplomatically. So, it looks as though the world still values appeasement and maintaining peace above all.

What new product/ technologies came out of World War II? Illustrate their use in modern day society.

Of course, when most people think of technologies that came out of World War II, they may think of the atom bomb. Robert Oppenheimer is well known as the man behind the bomb. This weapon and technology is till developed and manufactured today with war, death, and destruction as its intended use. However, in addition, nuclear power was also developed. Nuclear power is used in factories and for general power.

Computers were a significant product that came out of World War II. They were at first developed for the military in order to quickly determine firing ranges for weapons. These had been figured manually prior to the invention of computers. Transistors were used in computers. Now of course, silicon chips are used. Technology is constantly changing and improving. The computing capacity of a personal computer of today would have taken up a huge room back when computers were invented. Computers are used everywhere in today's world. They are in cash registers, homes, schools, libraries, cars, and about everywhere else you can think of.

Walkie-talkies were another technology developed because of World War II. These were essential communication tools for the military. They still are. In addition, walkie-talkies are used in businesses, warehouses, by the police and fire fighters, as well as by kids just having fun. The use of walkie-talkies ultimately led to cell phones. Cell phones are everywhere these days and now there are combination cell phones and computers, like the Blackberry.

All kinds of chemicals were developed as a result of World War II. They are used in chemical fertilizers. Some of these caused pollution and were later banned. Chemical warfare is also made possible thanks to the development of chemicals.

From World War II to the present there have been so many new technologies and inventions that have come about because of the innovativeness of the modern day world. The changes in society because of these technological changes have been as far reaching in this age as the Industrial Revolution was in the past.

Why does the Marshall Plan of Post-World War II still serve as a model of what Western Civilization can do today to offset global disasters of nature and/or man's own destruction?

The Marshall Plan was set up to counteract the damage and destruction in Europe from World War II. However, it did not provide any assistance to the Soviet Union. The United States believed that the Soviet Union would more easily spread communism throughout Europe if the European countries couldn't get loans or other help to make things better in their countries. Since the U.S. was helping western European countries, and gaining their loyalty, through millions of dollars in economic support, the Soviet Union began to control the Eastern Bloc countries more tightly. Western Europe, with this help from the United States through the Marshall Plan, returned to solid economies much quicker than the Eastern Bloc countries.

The Marshall Plan is still the model that the United States goes by to help countries in times of need. This is the case with natural disasters like earthquakes, floods and tsunamis. The United States provides loans and other support. This helps those countries deal with disasters. It also makes it more likely that those countries will then think favorably of the United States. Besides that, assisting a country in times of need after a disaster helps us look good in the eyes of many other countries. The United States also still loans countries money to help with their economic problems. This is one way that we remain a super-power. We lend countries money, and it helps them stay on our side. It also creates stronger economies. It helps some countries avoid conflicts, deal with disasters, and helps them solve many other problems.

In what ways have modern music and art brought the world closer together and will this influence carry over to the 21st century that we are currently in?

Modern art was like the modern music, radical experimentation. Most of the music that came after the war was surrealism. This means a compositional method where the order of music is set for values, pitch, loudness and units of time. Punk music was started in Great Britain and this fueled frustration from how things were going too far.

Even people that were educated knew how degenerate society was so they became punk as well. Pure punk was short lived. Music has more power to influence people than any other government, so it does bring people together. Mostly it makes society spiral down in a negative way/attitude. So it brings good and bad. It will only influence large groups of people in a good way if we take out of the Bill of Rights (the freedom of the press and the freedom of speech). I say this because people take their rights too far, and pollute our minds with garbage. But removing these rights will probably not happen in the U.S., at least for a long while.

The Arts were taking many forms in the 1960's and 1970's. Examples of this are radical ideas of rock structures like the spiral jetty and the Piazza d' Italia in New Orleans. The modern art movement was preceded by the neo-expressionism movement. This type of art helped bring some good out of evil by showing the negative effects on Jews by Nazism.

As far as the 21st century is concerned, the arts will both unite and divide people. The arts have always done that, and that will not change. A great unifier for the world has been artistic endeavors like Live Aid and "We are the World". Both of these made millions of dollars that were used to help suffering people.

Why is the International Space Station now being built so important to the future of Planet Earth and its environment? Is it essential that we next go back to the Moon and then on the planet Mars?

It is most thought of that we need to come together to be a people united if we want our future to be prosperous. In order to do this, we must think of the future. The future will consist of going to other planets, for exploration, or perhaps to live. We cannot do this unless we come together (Russia and the United States). We need each other's expertise and money in order for space exploration to be successful. If it is all competition, then war could result from space exploration, and we already have enough war going on here on the ground. The more programs or projects that the major powers of the world can cooperate on, the better it is for the world. When great minds come together, amazing things can happen.

I believe it is imperative that we go back to the moon and Mars to re-explore. We could find different things this time. New research could be done to stop war and natural disaster such as tornados, earthquakes, and global warming. (However, in my opinion, global warming isn't as huge a threat as people are saying it is). There are always more scientific projects and experiments to conduct. It is a very good thing that the big countries are working together on the Space Station project.

- 5 -

CRIMINOLOGY

Criminology taught me how crime is studied and how crime statistics are determined. The professor had been the chief of police for a town in Illinois.

What do we mean by the "sociological perspective"? How does this perspective help us to understand the origins of crime and possible ways of reducing crime?

The sociological perspective is the way we are all social beings. Crime is based on religion, race, and the poverty levels where people are located. This helps us to understand crime in a social origin. We can stop crime by looking deeper into past crimes, as well as how and why social levels of deviance escalated into crime.

In what ways are the disciplines of sociology and criminology relevant for each other?

Both criminology and sociology have similar disciplines in the study of both of them. Both have tests done to uncover the reasons for why our natures are leaning to evil and what can be done to prevent unwanted chaos. Criminology relies on the knowledge of how a society works.

What are the advantages and disadvantages of using surveys to understand crime and other social phenomena?

The advantages of using surveys to find out about crime and other social phenomena are numerous. People can gain information and use less money to perform mailed questionnaires. Telephone interviews can provide valuable information from foreign countries. Recording data to determine the statistics like suicide can be very useful to stopping crime. Studying crime trends can provide ideas for types of crime that need focus and attention. Developing new laws that benefit everyone can also happen. Durkheim also did a study to get results. This can be, in my opinion, a little trickier than surveys or interviews.

Disadvantages of using surveys generally include the same risks as there are with any test of human behavior. The questions can be hard or confusing to answer. If the survey is flawed, the answers will be. For example, for a survey about violence, the person may have to answer something that is only on the list of selections. In addition, people being surveyed may lie to protect themselves from punishment.

56

What are the three legal defenses to criminal liability? Do you think these defenses should exist, or do you think they have been exploited by criminal defendants?

Duress, entrapment and ignorance are all defenses to criminal liability. I think duress and entrapment are good defenses, but ignorance of the law is no excuse. The reason for this is that everyone could use that defense, whether it was for drugs, violence, or even passing in a school zone in the state of Arizona.

Explain the UCR- NIBRS systems for crime reporting

NIBRS is better in the broader sense in finding data for crime reports. Comparisons are presented in what can be learned from police data and not other sources. Some problems occur in the NIBRS, in how data is designed, organized, and produced.

The UCR began in 1929 and is part of the FBI. The UCR collects data about crimes reported to the police. In 1982, the FBI sponsored a study of the UCR so they could revise and update it for the 21st Century. This five year redesign effort brought about the NIBRS. The NIBRS collects data on each reported crime incident. Before, authorities gathered crime information by type and sent it to the FBI, but under the NIBRS, all accounts are individually recorded. The UCR provides limited information on the eight Part I Crimes including: homicide, forcible rape, robbery, aggravated assault, burglary, larceny-theft, motor vehicle theft, and arson. UCR provides limited information about offenses. They are more generalized than the NIBRS.

The NIBRS provides the FBI with offenses from a list of 43 individual offenses, 8 Part I crimes, and 11 lesser offenses. Information will have multiple victims and offenders. Locations will be kept on record, and so will small details, like a perpetrator being a stranger. The UCR only gets detailed information for homicides. Weapons used in rape are not recorded, but are in the NIBRS system.

In 1994, software was designed for the 75 agencies involved that converted LIBRS to NIBRS. The states also provided the agencies tools for more enhancements. A big benefit of NIBRS is that it enables the state program to transform the NIBRS incident reports to summary formats. This is useful in comparing old UCR patterns to the NIBRS data. The easier training that is a result of the simplification to one system leads to more confidence in the accuracy of local data. Many officers feel that the NIBRS is more user-friendly and more comprehensive. After the implementation of NIBRS, agencies found that officers logged the same amount of mileage while it lowered the crime rate. Detectives felt they had better follow-up information, and most NIBRS data is accessible in the police vehicles as well.

Police agencies saw an eye-opening difference in how to separate call for service versus actual crimes and traffic violations. The detailed information can help spot dangerous patterns early on. NIBRS is also a tool that can help build more crime investigative structures in the future. Still, in different states in the U.S., the incidents are sorted by type, but highly informative reports are far better than just categorizing crimes. NIBRS views all of a crime's components as an incident, and therefore is more efficient. In contrast, UCR only captures and lists Part II offenses if there is an arrest.

Background, heredity, and hormones as an explanation for crime

Sigmund Freud, the founder of psychoanalysis came up with the concept of the id, the ego and the superego. The id was based on the wants, both physical and mental, that was given to every human at birth. The ego is a sense of right and wrong based on rules and restrictions. This is connected to the id. The superego is a moral aspect on the human nature. If Freud's analysis is right, then our lives are shaped by these unconscious forces. Freud further says that the ego is the conscious mind. Knowing what the law is, and the consequence of breaking the law is a big factor in the human psyche. The primary motivation is "will I get in trouble?" when examining the ego. Subconscious feelings come from both the superego and the id. The moral codes and instincts that we were born with lie underneath the conscious mind, but they become more developed throughout life.

Bad things, images or situations can happen to a person. For example a violent upbringing has a lifelong effect on a person. Bad situations or events go into the subconscious and often do cause criminal behavior later in the person's life. The person might not have had the urge to engage in criminal behavior if other situations in his life had not gone wrong. People's behaviors are based on personality, how they think, act and feel. If a person has aggressive genes, he or she is more likely to commit a violent crime than someone who is not carrying violent genes. Argument says this anyway. However, a teenager with a tremendous amount of hormones, combined with a bad behavior or thinking process can be enough to send him over the edge unexpectedly. Bad behaviors and decisions can lead to a warped sense of ego, and thus make the person feel that he is above the law. When feeling above the law, a person can no longer decide to live with a sound foundation of principles and morals. Again, the roots of the person's criminal behavior began with his psychological condition.

Economic problems like poverty and welfare can make hope hard to find in the generation we have now. This hopelessness has led to poor psychological development, and warped morality, which leads to criminal behavior. Some crime occurs out of sheer desperation, such as an out of work person stealing food to feed his family. People need to have a sense of well-being and to be at peace. We all want peace, but some seek peace in illegal things. If the individual wants a bad thing from early on in life, then someone needs to be there, making sure that person will change his behavior. Rehabilitation can be a great tool. Some people, on the other hand, are not willing to admit they have a problem. They then subconsciously remain on the fringe of a mental disorder, and continue their criminal behavior.

Maturity and hormones don't fully form until around 21 years of age. Hormones automatically cause greater alertness in the body, which in turn makes it harder to sleep. People who have a job and school may be overloaded. This can affect their psychological condition, and decision making, too.

Psychological factors contribute to all of human behavior, including criminal behavior. Statistics show that more African Americans are arrested than whites. Lower income neighborhoods with single-parent homes are more likely to have higher crime rates. This is because of economic factors, but also because there aren't enough positive role models around. Many families have multiple generations of criminals. As these children are growing up, and their minds, morals and decisions are formed, they see bad decisions being made, and no good decisions. They begin to think of this as normal, and therefore "inherit" criminal behavior patterns. Overall, criminal behavior is largely caused by psychological factors, as well as heredity and hormones. Rehabilitation of the criminal needs to include addressing the psychological factors that helped to cause the behavior.

Self Control Theory

Self Control theory states clearly why crime is committed in social structures. The way parents put responsibility on to a child is going to affect a response from the child on different situations, according to Michael Gottfredson and Travis Hirschi. Evaluating this theory is like evaluating Sigmund Freud. Gottfredson and Hirschi have good points, but there are also loopholes as well. People do change over time. Deviance can be eliminated entirely from forces in our society. For example in areas such as employment, marriage and relationships, deviance can enter in or be eliminated. I believe this is a part of why people commit crime, but not the only reason.

I believe that even though a person might have a huge amount of self-control, the person might still commit an illegal act. This fact makes many aspects of the self-control theory invalid. Some peoples' spontaneous or extreme behavior may be illegal and to the rest of society these people appear to be without self-control. These people become criminals and over a period of time develop a malformed conscience. If a person *doesn't believe* that his behavior is bad, then the behavior is normal to him, thus creating no need for self-control, at least in his mind. However, to the petty offender, a great deal of self-control is thus required.

Controlling oneself is very important and necessary in order for communities to be crime free and for the economy to flourish. The definition of self-control changes slightly, resulting in the lack of self-control that criminals have as far as the non-criminals are concerned. But they might think other things for their lack of norms or anomie would be hard to abstain from. For normal law abiders, self-control can be reflected in things such as not running lights and not breaking the speed limit. In contrast, the hardened criminal wonders whose house to rob, or who he is going to murder first. In my view, both are using self-control, but the hardened criminal has what most people would consider a complete lack of self-control.

The reasons people commit crime might differ, but the outcome is still the same. For the equations in math to be a function, there can only be one y or output for the one input or x value in order for it to be called a function. In order for society to function, there can only be one legal system and everyone must follow it to obey the law. So many reasons, like ignorance of the law may be used as excuses; but the law has been broken, thus making the action illegal, criminal, and punishable.

If there are many routes to the same law or statute, then you can have relativism instead of an efficient system. Relativism can become chaos. Self-control is really defined by the norm of society. If the generally accepted norm is distorted, then there is a problem. This is why we need to conform to the norm established by the government. This assumes that the government is making good laws and exercising self-control. The lack of a norm is rebellion. Everyone would define what self-control is. This is not bad, but as Durkheim said we need the barrier of government to keep ourselves in check through the free will of self-control. We are one nation under God, and that implies knowledge of morals. There is one legal system for everybody, resulting in freedom and many good things. But a line must divide what is right and wrong. Each person's self-control should help ensure that the laws are followed. Checks and balances are very healthy for society. Crime keeps the law in check and therefore we pay taxes to support that democracy. The law keeps crime in check. Without checks and balances and accountability, chaos begins. Then lack of self-control spreads and fascism could begin.

Arguing for the Illegality of Recreational Drugs

The importance of ending this culture of drugs is to first end the routes in which people get drugs into this country. Efforts are always being made to stop this. It's hard to argue for the extreme control of drugs when the violence and rape are so prominent in society. But drugs can fuel this. For example; legal drugs most likely get a person caught in a downward spiral or in the under the table money. Obviously some things are not going to be evident to the user. He becomes infused with culture of greed, money, and drugs. The game is played not always a pleasant way. This could cause major problems at home or at work. Fear would be used to almost keep you doing it, (because the dealers want your money), and not to do the right thing. They don't usually press you but you are wanted for their business. On the flip side, as a buyer of legal drugs the only bad things are irresponsibility with drunk driving. Most 21 year olds can handle this beverage. Recreational drugs such as marijuana, crack cocaine, and heroin need to remain illegal in this country.

We must not end up like Amsterdam. If legalization of this drug were to happen we could tax the users and buyers immensely like the cigarette tax. Still this would be immoral and would open all kinds of doors elsewhere for illegal activity. Taxing would not solve the problem because people would still get angry and commit other crimes in order to get the money. If drugs were legalized even more people would use them. This has been the pattern for tobacco, caffeine, and alcohol. Drugs have always been a part of society and are therefore hard to eliminate. Almost 50% of Americans have tried drugs once in their life. The others are the regular users. 80% of drug arrests are for use not for selling. This means there are a lot of dealers but also a lot more users than dealers/users.

I think to stop the problem the police should ask users the name and location of the dealers in exchange for a lesser sentence or for first time users the punishment should be a couple of months in a rehab with a counselor. Then if the person screws up once more lock him up for good. This may provide a better way to stop the dealing and to give the kids a chance with first time offending. This would create a communal bond with the society we live in and the police. I think drug laws should remain very strict but also give first time offenders a break. Why wait to find out if the kid will change in 2 years if he can be persuaded to do it in several months. For first time offenders they are going to probably continue to screw up if that's what they intend to do. Cut the wondering time in half and see if they are a real person of character. If not, that's one less criminal on the street. Strict but fair is the best way to deal with the situation. How far you can limit sentencing and be reasonable is a good question. Long term users may not cooperate with information unless given a lesser sentence. I think the judgment of the legal system will prevail.

PHILOSOPHY: YOU CAN UNDERSTAND THIS!

POSITION PAPER: DEATH PENALTY EXAMINATION

This paper explores the argument involving whether the death penalty could possibly be ethical. The pro-life position is that death is presumed to be a natural process, as is life. The Oxford Dictionary states that ethics relates to morals. Are persons, then, expendable using the death penalty? The answer to this must be developed exploring the various philosophical theories, in order to understand the reasons behind the value of persons and the role of government.

Where does this value exist in the human person? Are ethics relative if they come from distorted human nature, rooting from God originally? Are humans capable of ideals that are universal? To answer this, I will begin with an example of utilitarianism. Suppose this semi-relativist view was applied to a world with no God or Creator at all, for argument's sake. The function of things, according to John Stuart Mill, would still work better if all creatures were treated in the way that they know is right. It would be in the best interest of the people. Utilitarianism uses as its guiding force whatever will bring the most happiness to the most people. Thus, utilitarianism would state that the death penalty would be appropriate, as the death of the convicted heinous criminal would supposedly bring happiness to the rest of the people, because they would no longer face the threat of that person.

Universalists state that there are overriding universal principles common to most religions that basically define our existence. Furthermore, these principles should define our decisions and the way we live. If creation were mere chance, then it still would be just that. It would still be something. I will agree, in that we are free to make choices, but we don't have the freedom to stop making choices altogether. Just as with universals, we need a point of reference, or a base, to make sure human persons are incommunicable in every way and aren't connected to chance or arbitrary existence.

We can use deism and natural physical laws to form a solid argument. Deism focuses on natural human experience and science rather than teachings and scripture. God might have left us on our own after creation. His ultimate incommunicability suggests that it is in His best interest to want to share the experience with someone. With Deism, people's own experience of God completely defines their knowledge of Him. Thus, specific teachings and commandments wouldn't define people's stance for or against the death penalty. I think this can gradually evolve into the moral relativism which is quite prevalent in our society today.

The Platonic view and school of thought looks at government with a critical eye. It is well known that Plato felt that it is better to be ruled by a bad tyrant than by a bad democracy. However, Hitler proved that although he was the bad tyrant, actually the cooperation of the rest of the people is what enabled him to accomplish great evil.

God's nature is incommunicable. He has specific attributes that He did not pass on to us. However, there are many attributes we were created with that come directly from Him. Thus, I understand that our nature is derived from our being and not from our ideals. Our ideals commune with our personhood. We have a disordered passion and Eros and nature, but we still should punish the wicked. I agree thus far. I think that our attempt at truth and goodness from the universals is there, but we can't achieve it. I haven't made an argument in this, just an observation. Tying into my argument, I don't see a person having separations from their being. Body and soul are one, and if the soul is meant for immortality, how can one use a set list of rules for the material world that denies the immortality of the soul? This means that we must not use the death penalty. These rules assume that incommunicability comes from our unique nature and personhood which God endowed in us.

I'm not being dualistic, but I think it unfair to have the natural order of the cosmos be sustained if the government was expected to serve the natural order of the cosmos and intellectual or personal rights and dignities. So let's say it's not the job of the government to do these things, but you still say that it is fundamentally wrong. Well, fundamentally wrong things could not exist with the creation of good laws using reasoning and sense to counteract bad excuses for laws, and vice versa as well. Laws have to make sense and be ethical to be a valid law. Using the chicken before the egg argument doesn't work here, because we are talking about natural laws with the boundaries and constraints of time. Thus, before passing a law the underlying ethics must be concerned. Do the ends justify the means?

The only way to use our intellect or psyche is to perceive things through the natural world, which means that the temptations we all go through can be seen equal to the decisions that we make. One could not exist without the other. If our senses were deceiving us, this would also not work, because that would take away our option for an all-good and ethical God, or concept of the person in an ultimate ontological sense. The parts of a person (or of God) cannot exist on their own, separate from the whole.

The government can "get away" with killing if it is in the name of protection, freedom or justice, but they are lacking something they see in the natural order of society. This is taking your natural order jargon, and saying that wrong and right are on the same plane for a moment. The danger in keeping right and wrong on the same level is that natural order works because according to John Mill, men treat everyone with their best interest in mind, regardless of morals. So nature needs a Creator, but doesn't need the human person to claim ethical order to prevail. Love was what put us here, and love is a decision, which I will get into later in my argument.

Although people are irrational, and looking out for their own agendas, I can see that an unethical law can be created for an ethical reason. I think that necessary evil exists. If humans are incommunicable, then looking at a non-religious scenario will help us understand something. Let's say that our values and dignity are incommunicable. How can the death penalty laws that were made by few represent the masses, especially the people that don't agree with killing no matter what the reasons are? Well, by nothing more than keeping the good and the bad in society in line; protection of the weak and innocent. If not taking a moral position is unethical, the people can change the laws. But our empirical goodness calls into question how we as a people become swayed by excuses. This impairs reason.

If we assume that ethics were needed to stop chaos and evil, this means that there is a universal good and that good existed before evil. Summed up, I would say that this disproves the concept of the equality of good and evil, and the fact that it is necessary to suggest it has an Eros for the forms; furthermore, if evil was necessary, and then all evil would have to be necessary. Good and evil cannot be, and are not, equal.

Defining evil and safety is relative. Even in a world of no God, natural law reveals a sense of affinity. Evil is similar but is universal. Taboo and law show how we feel about what is evil. They are our points of reference. Killing in order to create a supposedly safer world via the death penalty can achieve that end. In a way it contains dignity in that it is making a point to criminals through the use of natural deterrence. Can God accept our concepts of safety and evil if He knows that we have a fallen nature? The answer is that He cannot fundamentally do this, because He is all good, truthful, and fundamentally incommunicable. Therefore, He can understand, but He does not accept.

The problem again is that media doesn't accurately cover these death penalty deaths, which could work in favor of the argument. Natural deterrence is different from the impact of seeing a cop pull over a speeder. Morality is a concept that exists without approval from the government. The government should be a vehicle or a means to a desired end. There will always be an authority over us. This is good and necessary.

Christian teaching need not be applied in order to prove that natural order makes a good point. This is the point that when one species is on top of the food chain, it won't be that way forever. The reason would be either through extinction or lack of survival skills due to climate change or other acts. We, however, are not animals and have a different telos than them. We could use the atheist as an example of the government. It fails to consider the moral aspect of death. The goal of having safer societies may be an elusive goal. Do we really want morality in the government? Governments deal with money, power, war, taxes, and death. There needs to be a group like the government to keep us protected and to let us protect ourselves.

The Cappadocia Fathers' view was that the concept of a person is an ontological one in the ultimate sense. The real unethical thing to do is to look at human life and its values of ontology through the eyes of ethics. For example, doctors who perform abortions are not right, but no one is. Some just have a little better understanding than others.

The analysis is that if humans stopped obeying the laws, or the government changed its laws every time an irritation occurred, then there would be no consistency. Thanks to democracy, however, we have the opportunity for a frequently changing society, or system of laws. Changing keeps the checks and balances, even though the results might not be fair to some. Using the word fair implies that the root of goodness is root goodness in our world. Human ethics is needed to make all other forms of goodness possible.

The best argument for the natural dignity is that we are living in a time where we admit our own faults, and this leads to no one else but God on the table of incommunicable hierarchy. The inclusion of God is the only way to justly handle the government. We are part of this and so our incommunicability can start to be understood. Evil will always win if good is absent. But good cannot exist without reasons.

This statement supposes that God is all good and that in order to increase human progression and not hinder it, one must see that we are all, in fact, incommunicable. Since this is so, we often see the government first and ourselves last. Seeing the government in an extreme good way or bad way reveals traits that make the person feel a certain way. It can, however, open us up to twist our own concept of truth. Persons cannot exist in isolation. God isn't alone either. Love is not a feeling, but a breaking down one person's will to submit to the other. It is the other people around us and our otherness that gives us a point of reference.

Ontological irreplaceable entities are what humans do and are. Personal identity can only exist where love is freedom and freedom is love. One cannot replace a person but just the communicable nature or species. Human nature is inseparable from its person and dignity.

These points all dovetail to the summary of my argument. What if the government does not know how bad the death penalty is? This still means that their decision is wrong and flawed. Ignorance is no excuse. Everything happens for a reason, so does reason include itself to wrongful acts? Yes, but you need truth and goodness in order for there to be the ethics of the human person. It seems to me that people who are criminals became criminals when they wouldn't conform to the laws of society; but actually they can't conform for various reasons. It also seems such an extreme case of two wrongs making a right. With this mentality, it shows that power from the higher authority (laws) can make people afraid to speak out against the authority. So if someone puts a needle into another human to kill them, and the knowledge was there that the person to be killed wanted to die because of painful cancer or some deadly disease, could an exception be made to end the life without euthanasia coming into play? This is where a third thing needs to arise that is greater than both acts. If love lacks knowledge, then it is not loving to end the agony of the possibly innocent man or dying man on death row. I can also see how a possible duress by a corrupt government would excuse the killing of another person.

Ethics derived from personhood and ideals looks at truth and goodness through the lens of the incommunicable person. The question is: how does one separate any person from their being? The answer is that you cannot. We cannot be separated from our essence, our souls, what makes us created in the image of God.

Laws are inherently subject to change. Laws reflecting humans show weakness. Distorted laws or wrong laws don't count for laws at all, and yet they still need to be followed. Greek example shows that we are all part of a whole. Plato mentions that natural order and proper behavior might prevail through justice that holds the universe together. Thus, our Incommunicable Individual Dignity must be preserved.

Affinity says that the universals all are good and true. A material ball is different than a human person in that nature and intellect are composite and are held higher than animals. If we suppose there is a God, then we must say that a ball must be geared toward a higher universal. God cannot make bad forms even if He tried. It goes against His nature to create without value or meaning. Let's suppose God created one globe. The globe would derive its goodness from God. So, though a ball comes from a rubber factory and a tree, there is a starting point of creation for all of these particulars that roots back to the universal forms. Parts must come from non-parts. Our parts exist through universal force. Our psyche is our life force. Humans have ontological primacy. Our ontology is monotheistic, Trinitarian and biblical.

Many believe that the goal of government to ensure safety, security, and orderliness can certainly be met using the death penalty. However, the existence of the death penalty has not eliminated crime. In addition, the same security could be met without the death penalty if these same criminals were kept in prison for the rest of their lives, without being able to get out on parole. Doing this would preserve the inherent dignity of persons and honor their communicable and incommunicable attributes and God's. We as a nation are, by definition, one nation under God. To take over His job of deciding when life should end is wrong, even in the interest of safety and security.

READING ANALYSES: PHILOSOPHY OF ETHICS

Analysis of the Alzheimer's Movie

The movie covered how the lives of a mother and her daughter are affected by the fact that the mother has Alzheimer's disease. It went into great detail showing some of the things that the mother had forgotten. For example, the mother had forgotten that her husband had died. However, despite the fact that she had forgotten many things, she could still function well. She could only remember her childhood. The daughter started playing along with the content of the conversation to keep her mother from getting upset. The daughter says that her mom's independence is more important than protecting her all the time. Various events were covered in detail including: the podiatrist, social security, the ticket and the banana. The mother felt much self-doubt and hatred.

I think that the mother who is going in the direction of Alzheimer's disease should be an ethical egotist. This is different from being selfish. Ethical egoism says that we should look at only ourselves and be selfish. It also says that everyone should do this. It is a normative theory. We see that the mom who got Alzheimer's disease is dealing with anger, and self-doubt. This in my mind can take two paths. She can use this anger to lash out at others and break down mentally to not care about others. When we really look at this situation, ethical egotism seems inevitable for her. The mom needs to care deeply about herself, which would then cause the daughter to feel good about herself and her mother. Ethical egotism seemed foreign at the beginning of the film. If everyone was an egoist, who would you compare yourself to (that was kind hearted) to know that you were fulfilling the role of an egoist?

The first thing I notice is that the mother (who was losing her memory) couldn't multi-task very well. The daughter interviews and tries to use white out to stop mother's obsession with note taking. Multi-tasking wasn't necessary for the mother. One could argue that for her it was necessary to obsess and multi-task in order to deal with her memory loss. We can assume that she still had great love for the people in her life, as was made evident in the movie.

The daughter was wondering if she was going crazy. She would white out her mother's notes because the notes seemed to be a distraction for the mother. This is basically summing up how the daughter feels. She is scared that she is caring too much, or caring in the wrong way. The daughter's self-doubt was kind of supported by the mother. The mother actually was the vessel to help her daughter feel like she had a purpose.

The journey itself creates purpose if one can take the opposite of ethical relativism and the opposite of ethical egoism, and live life with the inclusion of others. I think the fact that Alzheimer's disease attacks the mind slowly is more of a blessing than a curse. It's different from the onset of other diseases. After all, it takes more time to affect you than a scraped knee! It seems that memory loss is unique, in that it politely forces family members to care for the person with Alzheimer's disease. The mother seems perfectly guilty and innocent of the change that is taking place in her daughter. The daughter is realizing that she can be perfectly happy with a mother that has Alzheimer's. In philosophy we are free to make choices but we are not free to take those choices away (from ourselves or others). Since the mom is losing her memory, she doesn't realize that she has choices.

Ethical egoism is self-contradictory and has no moral weight. It also has people conflicting with cross purposes, because each is looking out for their own desires. There is no conflict resolution whatsoever, because each person is only looking out for himself; thus no one is ever wrong. According to ethical egoism, each man ought to look out for himself. In the context of the movie then, is the daughter looking out for herself? The mom obviously only does what she wants, because it is all she can hold in her memory. The daughter in a way looks out for herself by taking care of her mom, but actually this is more altruistic than ethical egoism.

Socrates answers Plato that an unjust person cannot be happy. Reason, will power, and desires are the three things that need to be in balance (as do power, virtue and pleasure). We can observe that creating circumstances to help people and yet not breaking the law reaps happiness. (This is the opposite of ethical egoism, because you are supposed to want to help yourself). The mother is upset because she is not fulfilling the social norm of politeness, kindness and caring. Losing her memory is like the disease and the antidote.

Life is about finding that one moment that makes you stop and never stop thinking. It is rare when a memory loss can inspire hope. It took the daughter's feeling of sadness and turned it into acceptance and joy. This constitutes a moment that I see as life defining. It isn't possible for her to be an ethical egoist, because she is putting her mother's needs and conditions foremost in her mind. She does it because, in her subconscious mind, she must. This is altruistic.

This in turn brings into play a higher being like a God who would give you what you can handle but no more. We need to realize that people are precious. If it wasn't for them, we could not possess the bad moments in our life, which transform into good ones. This also assumes that we are all human and have human nature. Our thoughts are usually the more disturbing than the actual events. The reason for that is human anxiety, which points to affinity and eternity. Ethical egoism only applies to the basest part of the human condition. If I as an ethical egoist had to care for someone with Alzheimer's disease, it would then be fine for me to refuse to help. This ignores the fact that our deeper selves prefer some degree of altruism, some human kindness. This is where Plato said that true happiness comes from.

Find other stories with a similar message: It is the inner beauty and truth that count, not the external appearance. Evaluate the message: Is it always true? Why or why not?

The movies *Pinocchio, The Little Mermaid, Rain Main, On Golden Pond,* and *Batman, The Dark Knight* all have the message of not really knowing anything until you have explored the mind. People can observe that the mind has much capability. In the case of the character Shrek, he has become so accustomed to the fact that he is green and ugly that he just walks around somber all the time. The donkey is thrown in his path to make Shrek reevaluate himself. This unfolds into saving the princess. As I was saying to my mom the other day, beautiful people have a burden that ugly (to us) people don't have. That is why Shrek was able to go in place of the prince. This action was all it took for Fiona to look past Shrek's physical appearance.

If you have seen *Shrek 2* (2004) and *Shrek the Third* (2007), you may want to weigh in on the further story: Is it a Socratic journey to find the inner truth, or has the theme changed? *Shrek 2's* theme is, above all, the choices we make for love. What might love's choices have to do with seeing the inner truth?

Abstract forms that are hierarchically higher than worms are those things such as love and ideals. The good is the highest form. It is true that the good is hard to describe or define in philosophy. Love continues to keep growing for the other, and so does the mind. Action by choices uses the Reason, willpower, and desires to show love, in this example. By having a balanced soul, one can share in an elevated part in the forms.

The Branch Davidian Analysis

The Catholic Church believes that one should live in the world, and yet not be of the world. An argument against this and Kantian perspectives is an individual who receives freedom from society is capable of doing things that societies are not used to. If the government looks at "what is a culture", they have no grounds there. Everyone at the Davidians' complex had a common purpose, and weren't bigoted, because one can't prove they had racial issues. For instance, threats weren't mentioned in the film of Waco. Furthermore, soft universalism would tell us that we all have common threads of code of morality, or that we should. I see the Davidians following basic rules. Equal treatment for equals would tell us that these people are not normal, but there are loopholes that should prevent governmental action. For instance, the Declaration of Independence was great for America but wrong in the eyes of Great Britain.

The flat earth argument against ethical relativism says the earth is round, and some did not believe this for some time. Facts are just facts sometimes. Did David Koresh use religion as a veil for his vices and corruption? Are miracles meant to undergo the inspection of tedious analysis and science? I ask this because even though religion has truth in its hands, it doesn't proclaim its truth immediately. Does this make it untrue? No. It just means the church is doing its job and being careful.

What if David was just a gun(s) owner, but had no religion or values? Or what would be the final outcome if no tear gas had been used, or a wall had not been bulldozed down? Then would we see him as a worse individual if he had no outrageous religion? If religion of any sort hinders us from invading property and killing, then the absence of religion should make us realize that religion had a big part to play in the ATF's decision. My theory is that the ATF intended to go easy on the Davidians because religion was involved. By this I mean that the ATF could have gone in during the night, risking an even more deadly outcome for the Davidians. The daytime strategy initially gave the Davidians a chance to save face.

Next I will discuss Dworkin and a previous point that I made. I will conclude with Socrates' theories. Dworkin would say individual rights can't be compared with social goods. In my mind, the Davidians' guns were the social goods, because they weren't using them to kill anyone prior to the raid. We are dealing with an unusual and unintelligent person, but not dangerous. The second amendment also doesn't say that potential criminals can't buy and sell guns. In conclusion, to Socrates' model of the soul, I will say that we are all many parts, but we are all one body. Socrates assumed his idea of the soul was correct for an individual and a society's behavior.

MASS MEDIA

RESEARCH PAPER ON CHURCH AND MEDIA: MORALITY IN MEDIA

The Church and Media course provided multiple opportunities to discuss and analyze media through the lens of the Church and morality. The final topic examined whether secular movies that deal with life issues are commendable for conveying a good message, despite the crude content that often accompanies them.

The Final Round

Here we are, with cramped fingers and fried brains, in our last attempt to be the "voice in the desert" crying out so that all may hear the good news of the future of the film industry. We hope our guidelines give insight to those searching for wholesome yet hilarious entertainment. We believe that the conclusions we have come to and the guidelines we are presenting regarding what an ideal secular movie that portrays life issues are a good starting point and framework for professionals who wish to make a difference in the film industry by reaching the audience through humor and real life, pertinent situations.

The Family

After long debates both in and out of class, it is now obvious that there are going to be persistent disagreements concerning these movies between the opposing team and ours. The strongest of these disagreements is the opposite view our teams have concerning the portrayal of the family in the mentioned movies. First and foremost, we agree and reaffirm what the opposing team said concerning the Church's teaching on the family. The Church even calls the family the *"original cell of social life"* (The Catechism of the Catholic Church, 1993, paragraph 2207). The Catholic Church places an importance on the family and stresses society's role in strengthening and protecting it. Secondly, our team agrees with the opposing team that, "the institution of the family is important when trying to convey a pro-life message" (Dickey & Fisher & Hauge, 2008, p.6). Both teams agree with the Church's teaching and the importance of family in the pro-life message. While the opposing team sees these movies as negative or blurry portrayals of the family, our team sees them as accurate portrayals of the modern family that stress the importance of family and demonstrate the struggles and problems found in the modern family.

Knocked Up

The opposing teams says that Ben and Alison, "…immerse themselves in regular premarital sex and pornography, and dare I mention the countless number of crude language. How does this create a 'good environment'? This is not a family environment in which to be raising a child" (Dickey & Fischer & Hauge, 2008, p. 7). The word "immerse" is quite strong considering there are only two sex scenes between Ben and Alison, one in which the baby is conceived and one during the pregnancy. Also, the couple do not "immerse" themselves in pornography. Yes, at one short scene in the movie Alison is watching a movie along with Ben's friends and calls out the moment she sees a "boob." However, towards the end of the movie, Alison is no longer actively participating in Ben's friends' "nude scene" business. Furthermore, Ben quits his "job" collecting nude scenes in movies and gets a real job. He also moves out of the house where his pot-smoking, deadbeat friends live and buys an apartment in which he builds a simple yet loving nursery. At the very end of the movie, Ben and Alison are together and the credits show the two happily playing with their child.

Juno

Another issue the opposing team raises is the portrayal of Juno's parents. They state that, "They [Juno's parents} casually accepted it [her pregnancy] as if it was the next obstacle in their lives that they had no choice but to face, and instead they should have taken this incident and taught Juno a lesson in some manner, not harshly, but in some way" (Dickey & Fischer & Hauge, 2008, p. 7). Considering the circumstances, it is fairly obvious Juno has already learned her lesson. When the girl offers Juno a condom at the abortion clinic, Juno looks at her in slight shock and says, "No thanks, I'm off sex." In another case, Juno and Bleeker are arguing and Juno says, "Are you ashamed that she did it? "Cause at least you don't have to have the evidence under your sweater." Juno has learned her lesson and has accepted the consequences of her actions, without her parents having to sit her down and lecture her about premarital sex.

The Catholic Church says parents are responsible for, "…creating a home where tenderness, forgiveness, respect, fidelity, and disinterested service are the rule" (The Catechism of the Catholic Church, 1993, paragraph 2223). Juno's parents treated Juno's pregnancy with tenderness and forgiveness. They respect Juno's decision to give the baby up for adoption. Juno's step-mother shows her fidelity for Juno when she staunchly defends Juno against the ultra-sound technician. Furthermore, both parents are examples of service. Mac, her father, brings her to the house of the adoptive parents, gives her advice on love and relationships, and loves her unconditionally. And Bren, her step-mom, takes her to the ultra-sound, holds her hand in the delivery room, and on a lighter note, has even pushed aside her love for dogs because Juno is "allergic to their saliva."

Waitress

Although the movie was horribly made, we still disagree with the opposing team that Jenna should have gotten an annulment in the movie. Yes, as Catholics we would prefer that she had the marriage officially annulled. However, we must remember the setting of the movie and the characters involved. It takes place in the south in the middle of nowhere. The reasons for why they got married were not addressed, and neither were the religious practices of any of the characters. Furthermore, a scene in which Jenna gets an annulment would be awkward for the flow of the movie. We must also remember that not only does Jenna leave her abusive husband; she also leaves her affair behind. She could have easily started fresh with a new man. Instead, she starts a new life with only herself and her daughter.

Reality of the Modern Family

The families portrayed in these movies are realistic to the modern family. Like Ben and Alison, there are people who have children outside of marriage and before they are ready. Ben and Alison show an example of two people who accept responsibility for their actions and try to improve themselves for each other and their baby. It is a reality that there are single mothers like Jenna from *Waitress*. She leaves her abusive husband and her affair in order to make a better life for herself and her daughter.

Furthermore, teen pregnancy is a reality. *Juno* not only offers an example for parents to approach the situation with tenderness and love, but the movie has also been used to bring adoption back into society's view. Less than 2% of all pregnant teens give their babies up for adoption (Koch, 2008). In an article in USA Today called *Movies open door for adoption advocates,* Thomas Atwood, President of the National Council for Adoption says, "We see the movies [Juno and Bella] as an opportunity to promote adoption awareness" (Koch, 2008). A movie such as *Juno* has the ability to bring the option of adoption back into the picture.

Divorce is also a theme in *Juno*. Although it is a sad reality, divorce is a more than common occurrence in our society. According to the U.S. Census Bureau, the average divorce rate in 2004 was approximately 43% for all marriages, and this number has been speculated to have climbed towards 50%. In 2004, out of all male U.S. citizens over the age of 15, 20.7% had been divorced at least once. Also, for all U.S. women over the age of 15, 22.9% have been divorced at least once. The opposing team says, "We are not refuting that there are no families with difficulties and pain, but rather that the movies *Juno* and *Knocked*

Up suggest that the brokenness is okay and doable, and instead of being depicted as broken and unhealthy, they are brushed over lightly" (Dickey & Fischer & Hauge, 2008, p. 7). If the brokenness of the family was "brushed over lightly," the opposing team must have watched a different movie. The idea of familial brokenness is one of the deepest conflicts in Juno's life. She tells the audience early in the movie that her mother left when she was a little girl. When she finds out that Mark Loring is going to leave Vanessa (the adoptive mother), she pulls over on the side of the road and cries for the first time since the beginning of the movie. Later, when Juno goes home, her father asks what's bothering her. Juno responds saying, "Just losing my faith in humanity," and also says, "I need to know if it's possible for two people to stay together forever." The idea of a broken family is not addressed lightly in Juno, but rather with sensitivity and insight.

Difference of Interpretation

Although our team and the opposing team strongly differ on the issue of family in these movies and on other issues, we also realize that one of the underlying causes of these disagreements is a difference in interpretation. Like paintings, books, and poetry, film is an art form and open to interpretation. When it comes to artistic interpretation there will always be differences and similarities. These differences can stem from both personality and life experience. Our team sees that there are differences central to the issue at hand. We feel these differences will not be solved through this debate.

The *Knocked Up* Conclusion

After discussing the matter as a team, and with the opposing team, our team has drawn a conclusion concerning the movie *Knocked Up*. Although the movie has moments of goodness, truth, and beauty, we have come to the conclusion that the profanity is far too excessive to fully commend the movie. The nudity is beyond ridiculous; one example of this is the exposure of six different women's breasts. Also, the language exceeds simple curse words; some entire conversations are blatantly inappropriate. Although we still believe that some people will come away from the movie with a greater respect for life, we also see the dangers in the rest of the movie's material. *Inter Mirifica* discusses the portrayal of moral evil in the media and says, "…such presentations ought always to be subject to moral restraint, lest they work to the harm rather than the benefit of souls, particularly when there is question of treating matters which deserve reverent handling or which, given the baneful effect of original sin in men, could quite readily arouse base desires in them" (Paul VI, 1963, paragraph 7). *Knocked Up* has the great potential to harm rather than benefit the soul; we cannot commend *Knocked Up* as a whole. Rather we commend the beautiful moments of truth found inside the core of the movie's message.

Guidelines

The rest of our paper will focus on constructing guidelines for those Catholics who desire to make life-issue films in the secular world, though the guidelines will also apply to Catholics who simply want to watch secular life-issue movies. How should we make them and which ones should we watch? When does the bad outweigh the good, and how do we discern when a movie has crossed the line?

Portrayal of Reality and the Pro-Life Message

There is a saying that goes like this: "you can't show the good without showing the bad". Whether or not this holds true for everything, it's certainly a fundamental aspect of storytelling, because every story needs conflict. If *The Lord of the Rings* had no representation of evil, for instance, would there be a lesson in Frodo's goodness?

In a story about life issues, the opposing forces, or the obstacles have to be shown in some capacity. Society today happens to be one of the pro-life advocate's greatest opponents, and thus it is important that filmmakers portray society accurately and relevantly. This doesn't mean they should indulge, or greatly expand upon, any particularly sinful aspect of society in order to 'talk' about it – such as Knocked Up does with its gratuitous sex and drug-related scenes. Rather they should apply *Inter Mirifica's* instructions:

> Finally, the narration, description, or portrayal of moral evil, even through the media of social communication, can indeed serve to bring about a deeper knowledge and study of humanity and with the aid of appropriately heightened dramatic effects, can reveal and glorify the grand dimensions of truth and goodness. (# 7).

The Catholic filmmaker should seek to be honest and realistic, painting the whole picture in a way that will strengthen and nourish the morality of the viewers. The movie must highlight the good and cast the evil into shadow, in order to glorify that goodness. Furthermore, movies must be realistic if they are to increase our understanding of humanity and the world. Movies like *Mom at Sixteen*, *Too Young to be a Dad*, and *Fifteen and Pregnant* are in danger of turning viewers away because the characters within may seem contrived and the atmosphere warped or overly biased. The belief that they are conveying the real truth is lost; at its simplest, then, 'being realistic' means to portray things the way they truly are.

Nevertheless, such presentations ought always to be subject to moral restraint, lest they work to the harm rather than the benefit of souls, particularly when there is question of treating matters which deserve reverent handling or which, given the baneful effect of original sin in men, could quite readily arouse base desires in them (*Inter Mirifica #7*).

As mentioned earlier, the scenes depicting immorality in *Knocked Up* went too far and ended up having a negative influence on the audience instead of a positive one. Thus, when portraying evil, the ever-proverbial 'line' can be drawn at the precise point when the evil begins to tempt the viewer, rather than repulse. When a certain scene in a film arouses 'base desires,' it is not fulfilling its purpose to enrich the soul of the viewer or to illustrate the triumphant nature of truth and goodness; it is merely flirting with sin. All movies must have a conscience. Moral evil must always remind us of moral good; it must *never* cause us to forget. When the audience has forgotten that the evil presented is evil, the film has lost all merit.

Portrayal of Sex

The portrayal of sex in any media is probably the touchiest subject to audiences, especially Christians. As Catholics, we believe that sex is a sacred act in which two people experience union with one another and with God. With regards to the sanctity of sex, it is morally offensive to see it perverted on a movie screen, reduced to a mere act of pleasure and objectifying both the man and woman. Because of this, it is absolutely necessary that sex scenes in movies are not pornographic. The Catechism of the Catholic Church states that pornography "does grave injury to the dignity of its participants (actors, vendors, and the public), since each one becomes an object of base pleasure and illicit profit for others. It immerses all who are involved in the illusion of a fantasy world. It is a grave offense" (CCC 2354). However, the purpose and means by which the sex scene is portrayed must be taken into account.

Grossly explicit sex scenes are never necessary for any reason and should always be adamantly discouraged. Audiences should "avoid those [media] that may be a cause or occasion of spiritual harm to themselves or that can lead others into danger through base example, or that hinder desirable presentations and promote those that are evil" (*Inter Mirifica*, # 9). However, as stated earlier, # 7 of *Inter Miricfica* states: "The narration, description or portrayal of moral evil, even through the media of social communication, can indeed serve to bring about a deeper knowledge and study of humanity and, with the aid of appropriately heightened dramatic effects, can reveal and glorify the grand dimensions of truth and goodness." With this in mind, we must consider those circumstances in which a sex scene, though intrinsically morally offensive, may be used.

With respect to the movies, the character development and plot are essential for success. Sexual content sometimes plays a key role in this development, but careful attention should be given to whether or not the content is gratuitous. For example, in Juno the opening sex scene is fundamental to the plot of the entire movie and acts as the basis for the ensuing relationship between the two main characters. The act is not explicitly shown and only lasts long enough for the audience to begin realizing the situation that Juno and Bleeker had. Conversely, in *Knocked Up,* much of the sexual content became gratuitous when it was no longer providing new developments of the characters of the plot. The sex scenes in *Waitress* that show Jenna's affair are unnecessarily explicit and ultimately gratuitous. In all possible cases, it must be encouraged that sex scenes are implicit for the sake of the actors and audiences because "such presentations ought always to be subject to moral restraint, lest they work to the harm rather that the benefit of souls, particularly when there is the question of treating matters which deserve reverent handling or which…could quite readily arouse base desires in [men]" (Inter Mirifica, #7).

Profane Language

The use of profanity in movies should not be judged by the precise number of times certain words are said, but rather by what purpose they serve. Language is essential to creating the environment of a story, and the way in which characters speak and relate to each other through dialogue is very significant. The reason that there is an emphasis on language is because it is an element that greatly contributes to the "realistic" aspect of stories. It is therefore necessary to correlate the need for realistic situations in these movies with the need for language that realistically helps the development of the story and its characters. Profane language must not be gratuitous, and under no circumstances should derogatory language be used for the sake of humor. Again we can turn to *Juno* as an example where the language in the film contributes to the entire persona of Juno and her sarcastic, witty attitude, as well as to the sense of reality for the audience (every character's language reflects how many people in society speak). We do, however, acknowledge that in some instances there were dirty jokes that were not necessary and instead only provided humor, but that is why *Juno* cannot be taken wholly as a perfect example. Some of the language, however, satirized different stereotypical groups in society, like abortion clinic workers and sex education teachers, and though it provided humor, these are examples of the proper use of crude language for humor.

The Appropriate Audience: Judgment of the Parents

When facing the question of what age a child or adolescent should be permitted to see films such as these, the answer is not a simple or a definite one. There are so many variables that come into play. Most importantly, we must consider the vast differences in every family and every child, each from different backgrounds and cultures. What is old news to one child or teen may be shocking, terrifying or scandalizing for another. Since there are these variables, who can rightly say what a child can watch but his parents? *Inter Mirifica* states that "Parents should remember that they have a most serious duty to guard carefully lest shows, publications and other things of this sort, which may be morally harmful, enter their homes or affect their children under other circumstances." Parents need to ensure that they educate themselves and stay aware of what their children are watching and what is in the recent films.

There is a fine line that parents need to be aware of between protecting their children from truly morally offensive films, and sheltering their children. The Catholic Church urges us, in regards to the media, to take a threefold part of "formation, participation, and dialogue" in *The Rapid Development* by Pope John Paul II. This can be useful for parents when trying not to shelter their children because if they choose to let them see a movie that may contain some "tough" issues, such as teen pregnancy, premarital sex, or broken families, they can talk about the movie afterwards and make sure that their children understand the Church's position on these issues and what attitude to take on them. By educating their children in this informal way, they are arming them with the tools they will need later in order to make their own judgments. Article 10 of *Inter Mirifica* states:

> Those who make use of the media of communications, especially the young, should take steps to accustom themselves to moderation and self-control in their regard. They should, moreover, endeavor to deepen their understanding of what they see, hear or read. They should discuss these matters with their teachers and expert, and learn to pass sound judgments on them.

The fact that the older adolescents are the more they are able to judge what they see was confirmed in a study that was done and published by the Journal of Sex Research entitled "Adolescents' Contact With Sexuality in Mainstream Media: A Selection-Based perspective". Part of the study says that the age that the adolescent is exposed to media with sexual references of or images plays a large part in what their attitude towards it is. They tend to evaluate what they see and weigh it against their own beliefs. Taking this into consideration, parents should feel confident in allowing their children, as they grow into teenagers to make their own judgments on what is appropriate to see and what is morally offensive. Parents need not be afraid to let go of controlling every entertainment decision for their children once they are confident that they have done their duty in arming them with the truth.

The Appropriate Audience: Media Practice Model

The Media Practice Model as outlined in the article entitled "Teenage Sexuality and Media Practice: Factoring in the influences of Family, Friends, and School" helps shed some light on the question of what age a child or adolescent can see some films. The study is based on the research that shows that a teens own self-image and sense of who they are affects what kind of encounter they have with the media, especially media that involves sexual themes. This study revolves around what kind of upbringing the teen has had and who he has been surrounded by and influenced by. This gives further confirmation to our conclusion that we cannot definitively give an age range that these movies are appropriate for since each person's evaluation of, and reaction to the film differs depending on what they were taught and who they were influenced by.

Conclusion

Catholics must uphold their values in whatever they do, including making movies, watching them, or sharing them with others. Likewise, when a Christian filmmaker is trying to reach a secular audience, he cannot merely restate his Christian values and go home; he must show, not tell. He must integrate, or apply, his Christian values to real-life situations when crafting his characters and his storyline. He must be willing to show the world in as honest a light as he can. He must show the truth first, before he reveals the religion, if he does indeed choose to reveal his religion as a source for his ideas at all.

Over the course of this debate, we have argued the merits of four movies, claiming quite firmly that all four were commendable for their pro-life messages, despite their crude content. We were wrong about *Knocked Up*, a movie we have come to see does, in fact, cross the line. Its crudeness makes it ultimately immoral, and no good message within it can redeem it. Comparing it to the other films that remained within the boundaries, especially *Juno*, we then came up with a set of guidelines that were in keeping with the teachings of the Catholic Church, and (we hope) accurately judge the morality of a movie. These guidelines can be applied not only to life-issue movies, but to all movies Christian or secular, kid or adult, action or drama or any movie at all in any situation.

References

Hawk, S., Vanwesenbeek, I., Hanneke de Graaf, & Bakker, Floor. (2006). *Adolescents' Contact With Sexuality in Mainstream Media: A Selection-Based Perspective.* Journal of Sex Research, Vol. 43, Issue 4. Retrieved Sunday, April 20, 2008 from the EBSCO database.

Knock, W. (March 10, 2008). *Movies open doors for adoptive advocates.* In USA Today. Retrieved April 20, 2008. http://www.usatoday.com/news/health/2008-03-09-juno-adoption-side_N.htm.

Rapid Development.

Steele, J. (1999). Teenage Sexuality and Media Practice: Factoring in the influences of Family, Friends, and School. Journal of Sex Research Vol. 36 Issue 4, pgs. 331-341. Retrieved Sunday, April 20, 2008 from www.findarticles.com.

U.S. Census Bureau. (2004). Divorce rates. Retrieved April 19, 2008. http://www.census.gov/population/www/socdemo/marr-div/2004detailed_tables.html.

Vatican II. (1963). Inter Mirifica. Retrieved April 20, 2008. http://www.vatican.va/archive/hist_councils/ii_vatican_council/documents/vati-ii_decree_19631204_inter_mirifica_en.htm.

PUBLIC SPEAKING

This, like most public speaking courses involved learning the dynamics of giving a speech, of course. However it also examined the concepts behind public speaking and improving everything about your communication. This meant even examining your own role as an audience member – whether in a class, a business meeting, or even the performance of a play. Throughout the course I researched information for each of my speeches using the same research and writing skills as I do for a paper. However, there is a difference: each word spoken and each visual aid must take into account the audio/visual impact upon the audience members. To learn about being an effective audience member, I attended and analyzed the play Edwin Drood.

REVIEW OF A PLAY: THE MYSTERY OF EDWIN DROOD

Charles Dickens liked to interweave his characters. This play was no exception. I enjoyed the play, the use of accents and British language characteristics, with hints of modern day pronunciations. The way the production was done was transporting. The production created the feeling that the audience was at an auction that was meant for suspense, not valuables or money. The actors all seemed comfortable with their roles, yet fresh to the stage for every new set of audience members. It was fast paced in some parts, and slow paced in other parts. I think there was great talent, as I could see from the reading the program descriptions about actor and actress.

It is very hard to draw audience members outside themselves, especially when the known facts about what Charles Dickens intended is limited. For example, some actors and actresses sat in the dark, not invading the stage or main performers. Yet, they looked emotion-filled at times when the audience might have seemed bored. They provided facial expression in an atypical way, which created a sense of urgency and credibility. Although this seemed rehearsed, as it should, it also seemed relaxed. In order to get this combination of rehearsed and relaxed, or extemporaneous and impromptu, takes some doing. For some odd reason, television tricks the brain into being very real. When we are at a live play we want to be tricked into a fake non-candid presentation. In other words, the story line needs to have elements that speak to the lives of the audience members, but then makes you forget that you heard something emotion-based. Hence, credibility needs to be established. The narrator did this very well. Another lesson the play did a great job conveying is that if your audience does not know the details or specifics that the author intended, it is still possible to establish credibility by providing general knowledge to them. The night that I attended was Friday, March 13. The audience got very involved in the play, and that made it a very effective show.

The question then becomes the classic "Who done it"? Dickens never finished the play, so his answer is unknown. Each performance differs as the audience votes to decide who committed the murder. I believe that my fantastic view is correct. I first thought that Rosa Bud did the killing, which happened to be correct that night. Further thought made me think that Princess Puffer did it. She wanted to gain leverage against Edwin Drood, and she used Jasper and Neville to do it. The history described during the play tells us that the romance of Edwin Drood and Rosa Bud was decided by their families while they were young children. I believe that this arrangement did not meet the approval of Princess Puffer. At the time, she was Rosa Bud's nanny. Unfortunately for Princess Puffer, she had no control over her daughter-like figure's future romances.

My theory is that Princess Puffer created the plot to kill Edwin Drood. She created the plot in Jasper's head when she drugged him. That was the reason for the scene with Jasper in her opium den. She influenced Jasper to search out Neville and destroy him. This was because Neville wanted Edwin Drood out of the picture to claim Rosa Bud as his. I note here that Jasper did not like his nephew Edwin, but at least found him bearable. He was willing to associate with Edwin, because it gave him another way to associate with Rosa Bud. Secretly, Jasper liked Rosa Bud; so the story goes. Neville more or less overtly doted on Rosa.

Now the stage is set for Jasper to be primed to kill and Neville to want Edwin dead. It is important to note that much of the play had an unwritten intention and non-read script happening in the background. Charles Dickens died, leaving us with a hilarious yet disturbing entanglement of characters. Any one of these characters could have committed the murder. Princess Puffer seems the most suspicious to me.

It is important to examine what occurs when Edwin goes missing. Neville goes looking for Edwin, seeking an opportune time to commit murder. Jasper goes after Neville, trying to fulfill his opium brainwashed dream of saving his nephew, while destroying Neville. Note here that Princess Puffer probably wanted the uncle (Jasper) to want to save his nephew. That way he couldn't blame Princess Puffer for the drug induced murder that is about to take place. I think that Jasper thought he saw Neville, but it was actually Edwin. Jasper pushes him off the cliff. Although she didn't actually push Edwin, Princess Puffer brainwashed and drugged the killer, so she is in essence, the killer. Meanwhile, Princess gets Neville and Jasper suspecting each other, and gets off scot free.

Princess could even want money from Jasper while she does detective work for him while trying to find Edwin. Perhaps she believes that she could get money as an installment from the dowry (which surely must exist) from the marriage between Rosa and Edwin (unaware that the wedding is cancelled). Although I could be wrong about Princess Puffer and her motivations I definitely enjoyed the play and got something out of it.

FIGURE OF SPEECH EXERCISE

In the movie *What About Bob?*, being Bob is like being a baby who spills his milk 7 days out of the week and then becomes a responsible rug and tile expert. (Simile). Getting on an elevator, on a medication, or on a doctor's nerves can be scary for Bob Wiley. (Parallelism). Dr. Marvin is as full of himself as a hot air balloon that's full of helium. (Simile). While setting his vacation and interview up he says, "It's a real shot in the arm for my book." (Personification). The book is a key part of Bob's success, but mostly it's the "horse sense of the guy" "that just gets you." Bob missed Dr. Marvin so much that he could have broken into pieces like a twister game gone bad. (Simile). At Lake Winnipesaukee Dr. Marvin starts relaxing like a person just starting a diet; happy to lose the weight but waking up to the grim reality of eating habits. (Simile). Bob spends the night never to leave the darkness of the doctor. (Antithesis). After the interview goes bad for Dr. Marvin he can't even turn his patient in to the mental ward. Dr. Marvin foreshadows his own fate of insanity. So, Dr. Marvin tries to kill Bob, but Bob, being very naïve, gets free of the explosive death trap. Dr Marvin was so happy to be free like the previous psychiatrist, that he could have eaten Bob's goldfish. (Hyperbole). Finally Bob finds love in the "fam" and marries Dr Marvin's sister Lily.

Tourette's, toothbrushes, and Teleprompters are the hilarious attributes of this screws loose, psychoactive, silly movie. (Alliteration). If your mentality ever gets off the chain, remember some people think huge problems are just a walk in the park. The irony here is that it made Dr. Marvin's ego the size of pixel on a high definition television. (Metaphor/Simile). Some people can't handle having no control of a situation. I guess Dr. Marvin never knew his limits. We can all relate to this super-de-duper classic Bill Murray film. (Hyperbole).

ANALYSIS OF SPEAKER ANXIETY ARTICLE

The article from the website provides even more advice and information about handling speaker's anxiety than the textbook provided. In both sources, the overall point is that proper, thorough preparation is the key to overcoming fruitless anxiety. Besides researching the topic and repeated rehearsal, other strategies are provided. An interesting fact is pointed out in the textbook. "Physical changes caused by anxiety improve your energy level and help you function better than you might otherwise" (Beebe). This sheds a new light on the nervousness a speaker feels, and means that the endorphins the speaker feels from anxiety can beneficial to the speaker.

The website article provides detailed advice about overcoming speaker's anxiety. This advice includes practical matters that I had not heard before, such as to "number and staple together all pages of your presentation; and use large and bold type" (Zalaquett, Ph.D.). The preparation should include what the author called comebacks, in case the speaker gets lost. An interesting point made by the website article was to think through the disasters the speaker imagines could happen. This prepares the speaker for what to do if these things happen, and keeps the potential problems in perspective.

Excellent points were made in the taking care of yourself section of the article that I had not heard before. Dressing for success and de-stressing through tensing and relaxing muscles were presented as ways for the speaker to handle anxiety. The article also states that the use of physical aids like handouts and a pointer can help to reduce stress during the speech as well. This information is especially helpful, as it gives an outlet for nervousness that comes from being in a public speaking situation. I liked the advice about knowing your audience and looking for a friendly face. This is something a student should be doing on a regular basis. No man is an island, and that is an important thing to remember. Knowing the people in the audience will increase the likelihood of an effective speech. Most people won't notice a speaker's mistakes, or if they do, probably will not ridicule the speaker. Remembering that helps to calm a speaker.

Of course, the article had advice for during the actual delivery of the speech as well. I believe most people had heard the bulk of this advice before. Points such as introducing yourself, maintaining eye contact, moving around, providing colorful details, making clear points, varying both speed and volume, and using a powerful introduction and ending have been heard before. Two pieces of advice that were new to me were provided that I found to be both interesting and powerful. The first was to "release hanger syndrome tension" (Zalaquett). I believe that relaxing the shoulders before and during the presentation would be an excellent centering activity, and would greatly reduce anxiety.

Practicing your speech is a huge element of reducing speaker's anxiety. Even with rehearsal, when you are speaking, your voice may tremble. This comes from cortisol and other chemicals released into your body. The second new strategy mentioned in the article was to "let the tremor in your voice come in and go out" (Zalaquett). These strategies keep nervousness from overpowering the speaker. Overall, the web site article did a terrific job of leading the reader through advice to reduce speaker anxiety, while reassuring the reader that anxiety is both normal and something the speaker can readily handle.

Works Cited

Beebe, Steven A. and Susan J., <u>A Concise Public Speaking Handbook, 2nd Edition</u>. Pearson Education, Inc. Boston, MA, 2009.

HUMANITIES ESSAYS AND RESEARCH PAPER

Most colleges require a certain number of credits in the humanities in order to earn a Bachelor of Arts Degree. This gives students ample opportunity to become well-rounded learners. As a matter of fact, many colleges also require courses that provide a cross-section across the humanities. At my school (Ottawa University) this course is called Proseminar. The course teaches the students to apply humanities concepts to their lives. It gives them a wonderful lens to see the world and themselves. The essays and research paper in this chapter provide the reader with examples of exactly what this means. My advice is to write each day. Your thoughts will begin to gel and your writing will become self-revealing.

FROM SKINNED KNEES TO SHEEPSKIN: MY FORMAL/INFORMAL EDUCATION

Introduction

Education is a lifelong pursuit and a process that has formed and will continue to form me. My education has taken place in school, certainly; but there have been a wide variety of learning experiences that have taken place outside a traditional classroom that have served to teach me many lessons as well. All of these forms of education have helped to form my mind and my character. The formal and informal aspects of education depend on each other.

My Elementary School Years

There were many aspects to my elementary school classroom experiences. In general the teachers did not make the efforts to connect with students. I felt that this made it much more difficult for me to learn and emotionally painful to be there. However, there were two teachers that were an exception to that rule. The first was Mrs. Oxley who helped instill my love for reading and writing in me. The second was Miss Duncan. I felt respected by her and learned a lot as a result. She was a visiting teacher for the year and was from England. She made us work very hard, but when we did work hard, she gave us breaks during the day during which we could play cricket, or other enjoyable activities.

Another positive formal education activity during elementary school was gym class in the early years, because it made me feel competitive and the teacher was a man. I earned the Presidential Physical Fitness Award, and that was an accomplishment that meant a lot to me. Most kids don't have the patience to stick to a fitness program at that age, but it helped me have fun while I exercised. I wish I had been as health conscious then as I am now. I would have done even better.

One major aspect of my elementary school years that bothered me and got in the way of my formal education was the fact that the attitudes of the teachers completely revolved around rules and crowd control. The rules were not evenly enforced, nor were they explained. While this may seem like a minor thing to many people, at the time it seemed unjust. If I had understood the reasons behind the rules, they would not have seemed arbitrary or pointless. I had not developed the communication skills to explain my thoughts and feelings to them. I only knew that I was upset. Their teaching styles did not include an opportunity for participation or interaction. This made learning very difficult for me and became a major obstacle.

Students' attitudes at my elementary school were very cliquey. This made it very difficult for me because I often felt left out. I was very sensitive about this because I am an only child. I hoped that this fact would cause some of my classmates to reach out to me, but that did not happen. I believe the students should have helped each other reach the teacher's goals but the cliquey atmosphere did not lend itself to helping. Small group projects did not help me learn either, because it reinforced students' elitist and cliquey attitudes.

Outside of school there was a major informal education opportunity for me. This was the chance to learn about and practice my religion through my family and church experiences. At times it didn't seem like a positive, since it took away some of my play time. My religious experiences included confession, communion, and confirmation. These informal educational experiences through learning about my religion were very important in the formation of my character.

The other major informal learning activity that I participated in during my elementary school years was sports. I participated in soccer, basketball, volleyball, football, swimming, and horseback riding. I had to learn to manage my time as a result of the time I spent participating in sports. Sports were a lot of fun for me, and I excelled at them. My favorite coaches were the ones who took the time to show they cared about me personally. That helped me learn what they taught.

My High School Years

I completed high school in record time by using a home school program while living on a ranch in Wyoming. I learned all of the usual subjects during this time. I worked very hard and finished high school in three years. This gave me confidence in my ability to learn if I worked hard. This confidence helped me to believe that I could reach the next rung in education, a college degree.

The informal things that I learned as a result of my situation were even more important. I learned to be self-motivated and self-sufficient. I learned not to be afraid to talk to adults. I learned to ask questions, respect authority and myself, set goals and follow through to achieve them. Through performing ranch chores I learned the value and meaning of hard work and working as a team. These lessons were invaluable and continue to help me to this day. That is when I started to think a lot more about the effect I have on others. That led to building character and patience. I learned that a person is never done growing up and must never stop striving for the ultimate good.

My College Years

The philosophy that works best for me is slow and steady wins the race. I learn best in situations where I can participate and so can others. Learning is something we do every day; but in the course of a lifetime we only get to do it once. I value that time. In my formal education, college is where I have really come alive. I have a passion for learning and believe in the concept of being a lifelong learner. Ayn Rand believed in the importance of focusing on oneself. She believed that this principle leads to the desire for education and improvement and allows the present and future to be of good use. I agree with that concept completely. Even President Obama spoke at Arizona State University's graduation about the importance of education for the student and society.

My informal learning during my college years took place on the job at a pet resort called Pete and Mac's. When I worked at the ranch in Wyoming I cooked for a large group, worked on tractors, trucks and fences. I developed a strong work ethic as a result. It was a nice change to work with people's pets and to see the value my employer placed on my ability to connect with the pet owners and on my work ethic.

Conclusion

Formal and informal education should eventually teach how and what to question in life. There is a concept called group-think, where a large or semi-large group of people share the same experience and profess to think the same way. This is where informal education really comes to play a part. Many questions come into play, and sometimes the questions and answers can interfere with my goals. How do I dress? What rate of speech should I have? How much should I worry since I am going to worry anyway? How do I handle other students so that the teacher respects my decision and I don't offend the student? Are people actually concerned with me enough to want my demise even though they don't know me? The important point is that I should permit no one to stop me from reaching my educational goals.

Most people have siblings and are not an only child. I have worked hard to develop humility and to fit into a crowd. People that have siblings haven't gone through what I have gone through. What they have gone through was, in reality, probably much more difficult. I know I have been abundantly blessed.

Regardless, each person deserves my acceptance and help before my judgment. I have learned this through my formal education activities as well as my informal education activities.

I recognize that my education should never end. Even after I earn my degree, my education will continue. At that point I would like to continue to work on the virtue of humility. My goal is to work on being forthright, but not being blunt to the point of causing self-doubt in others. I want to be a fatherly figure, either through marriage to a woman, association with the saints, or father of a congregation of church militants. I would also like to laugh more and be a stepping stool for others to laugh.

THE ARTS IN MY LIFE: MY ARTS/EXPRESSION ESSAY

Introduction

I have experienced the arts in various ways throughout my life. The way I have experienced the arts and what those experiences have meant to me have changed through the years. The important aspect of art and expression is that these experiences affect my whole psyche. The arts go with me throughout my life in many ways, even though I may not be aware of the specific experiences at that moment. An example of this is how I experience classical and jazz music. As a result of studying the history of jazz music, music fills my heart, mind and soul with peace and joy.

My Experiences of Art and Expression as a Young Child

From a very early age I was exposed to the arts. The walls of my home contained prints of paintings by Renoir, Monet and Michelangelo. My mother read books to me that contained beautiful artwork. We attended symphonies, opera, and plays in the park. At Christmastime we went to a performance of The Nutcracker Ballet. Going to these events were wonderful experiences for me.

When I was in elementary school my family took me to see the outdoor play *Tecumseh*, which was a very exciting play. The Indians battled right in the audience and on the stage. The Indians even rode horses through the aisles of the amphitheater and onto the stage. This was a thrilling way to experience the arts through theater. We also attended two performances of Shakespearean plays at Shakespeare in the Park and saw a performance of opera music by the Metropolitan Opera. These were such thrilling events!

Pre-College Arts Learning and Expression

Art and music classes in school during these years were focused on proper technique and copying the artwork of the great Masters. While this taught me drawing with perspective, how to work with the tools and mediums, it limited my creativity to a certain extent. It did give me a large base of knowledge about specific periods of time in art history, especially the Impressionists.

To express myself artistically, I took piano lessons and drama lessons. In both cases I was a quick study and enjoyed the practice and performance. I also taught myself how to play the guitar. Guitar, piano, and jazz music have influenced my life. The countless bands that pop up that no one really is aware of are what discovering musical talent is for me. I think that is what inspires Americans to search for talent, not just wait for talent to come to them. A jazz musician said that people should be just as informed about the music as the composer was.

The Arts in College

My experience of the arts in college has been a deepening experience. I took a drawing course that really challenged me and helped me grow. This affected my drawing skill, of course. It also affected how I view picture composition, whether it is through drawing, painting or photography. What really improved were my photography skills. This carried over to my power point presentations as well. In addition to art classes, I took a history of jazz music course. This was an extraordinary class and very difficult, too. I gained a plethora of knowledge about jazz music and big band music. We were required to attend multiple jazz music performances and this was a wonderful benefit of being in the course. To this day I truly enjoy jazz music and big band music.

Art in a Non-traditional Genre

Although art is not synonymous with beauty, even things as mundane as cars are modeled to be appealing to the consumer. I think art has no hidden motives, contrasted with the technological and economic realms. I like that! My artistic talent and expression right now involves marketing and web development. I have a good eye and am very spatially oriented. In my marketing and web development efforts, I shouldn't shy away from growing more observant; but I have to practice patience because my overly observant nature can be a good or a bad thing. I need to use my talent to observe and create things. I shouldn't compare myself to people who are already in the field of marketing. Although there are already numerous ideas about marketing styles, there are still new styles to be discovered.

The Importance of Funding for the Arts

Cutting funding to the arts in times of economic unrest would simply make the possibility of the arts being available during the good economic times far less likely. Arts should not be looked at as something that is dependent on economic well-being. People always get more creative and unique during difficult times, so cutting funding would imply that economic growth could not be reached by the skill found in the artists and people's willingness to appreciate the arts. I would say the only reason to cut funding to the arts is if everyone in this country would be willing and able to successfully contribute their own time, talent and treasure to making the arts available. In this circumstance, people might become more giving. The premise of art is self-expression. Thus, self-expression through the arts is a way of giving. I believe we must continue to search for new talent so we can experience their creativity.

Two Significant Twentieth Century Artists

George M. Cohan and Frank Lloyd Wright were the greatest artists of the twentieth century, in my opinion. George M. Cohan was a composer, actor and dancer. He produced numerous Broadway shows and composed hundreds of songs. Through his music he influenced America and increased people's patriotism. Not only that, but through that music he gave people hope and courage during two World Wars and the Great Depression. He was awarded the Congressional Medal of Honor for his efforts. Many composers on Broadway have followed in Cohan's footsteps, but he was the pioneer. Frank Lloyd Wright was an architect and designer. He started a whole new concept and movement in the field of architecture (in both homes and commercial buildings). Architects to this day study the works of Wright and follow in his footsteps.

Conclusion

I can see that the opportunity to learn about and experience the arts is important for my psyche and for our society as well. It always makes me feel good to know there is a place I can go to escape from reality for awhile. The arts provide that wonderful escape or haven. I think art is just a different way of expressing what is already there inside each of us. That is why people enjoy it so much, because they can relate to it. I would even look at art that people think is kind of bad, and see that it still fulfills a need. Perhaps, if nothing else even bad art inspires good artists to be even better. Art is subjective as well. One person sees something that another doesn't see. Van Gogh only sold one painting in his lifetime, but that certainly does not mean he hadn't created art!

The bigger question for society becomes, what is valuable art? Humans by their very nature like to categorize and defines things. Art, though, defines humans. Why is this and how does this happen? There is something about art that cannot be ignored. This is because there is a spiritual aspect to all art. This is how the arts define us and changes us as a society. We must continue to search for the talent and arts that have been overlooked. The arts make the world richer.

SCIENCE AND TECHNOLOGY IN MY LIFE: MY SCIENCE/DESCRIPTION ESSAY

Introduction

Science should be a tool that aids in technology. It shouldn't be the dominating thing. I believe it should have a more noble purpose; to elevate society and inspire us. The sciences make me look at the world through questioning eyes. It is built on questions, observations, and data reports. Science is rigorous in its approach, to prove to the world what is knowledge and truth, but to also discover which theories are wrong. Scientists sometimes explore unpopular ideas in order to find the truth. An example of this would be the case of Galileo, who was ostracized from society for his discoveries and theories. Finally, I believe that you really can't take God out of any picture, even the sciences. Science doesn't try to encompass God's purpose or the salvation of souls. The goal of science is to ask what we know. The answer is quite simple. We know nothing. The challenge for scientists is to test, explore, experiment, and find new answers.

Significant Scientific and Technological Developments

Stem cell research is receiving a lot of scientific attention. In my opinion, stem cell research still has a long way to go. The morality and implications of stem cell research are heavily debated. The dividing issue is actually regarding embryonic stem cell research. Those who support embryonic stem cell research prefer to cast those who are against it as kooks who oppose stem cell research. In reality, most people who oppose embryonic stem cell research are against it because it kills the embryo. They do, however support adult stem cell research. The only true scientific breakthroughs in stem cell research thus far have come from adult (not embryonic) stem cell research.

Biodiesel fuel usage is more widespread than it used to be, but does not yet have widespread popularity. Willie Nelson uses and advocates the use of biodiesel, for example. Biodiesel fuel has political implications for this country. Increased biodiesel fuel can mean less foreign oil requirements. In this area, science can even serve our political needs as a country.

Solar cells are not a huge technical advancement, but the economic growth from solar technology has become huge and will continue to be so over the next few years. Going green is one of the big political and scientific discussions of our times. In Arizona it makes sense to use solar technology, as we have a plentiful supply of sunshine.

The recycling of electronics has grown in popularity and importance over the past few years. It has grown, despite the fact that there are difficulties in recycling these electronics. For example, electronics are not necessarily repairable any more, and have become throw away items. Recycling these items has grown in popularity because of the environmental impact of throwing them away and the economic impact of these electronics getting cheaper over time. Not only does this development help to keep lead from electronics out of landfills, it also protects our water supply as a result of keeping the electronics out of the landfill.

Regarding Fears and Anxieties

In our shifting paradigms, some people deal with their anxiety by simply not facing the facts. Some people will start movements in protest. As we can see, humor is one way people use to deal with anxieties about science and technology. The presence of lead in products and water as well as other toxins is a matter of grave concern to people.

Relating televisions back to chemical problems I will ask, where do we strike the balance? Do we compromise functionality for the sake of societal needs that are in reality merely wants? For instance, not everyone needs to buy a television from the store. Plus, some of the broken TVs that people don't resell go to waste. Manufacturers must continue to reduce the amount of lead, chemicals, and pollutants in TVs, laptops, and other electronics.

With the economy the way it is, we will either rise triumphantly and fix the problems, or mask the problems. Our country seems to be like a pendulum that swings from one side to the other. At times this keeps us from progressing as a society. One reason, among many, that America has prospered is that God protects us. I believe that our society needs to be more resourceful and less wasteful. We are in a time when people's rights collide with science and politics.

How will college help me?

I think my education makes me want more out of life. There are those that want material possessions, often without regard to the affect on society. Everyone is guilty by association in a figurative sense because of our fallen nature. Education pays off, even though it costs me money because it can increase my moral standards. I cannot be for education one day and against it the next. I must be either completely for it or completely against it. I am for it because there are not many things that can inspire me to compete in such a responsible way as education. School is a process; processes use logic, in some ways more than others.

Is science at odds with religion and philosophy?

Process and logic also apply to science. Science varies in degrees of logic as well. After all, God created science. I am concerned about the theological man that says that he is above science. This brings about the discussion of religion and philosophy and how it corresponds to science. I do not think they are at odds because science used to be considered a philosophy. The idea of religion and philosophy are good in themselves. But it is how people use them that can cause problems. The same can be said of science. Science is limited in some modern philosophy and present in others. I believe that people need to place a higher priority on forming their consciences and having good values. This can at times clash with the goals of modern society, as seen in the debate about embryonic stem cell research. Science, religion, and philosophy can and should work together. In my Catholic faith it is this kind of interrelationship in life that is even used to describe the Holy Trinity of God, coincidentally. The Holy Trinity works together.

Scientific method

In biology and physics classes I did use the scientific method. I think it is a powerful tool that governs man's perception of the world. It is slow and laborious, which is why some students, including me, felt rushed with projects in class. I have never used it formally outside the classroom, but I have used inferences, inductive, and deductive reasoning. The goal of the scientific method is to remove the possibility of bias from the experimentation. This is a good goal because it tries to keep the scientist honest.

Has Darwin influenced me?

Darwin influenced me in biology and philosophy classes. There is still no scientific explanation of the missing link, scientists just say it exists. They explain the gap in the evolutionary chain as the missing link. People of faith know that God is the unnamed missing link. I rely more on religion to help me when it comes to the origin of life. I don't like to think of limiting God's role in life. I think one of the apostles said "even if heaven doesn't exist, it won't hurt you to be a good person during your life." I think it's important to see that scientific discoveries should always support religion (even though scientists don't use the word God very often) because they work together even though religion doesn't always correspond to scientific fact. An example of this is the topic of miracles. Just because a person can't prove something scientifically shouldn't stop them from trying to prove it at all in the larger and more religious sense. I observe that God also only reveals thing to people when they are ready. A simple Bible verse to some might have vast implications to those who study religion on a regular basis.

Conclusion

One of the influences on my education was a physics teacher in college who was totally strict and yet totally reassuring. Never have I recalled seeing such an engaged and orderly yet down to earth individual. At first glance, she seemed not fit for the job, but I underestimated her. She was perfect. Another strong influence in my science education was an elementary school teacher that I had. She was from Great Britain and touched on all learning styles while she was teaching us about humans, animals, and plants. I valued her more because many other years at that school were horrible. Her teaching method showed our class that unfamiliar things seem comforting at times. To this day, her teaching methods help me when learning the sciences. I try to see a new way or see things through someone else's eyes.

This interest in science drew me to the field of psychology in college. I changed my mind about studying psychology, not by the difficulty level, but by a turn of events which showed me not to test people that inspired questions in me. It made me too uncomfortable. I wanted to work for my own needs first. Conversely, I am still happy for the existence of counselors, and psychologists, but it is not the field for me. I discovered that many other fields also offer the chance to help people.

Lastly, I think that we forget to be humble and considerate among friends, coworkers or other relations. I imagined, briefly, life without mirrors or televisions. Science has made TVs better. Mirrors help prevent car accidents. But we get so used to the fact that these outlets exist. These everyday items, although seem harmless, can get in the way of relationships. We need to rely more on other people and be more imaginative. That describes selflessness to me.

Further, science is very much like art. Bringing my previous point to light, I think art is not a mirror of what people have done, but a window. Science should be the same thing. A mirror shows you what you already know is there. Science should be a window as well, and the scientific method is the glass. There is something separating us from the material world. But it shouldn't obstruct us; it should be a filter. Science gives us a window to the world of discoveries, so do religion and philosophy.

This is exactly how science can serve society. Science doesn't always seek to help humans directly. Rather it seeks to help establish order and determine the consequences of events. I think science is likened to a strict teacher. They are not there to be emotional support but just to get you through the material. Lastly the act of the connection and emotional process is left up to each individual. This is why science is unbiased. At least good science is unbiased.

WE ARE THE WORLD: MY SOCIAL/CIVIC ESSAY

Introduction

I live in a country that is known for being a melting pot. This society has a wide variety of views and opinions about every subject under the sun. President Kennedy told us to ask what we can do for our country. This is an ongoing challenge. The United States was founded on the idea that we work together with the underlying principle being that we come to a respectful consensus while keeping in mind the rules of the Constitution. From a political and civic standpoint, I have been shaped by experiences (personal and societal) as well as people I have known and knowledge that I have gained regarding how the world works. The song *We are the world* eloquently said that we are each responsible for the world and the people in it. In other words, the song stated that we are all interconnected.

How Society Has Shaped My Political Views

In my lifetime there have been many firsts. In the 2008 primaries, we had the first woman as a serious contender to be a presidential nominee; and of course, the first African-American was elected President. On a personal level, an important first for me was when I reached voting age. My political views became especially important when I became eligible to vote. Some elitists would argue that the voting age should be raised. This seems wrong to me, as the ones who state that already have the right to vote, and now they want to change the rules. After observing the presidential primaries and seeing so many more people involved in the political process than in the past, I can see the importance of being involved in finding solutions to the problems our country faces.

The political process is often described by cynical people as a power grab. I do not believe it is always a power grab. For some politicians it is, and for others it is a way to make changes that they believe are for the better. The political process and the changes to our laws often seem to move slowly and carefully. This is frustrating to people who want immediate change.

There has been a reawakening of political activism, which has been an inspirational event for me to witness. In past primary elections, voter turnout was not very high. In more recent elections, especially the past presidential election, people were very much a part of the election process. I know I was very involved and interested. The message to elected officials has been that they work for us. This has made me feel part of the process, and not shut out of the process.

I have come to believe it is important that people don't just vote for a candidate because of the candidate's party. It is important to look at the views of the candidate, not just to which party he or she belongs. After the last election, I believe that when only the two major party candidates are considered, the system becomes less workable. By this, I mean that it is important to consider candidates from other parties, such as Libertarians and other third party candidates. Furthermore, the voters try their best to elect representatives and senators who will make the decisions the voters want. Sometimes elected officials make bad decisions. Then the voters can replace them.

Change has become a significant part of the political process, or at least part of the political talk. I personally would like to see a woman elected as president. This is partly because it is a change, and after this last election it is obvious the voters wanted change. They wanted change and elected Obama. He promised during his campaign that he would work in a bipartisan way. It took a long time for him to say that he wouldn't listen to ideas that don't support his agenda (especially his health care agenda). Most people still don't have the changes that they wanted and thought they had voted for. I would summarize that some Democrats have begun to think like Republicans, and some Republicans have begun to think like Democrats.

I tend to only believe in myself when others are happy. When others are sad, I tend to try to step into their shoes and believe in the other person more. This drives my views about politics and as a citizen. We are each other's keeper. There is still so much I do not know about our society. I realize that being a positive example at this point in history is difficult. During difficult times and the everyday problems of life it is important to look for the good in people. When you look for this good in people, good people will find you. If we each do that as part of our being citizens, the political issues will translate into positive change. I would have to say overall that increased political awareness has been a positive change in my life.

Crucial Social and Political Issues

In addition to political process issues I have already discussed, there are other critical issues that have shaped and continue to shape me. Global warming is one of the hot topics today. I conducted a study on how building sustainable homes could impact global warming. During the course of my study I went to a store that sold "green" supplies such as carpeting and flooring. There was a general elitist feeling in the store. By this I mean that the workers were snobby when I asked questions. For change to occur there must be a welcoming stance, not an elitist stance. Many people are in the dark about sustainable products, and cannot gain knowledge about sustainable building without asking questions. Unfriendliness can sink a movement. People will vote with their wallets. It is my belief that when people can afford to spend more now to save money and resources in the future, they will. My research on sustainable building taught me that we live in an interconnected world. It created questions for me about the wisdom of solar energy when nuclear energy is cheaper, cleaner, and more efficient.

The issue of legalizing gay marriage has been very divisive in society. I wish there wasn't so much hate talk about the issue from both sides. I think we need to keep discussions going. The country cannot solve the issue quickly to everyone's satisfaction. This is because society is complex. In my opinion, legalizing gay marriage has a negative effect on society. I believe one point of marriage is to reproduce. If you theoretically cannot reproduce together, you shouldn't be able to marry and raise a child together. That being said, I still believe adoption is great and an option here, because I was adopted. But I was adopted by a mother and a father.

Deforestation is another issue that has affected me, but more on an intellectual basis. Deforestation to create charcoal is mostly taking place in poorer nations. This keeps them in poverty. They continue to be exploited by their enemies. At the same time, recent advances in methods have brought about more research and biological soil development. This is an issue that has affected me indirectly, and the issue was brought to my attention as a result of an environmental biology course that I took. Even though I haven't personally grown up with deforestation, it occurs in the world and does ultimately affect me.

The issue of property rights affects me, and affects us all. It concerns me that people are depleting natural resources that can never be replaced. I see a bigger picture and a higher level of interconnectedness than I saw as a child. The way people treat property, resources, and people affects others. All resources should be treated with respect. This belief has even had an impact on my views on hunting. Although I do not think hunting is immoral, I think people who hunt just for sport should not be allowed to hunt. This excludes people who need to hunt in order to provide food for their family.

The Gift and Responsibility of Freedom

Freedom can be a means to an end. In Proseminar class, it was said that in our pursuit of happiness, it is good to just stop and be happy. In philosophy class, I read about many insightful views on freedom as expressed by Plato and other philosophers. We do not have the freedom to take our choices away completely. However, we do have the freedom to let a hedonistic nature prevent the real freedom of pleasure take place when we die. I do not think people necessarily understand that cost.

If freedom feels like a burden for some, that is understandable. I think it is because our human freedom comes with the sacrifice of military service. The question is: if the majority of soldiers enjoy their job, has freedom come with a true cost? What is that cost? In other words, can the families of a soldier care more about their soldier's fate than the soldier cares for his own fate? Yes they can and do. I remember that the freedom to care for someone also includes pain.

Other Societal/Cultural Experiences That Shape Me

Fortunately, I have had the opportunity to experience many cultural parts of society, such as libraries and museums. I enjoy libraries and enjoy their online resources, too. I am very much a people person, so it is sometimes simpler to ask a librarian rather than use a computer. Libraries are an important resource because they also give people without a lot of money access to books and other information. My love for reading and learning has been nurtured at the libraries I have visited.

Museums have been fascinating places to me throughout my life. During regular visits to Chicago, I have visited the Field Museum of Natural History and the Science and Industry Museum. One Science and Industry Museum exhibit was a new sustainable home. They had built the house using energy conservation and sustainable building materials. Museums these days have many hands-on exhibits. This is very important, because it helps me learn about the world. In visits to Columbus, Ohio I always visited COSI. This is a renowned science and industry museum as well, and is chock full of hands on exhibits. I absolutely loved that place!

Besides museums, I have seen historical sites that are truly living history museums. For many years, I lived near Philadelphia. We took every out-of-town visitor to see Independence Hall and the Liberty Bell. This was especially important to me, as that is really where the United States began. In even saw and stood in the defendant's box in Independence Hall. This gave me a concrete example of how court cases were handled in those times. Seeing the room where the Declaration of Independence and Constitution were signed brought history to life for me.

Freedom, Education, Involvement, and Experience Dovetail

As I have discussed, my involvement with the world around me has helped me to become politically, culturally, and civically aware. I am politically involved. The last local election in Gilbert was very real to me. I knew how important it was to be involved in the campaign and election process. I helped by putting signs in our yard for town council candidate Erin Scroggins. He almost won. I have attended a political rally for town council candidates, a tea party event, and even went to our congressman, Jeff Flake's town hall meeting about the health care bill.

My community awareness motivated me to connect with my community. I put my faith and heart into action by volunteering at our church's food bank. I continue to be very aware of various charities and help them when I can as well. I plan to help to raise money for our church's food bank through the company that I founded. I know that concern for social justice is a part of good citizenship.

Travel has broadened my views. I traveled to Ohio and discussed politics with my grandmother. Her views differ from mine and yet we can civilly discuss matters. I have been to Minnesota where people are very concerned about health care and other social issues. I have gotten a glimpse of some other views as a result of my trips to California. I know through my education and life experiences that we are all connected and interdependent.

Conclusion

My education and experiences have taught me a lot. I now believe that stereotypes and extreme view come from too little knowledge, not an excess of knowledge. Through social networking and research on the internet it is easier to keep your culture alive, but this in turn also increases the need to accept others' cultures. I am a citizen of the world. Thomas Jefferson said, "Our greatest happiness does not depend on the condition of life in which chance has placed us, but is always the result of a good conscience, good health, occupation, and freedom in all just pursuits". I believe in that freedom. It belongs to each of us.

AWESOME GOD AND AWESOME LIFE: MY VALUES/MEANING ESSAY

Introduction

My values and faith have grown and deepened throughout my life. I think the hardest part of growing up is finding the joy when others around you are not joyful. I choose one action over another based first on God's law, then family, then the laws of the nation and state. After taking these aspects into account, I clear everyone aside and determine if I can live with my decision. Part of living with my decision includes considering the effect my decision will have on others.

Values and Meaning through Faith

Faith in God is at the core of all values and meaning in my life. As people grow up they do things that cause tension and hurt. Through my faith in God, I learned to forgive people that have hurt me. I now can see that only one person has the right to complain. His name is Jesus. My faith and religion taught me it is possible and necessary to grow, change, and forgive. My love for God doesn't grant me a seat in heaven. I must change my life and live for Him. That is why when I have mortal sin on my soul I do not receive the host at Mass. I do this out of respect. Changing my life as my faith grows has meant I must continue to find ways to improve for Him and serve others.

One of the ways religion has influenced my actions is that I don't put myself down for sinning. Instead I have learned how to analyze my faults and move on. In this way I can grow and change. It can be crippling if someone doesn't know what a sin is. They might lash out at others because of the natural guilt they feel. Through dedication and self discipline I have grown and changed. I work on my faults on a daily basis, and try to keep in mind God's eternal laws.

Value and Meaning through Relationships

When I deal with social interaction I try to play to people's strengths. I know I have been treated better and am more consistently happy than most people. As some kids grow farther away from their parents when they have hardships, I grow closer whenever possible. There are no foolproof instruction booklets on how to be successful with people, so I just use patience. An example of this is if I am driving and someone cuts me off in traffic I remain calm most times. I do this for one reason. Judgment will be given to each person accordingly. I honor God by letting Him judge, rather than letting myself be judgmental.

I try to be non-elitist, and instead be gentle and humble. It is important to me to be compassionate and kind in my dealings with others. After a failed relationship with a girl in Ohio, I left part of myself behind. The pain I experienced from her from that breakup taught me how not to treat someone. It also taught me I cannot please everyone if I cannot please myself. This concept is not the opposite of wanting to please God; it works with it. Why? I please myself when I please God.

My purpose is also to be the purpose for others. I want to be of help to them even if it is only once when I am old and about to die. I want to bring hope to the children of my family and friends. They need us, of course, but we also need them in a more distinct and sacred sense. Serving people is a big part of my purpose in life. Relationships with others add meaning to my life, and I hope to theirs as well. I believe we all need each other, and we serve God best when we serve each other.

My Obituary

In my obituary I would tell people that they should ask questions in life just to ask them, and not just because there will be answers in reply. I would also tell people if they had known me, I would hope they wanted to change their life forever. Some people do not want to change and improve. A willing spark of conscious intellect between two people is all the world needs in order to recover from its over-modernization and reduce disconnectedness between people. Furthermore, I would say that once people realize they are not the center of the universe they can become so happy that their soul will smile, and so open that they will truly hear human voices for the first time. I would tell them they can then begin to expect the kindest voice without knowing why. That voice will be God speaking to them, through them, and through others.

I hope people will remember me as someone who helps them know the God that remembers them above all. I want people to know that I have learned how to live even though some days I am a complete basket case! Life is too short not to poke fun at our own faults. I want people to know that God's heart is saddened by the actions of humanity. I would tell people I know without a doubt that God exists, and that life is over before you know it. If you could find happiness even in your subconscious, you are happier than most of mankind. I want people to know that God is not just an emotion. In fact far from it, yet being a human who loves God is the most worthwhile pursuit.

Conclusion

The values and meaning in my life stem from my faith in God. Certainly the values I learned from my family stem from our shared faith. God's eternal laws are what drive me to become a good and kind man, as well as a law abiding citizen. God is love, and thus I am called to love His people. My faith has grown either despite or because of pain and suffering that I have experienced. Regardless, I will continue to be dedicated to my faith and God. I will continue to strive to fully form my conscience and character.

RESEARCH PROJECT: VERBAL/SOCIAL LEARNERS

ABSTRACT

The study of learning styles has shown the strengths and weaknesses of each learning style. Teachers have learned that teaching geared toward multiple learning styles can increase the effectiveness of student learning. Students with verbal/social learning styles require some reflective time and some interaction time in order for them to learn effectively. Verbal/social learners must take charge of their own learning and make adaptations to make the lesson or course a better fit with their learning style. These adaptations include making time for reflection before or after class, interacting with the teacher or fellow students, and making outlines and flashcards. By recognizing their learning style, its strengths and weaknesses, and making adjustments and adaptations, these learners maximize their potential.

VERBAL/SOCIAL LEARNERS RESEARCH PAPER

Introduction

The study of learning styles in order to learn and teach better has become a popular topic in the field of educational psychology for educators, students, parents, and the general public. Suarez (2006) stated that there is a definite advantage to homeschooling because homeschooling families can and often do adjust their teaching methods to meet each student's strengths. To emphasize this point, Ralph Waldo Emerson wrote, "each mind has its own method" (Suarez 2006, p. ix). Homeschooling families realize that "each learns at his or her own pace; each grasps concepts and learns needed skills in his or her own way. Some children learn better in groups; others fare well with independent studies" (Suarez 2006, p. 1). Teachers are beginning to adjust their teaching methods to meet student learning styles. (Felder, 2009; Felder & Soloman, 2009). The goal of this adjustment in teaching methods is to increase the chance for student success.

According to Howard Gardner, "there are a number of distinct forms of intelligence that each individual possesses in varying degrees, and include seven primary forms: linguistic, musical, logical-mathematical, spatial, body-kinesthetic, intrapersonal and interpersonal" (Francis 2000, p. 44). These various intelligences become learning styles.

The scope of this research paper will be to explore the characteristics, strengths and weaknesses of the learner that has a combination of both a verbal learning style and a social learning style. This combination learning style (like any learning style) has an impact on how effective the verbal/social learner is. This paper will describe how the verbal/social learning style works as well as how verbal/social learners can succeed through the methods the teacher uses in class and through the actions of the verbal/social learner in class and outside of class no matter which teaching style is used.

The Verbal Learning Style

Verbal learners learn well from the spoken and written word (Francis, 2000). Francis explained verbal learners may have a difficult time determining which things should be written down, and which things are less important. The classroom environment is an important aspect for the verbal learner. Verbal learners have a high need for predictability in the learning environment so they can fit new concepts or material into a logical sequence, and then connect the information to past concepts. Furthermore, they believe it is important for verbal learners to have some reflective time during the lesson. Their reasoning is that it gives verbal learners time to process and learn the information and formulate appropriate questions (Felder, 2009; Felder & Soloman 2009; Mooney & Cole, 2000).

The Social Learning Style

The social (interpersonal) learner values the interaction with the teacher and/or classmates. The social learner often values relationships and discussing concepts with the teacher (during class or afterwards) is often a key to effective comprehension for this learner. "Teachers who accepted them, had time for them, recognized their needs and strengths, and met their needs by providing opportunities for active learning and challenge contributed to their success" (Francis 2000, p. 136). Interaction with students is vital for social learners. Since they have the potential to reinforce concepts and help relate information to other ideas, classroom discussions and small group projects are important for students with a social learning style (Felder & Soloman).

These discussions and small group projects provide social learners with the active participation that helps them learn. The interactions must be based on personal respect and build relationships between social learners, their teachers, and the other students. Social learners' ability to learn is often directly related to the respect social learners receive from the teacher and fellow students whether it is during the large group or small group setting (Francis, 1996). If social learners perceive a lack of respect or risk of ridicule, they often choose not to interact; the lack of interaction undermines their own chance for achievement. It is this undermining that is at the root of underachievement for social learners (Mooney & Cole (2000).

The Combination Verbal /Social Learning Style

Most students have more than one aspect to their learning style. In the case of the verbal/social learner, the styles feed off of one another. According to Felder, the verbal aspect combined with the social/interpersonal aspect means that the reading and writing requires interactive discussion in order to be learned (2009).

By the same token, having classroom discussion with insufficient lecture and reading time, the same problem exists. In both cases, there would be no way for this student to establish connections of the topic to other topics (Felder & Soloman 2009). Kathy Kolbe emphasized that social learners are frequently active learners, rather than reflective. This translates into a high need for participation; in contrast, verbal learners tend to be reflective learners. They want to understand the topic before they speak or ask questions (Kolbe, 1990).

This causes a bit of a problem for students that are verbal/social, as they are both active and reflective. Felder and Soloman determined that note taking does not help these learners integrate the information. They must have interactive opportunities to help them make connections between the topic at hand and other information and topics (Felder, 2009; Felder & Soloman).

Teaching Method Issues in the Pre-College Classroom

In the pre-college years, the teacher spends a large amount of time on rules and policies which, from the standpoint of a verbal/social learner are just issued with no context. The reason behind those rules and the connections of those reasons to the outside world are rarely explained. Mooney and Cole emphasized that, even in the pre-college years, the verbal/social learner needs to make these connections and understand the reasons in order to internalize the rules (2000).

Small group work, if it exists at all, is project oriented, but interpersonal support to increase that learning is rarely emphasized. Sometimes the verbal/social learner holds back on participation out of respect for another speaker. Mooney and Cole discovered the group can make the mistake of thinking the verbal/social learner is either dumb or lazy, which works against the verbal/social learner's high need for respect (2000). Verbal/social learners tend to participate less when they believe the group has or will reject them; this creates a vicious cycle that works against that student's own needs.

Furthermore, the verbal/social learner needs to ask the teacher questions in order to process the information. Mooney and Cole pointed out that the questions may repeat the information just presented by the teacher. The teacher may interpret this as inattentiveness on the part of the student (2000). Nothing could be further from the truth. Instead the verbal/social learner is asking in order to understand the concept behind what the teacher presented. "As a result of the structure of most schools and their underlying assumptions and values, our teachers teach to a universal learning process for all children: one teacher, one way of presenting the information, one way to learn" (Mooney & Cole, 2000, p. 69). This universal (or one way) approach leaves out the students that do not have those learning styles.

The College Classroom

By the time verbal/social learners reach the college classroom discouragement may have set in. In contrast to the pre-college years, verbal/social learners can make great strides in the college classroom by making opportunities for social learning, no matter what learning style the professor favors. One strategy, suggested by Mooney and Cole, is if the class is straight lecture with little or no time for classroom discussion, verbal/social learners can change this by actively establishing a connection with the professor before (2000). This can be done before or after class, or during office hours. During these meetings verbal/social learners can discuss real world applications to the material, as well as connections between the material and other subjects (Felder & Soloman, 2009).

College students must take charge of their own learning. Even if the professor or fellow students will not discuss the connectivity of the subject or topic, verbal/social students can explore connections independently. Furthermore, Mooney and Cole determined students should take time to reflect on the lesson outside of class even if the professor doesn't leave time for reflection about the topics during class (2000). This strategy can make the difference between success and failure.

Study Skills that Maximize Learning

A change in study methods can help students succeed. The verbal/social learner will increase effectiveness by analyzing the connections between concepts, and exploring examples beyond the actual textbook and lecture. Helpful tools for the verbal/social learner include: creating outlines, flashcards, and making summary notes (Felder, 2009; Felder & Soloman, 2009; Mooney & Cole, 2000). The interpersonal learning style of this combination learner can be satisfied by engaging in active discussion with the teacher, fellow students, friends or family members.

The strategy for studying quantitative subjects such as mathematics, science, statistics, and accounting varies slightly from the approach for qualitative subjects. According to Felder and Soloman, the typical teaching approach for these subjects is visual and/or experiential (2009). The verbal learning style requires careful review and reflection (before and after class) to fully understand the concept, especially if the lecture will be largely geared toward the visual learner (Mooney & Cole, 2000). Practicing problems while using the correct procedures will help the student to succeed. Learning the reasons for the procedures will help the student own the information (Felder & Soloman, 2009).

Strategies for Teachers

Teachers that give students all the material while gearing the presentation aimed at all learning styles can help students with each learning style learn. "They do so by using a variety of teaching methods such as group problem solving, brainstorming activities, design projects, and writing exercises in addition to formal lecturing" (Felder, 2009). He described a study of engineering students conducted by Professor Peter Rosati in which:

> The results suggest that professors could improve engineering instructions by increasing the use of methods oriented toward active learners (participatory activities, team projects), sensing learners (guided practice, real-world applications of fundamental material) and global learners (providing the big picture, showing connections to related material in other courses and to the students' experience).

The participatory, active, and global styles are much the same as the combination of verbal/social learning styles. Again, this demonstrates the need of students and teachers to accept and learn from each others' styles, and shows that students will learn better through a spectrum of teaching strategies.

How Students Benefit

Even if teachers do not teach to their learning styles, students can benefit if they learn to learn in new ways or develop ways to compensate for the fact that the teacher ignores their learning style (Felder, 2009; Felder & Soloman, 2009). To learn this adaptation is a critical life skill. Once students with the verbal/social learning style learn how to make a lesson or course a better fit with their learning style through their own efforts, they own their future success. As an adaptation to make the lesson more verbal or social, for example, "ask your instructor for interpretations or theories that link the facts, or try to find the connections yourself" (Felder & Soloman, 2009). This will make any lecture or lesson fit the learning style.

Conclusion

The combination verbal/social learner has specific needs, strengths, and weaknesses. The verbal/social learner learns through the written and spoken word but also requires interaction with classmates and teachers in order to relate the information to other previously learned information. During class time the verbal/social learner needs some reflective time to process the information in addition to the interactive time. In math and science classes the verbal/social learner needs to understand the theories, not just learn the procedures. In all classes the verbal/social learner needs respect, understanding, and the creation of relationships.

Acceptance of the student's innate learning style is critical. The concept that a person's learning style must be changed is wrong (Kolbe, 1990). Kathy Kolbe explains that understanding personality types and learning styles is important. "Correcting a single misconception removes the greatest obstacle to effective parenting. It is that children don't become who they will be; they come as who they are" (Kolbe 180). This is as true for teacher and student as it is for parent and child. If teachers attempt to teach to all learning styles, it helps each student.

The most exciting part, however, about the analysis of the verbal/social learner goes well beyond defining, identifying or accepting what the aspects of the learning style are. Armed with this information, verbal/social learners can take charge of their own education and succeed no matter which learning style the teacher gears the lessons toward. They can adjust how they deal with the professor and their classmates to increase the opportunity for social learning. They can make time to reflect on the lesson and explore the connections to other subjects. Using this strategy because of their learning style places the keys to success right in the hands of verbal/social learners.

References

Felder, R. (1996). Matters of style. *ASEE Prism [Electronic version], 6,* 18-23.

Felder, R. and Soloman, B. *Learning styles and strategies.* Retrieved September 7, 2009 from North Carolina State University web site: http://www4.ncsu.edu/unity/lockers/users/f/felder/public/ILSdir/styles.htm

Francis, S.S. (2000). *Many ways to be smart: artisans in action.* Colville: Artisans in Action Press.

Kolbe, K. (1990). *The Conative connection: uncovering the link between who you are and how you perform.* Beverly: Addison-Wesley Publishing Company, Inc.

Mooney, J. and Cole, D. (2000). *Learning outside the lines: two Ivy League students with learning disabilities and ADHD give you the tools for academic success and educational revolution.* New York: Fireside Book Div. of Simon and Schuster.

Suarez, P. and Suarez, G. (2006). *Home schooling methods: seasoned advice on learning styles.* Nashville: Broadman and Holman Publishers.

INTERPERSONAL COMMUNICATION

Interpersonal communication is a course everyone should take, as the key to building good relationships and a positive community is through developing communication skills. The professor required two research projects in addition to learning the textbook concepts. The purpose of these research projects was to demonstrate how to integrate the concepts into real world applications.

RESEARCH PAPER: SPANISH BUSINESS COMMUNICATION

Abstract

Spain is now part of the European Union, and has an interesting culture. Since the death of General Franco in 1975, the country has gradually been making the transition to democracy. As a result of this transition, many companies in the United States already have begun to conduct business with companies in Spain. Businesses that had been run by the government in Spain are gradually becoming privately run businesses. This, too impacts how communications occur. Gaining knowledge of Spain's communications styles and customs in the business world will aid in improving communication between business people in these countries.

Introduction

Today, Spain is "an effective example of transition from authoritarianism to democracy" (Thomson, Gale 2007, p. 1730). This transition has affected the country's culture and continues to affect the interpersonal communication styles and customs in the business world in Spain. Understanding these styles help to ensure effective business communication. Assuming that Spaniards have the same interpersonal communication styles and customs as Americans will lead to great misunderstandings.

Statement of Purpose

The goal of this research is to discover the styles of interpersonal business communication in Spain. This helps identify ways Americans can improve communications when dealing with business people in Spain.

Research Question

Will developing an understanding of interpersonal communications styles in Spain help Americans that need to conduct business with Spain?

Thesis

Knowledge of the business customs and interpersonal business communication styles in Spain will improve interpersonal communication between American businesses and Spanish businesses.

Significance

For effective communication to take place between Spain and the United States, and businesses to operate well, it is important to understand the communication styles and customs in Spain. Understanding the Spanish culture is essential in order to avoid misconceptions and interpersonal communication errors.

Method

An internet search on the World Wide Web provided research information. In addition, various books were used as the basis for this research.

Findings

Spain's Background

Until the death of Franco in 1975, Spain had been a communist country. Its business dealings were mostly with other communist countries, and the businesses were largely government run. Since then, "Spain's accession to the European Community…required the country to open its economy" (Thomson & Gale 2007, p.1730). As a result of their efforts, it has been a fine example of changing from a communist form of government to a democracy. Communication styles have been changing as well.

Spain Has a Collectivist High-Context Culture

Spain is a collectivist, high-context culture, and Spaniards see the value of the social group. That keeps their spontaneity alive. They are collectivist when it is convenient to the situation. Spaniards value being a Spaniard as a good thing, as opposed to being the best you can be. Spaniards focus on the group they are a part of, and the personal relationships that have developed. For example, if someone they know and respect is a personal friend of yours, they will transfer that respect to you as well. Spaniards collectivist high-context culture comes way ahead of any personal responsibility for business problems or situations. "However, although they are proud of their regional identity, most Spanish aren't nationalists or patriotic and have little loyalty to Spain as a whole" (Hampshire 2006, p.480-481). Spaniards convey a lot of passion in their communications; because of their passion, things do move more quickly than the outsider would think; however timeliness isn't necessarily their motivation.

It is important for Americans to keep in mind that emotional statements and communication styles on the part of the Spaniard does not mean aggression or a know-it-all stance on their part. "More reserved cultures should be wary of equating emotional expression of ideas with lack of control or conviction" (World business, 2009).

Need to Know Basis

The "need to know basis" in business simply means that information is only transmitted to individuals, groups or departments that are thought to need that specific information. This is in contrast to transferring information based only on hierarchy and written policy, which is an American concept. It is important for Americans to know this, as it can lengthen the time required to conduct business. The manager in Spain might only communicate information to a manager in another department that he feels a level of comfort with. The relationship may very well determine who one manager decides needs the information.

"Business organizations tend to be structured along hierarchical lines, but the reporting and power structures might not ultimately closely resemble the paper version. Information, power, and delegation might flow along more abstract, unclear lines or relationship and mutual self-interest" (World business, 2009). This will complicate how Americans deal with various people throughout the organization, as they must continually make sure that various people are all on the same page.

Spoken Word More Important Than the Written Word

Spaniards put more importance on the spoken rather than the written word. "E-mails and letters should always be followed up with a phone call" (World business, 2009). Probably the reason the Spaniards don't appreciate the written word as much as the spoken one is because of the *mañana* syndrome. This syndrome means the person believes that the project can always be done tomorrow. As a result, papers are lost, workers don't show up on time and offices are open at strange hours. "Almost all museums, shops, and churches close for 2-4 pm or longer for an afternoon siesta. Most Spaniards eat lunch during their siesta, so restaurants open in the late afternoon. Most restaurants will start serving dinner by 9 pm, although eating close to midnight is very common in Spain" (Pacheco, 2008, p. 890). These hours will obviously impact when and how business can be conducted.

While this can be frustrating, personal conversations can help to counteract the syndrome, and adjusting time expectations on the part of Americans is essential. Since e-mails should be followed up with a phone call it also speaks of their relatively new arrival to technology. In addition, it is related to the fact that they are relatively new to democracy. To some workers it seems like any excuse to talk is better than working. An additional note is that emotional statements are valued rather than discouraged when they occur.

Value of Building Personal Relationships

Business culture and communication in Spain are both very focused on relationships. In Spain, business people value saving face and building strong relationships. As a culture, they do not take criticism lightly. All interpersonal communication is seen as personal, which means that it is essential to tread lightly. Things that may not seem like an insult to Americans can seem very insulting in Spain. Therefore, Americans must remember that every communication is seen as either adding to or subtracting from the relationship.

As a side note, on a societal basis, the Spaniards have been called racists, but they are not racist towards Americans. There has been a recent decline in the problems they had with gambling, drinking and drugs. Sensitivity to these preconceived notions about stereotypes is important.

It is essential to continually communicate that the relationship is valued even more than the business at hand. This has a large impact on business meetings, as a considerable amount of time is spent developing the relationship and discussing each other's life and interests before getting down to the actual business topics.

Furthermore, "be aware of going too far by pursuing arguments or points on purely technical grounds because (a) the interpersonal element is valued over the technical truth, and (b) a degree of modesty (*Modesto*) is valued over assertiveness" (Petersen &Petersen, 2009). This is in sharp contrast to the American emphasis on competition and being right. Ignoring this aspect can seriously undermine business communication when dealing with the Spanish people.

Timeliness and Schedules

Timeliness and meeting schedules mean a far different thing to business people in Spain than in America. This can be highly stressful for Americans that assume that a deadline is specific and guaranteed. Gaining gradual agreement to specific deadlines through building relationships and as a result of many conversations will help.

"Be aware that time is less linear and compartmentalized into units (monochromic), but more flexible and overlapping (polychromic) to serve a purpose or relationship" (Petersen & Petersen, 2009). Time in and of itself has a far different meaning to the Spaniards. Their approach to time and schedules is not a bullet point or checklist approach, as it is in America. It is more of an epic poem approach, which means that a large amount of time must be spent building the relationship and discussing the schedules in that context. As they see it, "although it is important to be punctual, it is far more important to place the correct amount of emphasis on relationships. Therefore, dealing with people is more important than punctuality" (World business, 2009). In all communications, the American business person must convey their belief that the relationship is important and demonstrate patience and consideration.

Conclusion

Spain is moving rapidly forward in the business world. Effective communication in Spain requires a large investment of time and a willingness to establish honest relationships. Building consensus is valued far more than proving a point. In business communications and dealings, Spaniards want to see how others respond to the unpredictable. Gaining an understanding of Spain's interpersonal communication styles and business customs are essential in order to be effective when dealing with businesses in Spain. Through building relationships with their Spanish counterparts, American business people can help to ensure a successful and positive business relationship.

References

Ellicott, K. (Ed.). (2006). Countries of the world and their leaders yearbook 2007. Farmington Hills: Thomson Gale.

Hampshire, D. (2006). Living and working in Spain 2006 (6th ed.). London: Survival Books.

Pacheco, I. (Ed.). (2008). Let's go Europe 2008. New York: St. Martin's Press.

Petersen, A., & Petersen, S. (2002). English communication for professionals. Retrieved September 7, 2009, from http://www.aspetersen.de.

World business culture: business communication styles in Spain. Retrieved September 7, 2009, from http://www.worldbusinessculture.clm/Spanish-Business-Communication-Style.html

RESEARCH PAPER: FAMILY COMMUNICATION

Abstract

Family communication strengths and weaknesses are determined by the same interpersonal communication principles as any other type of interpersonal communication. The family is the microcosm of society; thus healthy interpersonal communication in the family will have a positive impact on society. Verbal communication styles in the family should be nurturing and serve to guide each other. Non-verbal communication and paralanguage should match the verbal communication. Communication in the family will improve when family members understand the differences in how males and females communicate and the requirements due to role differences within the family. Just like meetings in the workplace, family meetings can be effective in order to air grievances, discuss rules and policies, and improve overall communication within the family.

Introduction

The family is a microcosm of society; in effect it is a community. Communications within the family are affected by the same things as interpersonal communication in the work place or in society. According to Le Poire (2006), "families serve as the cornerstone for our lives and provide a rich forum for every type of communication, from affection to conflict" (p.3).

Understanding how family communication can be made effective translates into a family that functions well. Family communication can be healthy or unhealthy and is affected by the choice of verbal communication styles, paralanguage aspects, gender differences in communication, and respect for impact of role differences play in communications.

Statement of Purpose

The goal of this research is to discover the styles and characteristics of interpersonal family communication in order to identify ways to improve communications.

Research Question

What are the characteristics of effective and ineffective family communication in the traditional nuclear family? How can understanding the verbal styles, paralanguage characteristics, nonverbal communication, gender differences in communication, and role differences improve family communication?

117

Thesis

Family communications are affected by verbal communication styles, paralanguage aspects, gender differences, and role differences. Through the use of effective interpersonal communication principles and skills and conducting family meetings, family communication can improve the cohesiveness of the family.

Significance

As the family goes, so goes the community and society. If we want overall communication in our society to be effective, family communication must be effective as well. It is only through the knowledge about and application of interpersonal communication principles and skills within the family that family members can then become effective communicators with each other. When this occurs, family members can then use these same skills in their lives outside of the family.

Method

An internet search on the World Wide Web and a literature search provided the research information for this paper.

Findings

Verbal Communication Style Choices

The choices a family makes about the verbal communication styles positively or negatively affect family communication. Effective managers have said it is how many people they serve, not how many people serve them. The same can be said in families. DeVito (2006) stated "The issue then is not whether you will or will not persuade or influence another. Rather, it's how you'll exert your influence" (p. 24).

When verbal messages do not match, conflict can arise. Many families struggle with the concept of language and interpersonal communication. There is often tension in a family unit. Families are formed by people who each bring their own biases and beliefs. Just as crazy religions and cults have many reasons for forming, but generally think they are improving on what already exists, so too do many people set out to form families. They can fall short if they are ineffective communicators. Verbal communication should be clear and nonthreatening. Clearly explaining thoughts and expectations, without demeaning the other person is the epitome of healthy verbal communication.

Healthy verbal communication should allow family members to learn, relate, influence, play, receive help, and give help. The goal of all family communication should be to both nurture and control, according to Le Poire (2006) "nurturing includes communication that is central to encouraging development, including both verbal and nonverbal behaviors that are encouraging and supportive. Control includes communication that is central to guiding, influencing, and limiting the types of behavior evidenced by family members" p.11). In other words, even though nurture and control are separate, they are also two sides of the same coin. The words that family members choose can either create a positive or negative feeling. Why not be positive?

Paralanguage Characteristics

Paralanguage characteristics are *how* the speaker says things. Paralanguage characteristics can create harmony, conflict or even confusion depending on whether family members have matched or unmatched styles ideas with lack of control or conviction. Tone of voice, speaking speed, and volume can convey warmth, coldness, anger or excitement. An example of this would include the use of a sarcastic tone in the voice.

John Gray wrote that family members have things they expect each member to do. These expectations become part of how family members expect each other to speak and convey their support (Gray, 2004). The worst is when someone does something to break trust when they haven't even realized it. This can happen through paralanguage choices. If one person has a sharp tone of voice, the other person could interpret that to mean the person doesn't want to talk, is angry, or something else. This may make the person feel they can't trust that person. The person offended by the sharp tone could then jump from being upset about the break in trust to being upset that the person doesn't even realize they have done anything. When this happens, the upset family member frequently resorts to the silent treatment. This creates further disharmony in the family environment. Obviously, discussing the matter resolves the issue more effectively.

In verbal communication it isn't uncommon for parents to avoid certain responses out of love for the child. The parents might care more about a child's grades than if he drinks or smokes occasionally. In that respect, the parents have made a conscious decision about how they will treat the child under these circumstances.

Nonverbal Communication

Nonverbal communication includes: gestures, eye contact, facial expression, clothing, jewelry, body language, and touch. A family member can nod his/her head when the other person talks, lean in to show interest, and use other affective cues. These are additional forms of nonverbal communication. Nonverbal communication makes up close to 75% of all communication. Nonverbal communication can be a source of conflict when verbal messages and gestures do not match. As a certain beer commercial stated "it's not too heavy and not too light, but just right." Physical objects can become a form of nonverbal communication as well. Since divorce and violence do plague our families, the simple mistake of opening a door in the house too quickly or slowly has the potential to upset a person. If they are upset, people could hold grudges.

Gestures, angry looks, and other similar actions can provide negative nonverbal communication. Smiles, nods, hugs, and reassuring looks can provide positive nonverbal communication. Emblems, a type of hand gestures that represents exact words or phrases, should be practiced in the family. Different cultures have vastly different emblems; thus emblems in the family should be kept in the family.

Conflict resolution techniques can be used to fix some problems. Someone who is happy, and sends that message through verbal and nonverbal communication may help an unhappy family member. However, they might not rub off on an unhappy family member. This is why: not only do time messages exist such as past, present, and future orientations, but people will put more emphasis on different parts. Add to that a physical, social-psychological, temporal, and cultural context dimensions and confusion certainly can thrive (DeVito, 2006).

Physical closeness can be used to show love. Families can use this to their advantage to help to fix problems. It is important for family members to give when they touch, never take. Family members need to be aware that actions that are acceptable with each other in public may not be acceptable with nonfamily members. Examples of this include hugging, walking along with an arm across each other, or just walking very close together. Although social kissing has become more common, one should follow the cultural and gender rules, which are discussed in the next section.

Impact of Gender Differences on Communication

Gender differences come into play with family communication, as males and females have different ways of communicating. A lack of knowledge and understanding of these differences creates conflict and misunderstanding. It is ironic that women will display more acceptable emotions in public than men. Here is why it's ironic. It is ironic because women tend to smile more (even at inappropriate times) than men do (Gray, 2006). This is why in the family it can be hard to decode the emotions and feelings of others. Tannen argued that "issuing orders indirectly can be the prerogative of those in power and in no way shows powerlessness" (DeVito, 2006, p. 127). The stereotype that women are more indirect than men is true, it seems. The classic example of messages varying in abstraction comes into play when a precise speaker gets tired and skips a word or two. If the speaker doesn't catch it and the listener does but is afraid to point it out, then upset feelings or confusion will probably happen (Gray, 2006).

The most common communication differences related to gender difference between males and females has been studied extensively by John Gray. He discovered that men often want to go off and solve the problem on their own, and women want them to discuss it. Women want to discuss their problem, but don't necessarily want the man to solve it. As a matter of fact if the man offers her a solution, she thinks he wants her to stop talking about it (Gray, 2006). Awareness and acceptances of these gender differences can help family members from ending up in disagreements, and to be more supportive in the ways that the person actually needs.

Being assertive is a strategy that family members can use. It is a non-gender action that allows respect for the other, but doesn't put either person in an inferior position. Someone who uses this in the family might find that an "I win-you win (win-win)" conflict resolution style helpful. A nurturing family lifts each member to a better place. People learn more from interpersonal communication (especially effective interpersonal communication) than any other media source (DeVito, 2006).

Impact of Role Differences on Communications

Role differences within the family mean different communication styles and needs. Families can learn to communicate effectively, even when there is inequality because of their roles. Gray's research (2006) showed that:

> Many men have denied some of their masculine attributes in order to become more loving and nurturing. Likewise, many women have denied some of their feminine attributes in order to earn a living in a workforce that rewards masculine attributes (p. xxxi).

This shift in attributes has shown up in the family as well. It has become less acceptable for the mother to be the only nurturing parent. This can translate into the expectation that all children learn nurturing behavior. Since children do grow up and leave the home, it is best that they develop skills in interpersonal communication. For real world success, the TWA Journal explained that "interpersonal communication skills are considered "key" in the office of the future" (DeVito 2006, p.2).

Shared living space is becoming more and more common. However, shared living space does not guarantee a close knit family. Families that communicate well have a healthy family dynamic. In a very real sense, the healthy family dynamic shows children and adults how to perform in the real world. A real life experience for me is related to this concept. A friend of mine lives in Minnesota. He did not take care of his parents or brothers. He did not have a healthy view of life. The point is that sharing time was not a part of his family. Although the culture in Minnesota values respect and family life, my friend did not value these things.

When one looks at family, people assume they are dealt a set of cards and have to play the hand they were dealt. This doesn't mean they must tolerate violence, of course. It does mean that families must learn to communicate effectively with each other. It does mean that even though the children and parents do not have equal roles, they all have important roles to play. If the parents and children follow communication rules and respect each other, stress will be less. Family connections will have a chance to grow closer, because people need the structure.

Benefit of Family Meetings

Just as departmental meetings in the workplace have the potential to resolve conflict, clarify policies, and improve communication within the department, so too can family meetings benefit the family in the same way. Gebeke and Bushaw (1993) researched the concept of the family meetings and defined them as having specific aspects:

- Family meetings are time set aside to promote meaningful communication and to provide for family discussion, decision making, problem solving, encouragement and cooperation.

- Family meetings can be structured and rather formal or flexible and informal.

- At family meetings, everyone has a part and something to contribute. No one is less important than another, and family members contribute according to their age and ability.

Family meetings show that the parents care and have been found to reduce problems. A great time for family meetings is during family mealtime. A major problem for families when it comes to communication is distractions. If family members do not give the eye contact a person desires, or remains silent, it can really bother the person. People must learn to use the entire body to convey their mood. Through family meetings, misunderstandings and miscommunications can be discussed, resolved, and corrected. After awhile, family members can then begin to see each other (spouse, parent, and children) as not just a role, a sex, or an age, but just there for each other to help each other.

Family meetings can be very helpful for managing conflict. Hesitations, too many intensifiers, disqualifiers and big questions can all show lack of power. These should be avoided. However, the use of active listening through back channeling cues lets the speaker in the family meeting know the family is listening. If family members don't tend to argue or discuss things when they are in public, the only place left to resolve problems is in the home. De Vito stated (2006), "because the territorial owner is dominant, you stand a better chance of getting your raise approved, your point accepted, or a contract resolved in your favor if you're in your own territory (your office, your home) rather than in someone else's (your supervisor's office, for example)" (p. 162). This means that conflicts are more likely to be resolved in a family meeting at home, rather than in a public place.

Something to watch out for (not only in family meetings but in family communication in general) is cues which take the turn away from the speaker, and miscues. An example of a miscue would be the speaker is looking for sympathy. The listener will act jolly to cheer the person up. The speaker is actually looking for understanding. The listener should always ask the speaker what they meant by what they said. It is not an insult to ask what the family member meant by what he/she said; it is a sign of honesty and respect. The overall benefits of family meetings are that they can clear up misunderstandings, explain what is and isn't acceptable to family members, and increase close feelings between family members.

People sometimes feel that a stranger has the potential to know them at a glance, more than their closest friends. If all of a family member's family relationships are just brief contacts throughout the day, then the family members might think or act like they know each other very well. By actually having a long conversation with a family member as takes place in a family meeting, they may come to discover they don't know each other very well at all. Hence, they need time to build relationships. Family meetings on a regular basis can help family members feel that their family knows them well and accepts them, even if they disagree. Through interpersonal communication (like a one-to-one conversation) a family member may find out more about all of the family members through that one person. If the family is large, and there isn't time for a one-to-one conversation with each family member, this may be a helpful way to know each other.

Conclusion

In conclusion, active listening is the best way to use back channeling cues. Healthy verbal communication, positive paralanguage, loving nonverbal communication, understanding of gender driven communication preferences, and knowledge that family roles play in communication help improve family communication. Conducting family meetings can help keep the family's interpersonal communication healthy. Active listening during these meetings through back channeling cues will help keep family meetings positive.

Remember that the more people speak and listen in public effectively, the easier it becomes to communicate in their own home and family. The opposite is true as well. Learning family members' signals can take more time. The television show *Supernanny* demonstrates this repeatedly. Communication accommodation theory says that speakers adjust their speaking style to gain social approval and to increase understanding. In the family setting, family members must speak to each other in the ways they want to be spoken to. If family members speak to each other as if they are a warm close-knit family, they can become exactly that. In other words, people sometimes have to fake it to make it. "There is a powerful tendency for communicators within families to reciprocate the communication behavior they receive. Positive communication behavior is more likely to be met with more positive communication" (Le Poire, 2006, p. 259). The goal of families is (or should be) to build stable relationships. Le Poire stated it best when she said (2006) "Thus, in families, thinking and communicating positively predicts more satisfying and more stable family relationships in that more positive evaluations and more positive communication behavior is likely to result and to be reciprocated" (p. 259). This is the quintessential motivation for improving family communication.

References

DeVito, J. (2008). *Interpersonal messages: Communication and relationship skills.* Boston: Pearson Education, Inc.

Gebeke, D. & Busha, K. (1993). *Family communications and family meetings.* (FS-522, May, 1993). Retrieved October 1, 2009, from http://ag.ndsu.edu/pubs/yfl/famsci/fs522w.htm

Gray, J. (2004). *Men are from Mars, women are from Venus: The classic guide to understanding the opposite sex (1st ed.).* New York: Harper Collins.

LePoire, B. (2006). *Family communication: Nurturing and control in a changing world.* Thousand Oakes: Sage Publications, Inc.

SMALL GROUPS: ANALYSIS AND SAMPLE PAPERS

INITIAL ANALYSIS OF MY SMALL GROUP

The small group that I am analyzing is my family. My family consists of my mother, father, and me. In group task roles, my mom is an opinion seeker, information giver and a big time recorder-secretary. My dad is an evaluator-critic. In group maintenance roles, my dad is the one who compromises. An example of this is before we shop or try to find a restaurant. He wants to build consensus, but my mom and I don't like to provide as much input into decisions that affect everyone. In this area my mom is an encourager-supporter and a tension-releaser, my dad is an on observer-interpreter and a tension-releaser.

In the area of self centered roles, occasionally my dad is a clown. Confessor is an interesting role. I share this at times when my emotions and feeling build up. I think most people don't know how to reveal themselves appropriately in certain contexts. I think the opinion-seeker goes well with this role. My mom, dad, and I are all opinion-seekers at times.

Regarding the roles above there is additional information that further explains my family. My mom always wants to know how I feel. She is compassionate. She also focuses on the small insignificant things I do that seem normal for me to do. This is probably normal in families, but it is still noteworthy. This would place her as an encourager-supporter and an opinion-seeker. She always tries to balance the conversation with her own perspectives. She is the information giver in the family, in the historical sense.

My dad, on the other hand, needs to be a gatekeeper and make sure the conversation will go well before I was able to talk. This is just normal to him. He is also historically informed, and sometimes will be an observer-interpreter by jokingly repeating something my mom said to me, knowing that it will make me smile, and in turn make my mom smile and laugh. He does paraphrase a lot. In fact, he recently told me that he confused people when he would recite his lines for a play, because he didn't say them verbatim. My mom has conducted safe environment training workshops, and is excellent at getting people to reach an agreement. She is an ice breaker and a harmonizer. That would also make her an initiator and a tension releaser.

It is interesting to see that my perceptions of my family are accurate. I think this type of exercise encourages moving forward with ideas. Just because a non-social family member doesn't see the value of the other family members doesn't mean the value doesn't exist. It doesn't stop there. We always need to keep re-evaluating our relationships.

Questions for Analyzing My Small Group

1. ***Do members use plural pronouns rather than singular ones?*** I would say sometimes, because we only talk collectively at meal times and during outings. Other than that we use direct language. I think because we are such a small group (my mom, dad, and me) it is strange to use plural pronouns.

2. ***Do members use language that acknowledges shared needs?*** Sometimes. We only use this when we are about to do something like shopping. Sometimes we use this when we are joking around; for example, seeing something on TV we can all relate to and make fun of, but still strengthen our group opinions. I think a distinction needs to be made between tag questions and assertive opinion seeking.

3. ***Do members solicit opinions and express the need for cooperation?*** Very often. We do this as a family, but my dad is more overt than my mom is about this. For example, my dad will get me to open up because he cares, but he will take his time because he doesn't like to put pressures on individuals. He knows that it means more if the answers to questions aren't forced. I'm not saying my mom does a bad job at this. I'm just saying they do it differently.

4. ***Do members talk to one another on equal terms?*** We do this very often. In our family, you have to work for respect. The Golden Rule is in place all the time. I think the only power differentiation is when there is referent power displayed by my parents. In other words, we don't like to be shy just to make the other person feel less intimidated. If one of us is feeling intimidated it is that person's responsibility to speak up and let the other person know.

5. ***Do members use casual language, nicknames, slang?*** Very often. We have a lot of nicknames for things. I differentiate between having nicknames for each other and things, and actually naming inanimate objects. On my blog I have a section that goes into worldplay a bit. My family and I like to engage in wordplay and are good at it. Personally, I have about 10 to 15 names for my dog.

6. ***Do members express empathy and liking?*** Yes, very often. However, we do like to use each others' titles when we are showing respect. If the situation is less serious, then we will use empathy and avoid titles. I believe that sometimes it is important to be fun when a family member feels down. If we matched each other perfectly with empathy all the time we might become socially impaired, and unable to either face or give criticism in public or elsewhere.

7. ***Do members express interest in solving problems?*** We do this sometimes. My dad is especially good at doing this. He has experience with a process called "scrum" at work. His small group uses it for project management and conflict management. We are all interested in finding good strategies to make things better.

8. ***Do members use a non-threatening tone and nonjudgmental language?*** Very often. The fact that we do this often as a group makes us finely tuned in as to when the other person is talking in a slightly judgmental way. We don't exactly ignore our differences to make them disappear; we just use prevention strategies. For example, I think we have an aura as a collective group that lets the others know when one of us is feeling upset. It is important to not interpret facial expressions as direct judgment or threatening. I have a general rule of thumb. If a person in our group didn't know that they appeared threatening or angry, I discount that I might have felt offended.

9. ***Do members paraphrase one another?*** Sometimes. I think it helps us see things from a different angle and is a fun way to communicate. I think that with paraphrasing you have to be good at interpreting the other person's signals and meanings so that you understand what the other person means. Sometimes paralanguage and tone, and inflection make a huge difference. Occasionally we will catch the other person saying something that the other two of us in the group didn't hear to begin with.

10. ***Do members ask "what if" questions?*** Rarely. I mostly ask these questions. To start off, both of my parents did not like philosophy until I made them see it is ok. My dad knows a lot of stuff and does philosophize, but that doesn't mean he likes philosophy. Actually, my dad will use "what if" statements when he is teaching math to me. Other than that, I don't see any of us using "what if" questions, unless we are joking.

11. ***Do members propose objective criteria for solutions?*** We do this very often. I think "objective" depends on the group members' feelings. I believe you could also say "I think we need to do this a little differently". It becomes objective if the person who said it rarely uses "I think" statements and if they don't take themseles too seriously as a person. I think the group can meet the goal of objectivity under the right circumstances without being explicitly objective. We do this a lot because we all like to hear the others' opinions more than our own.

12. ***Do members summarize areas of agreement?*** Very often. I think we do this most of all in our family. Generally we use summarizing questions to probe deeper into something.

13. *How well do members define and analyze the problem?* We have become satisfactory with analyzing problems. The more input I give to our problem-solving strategies, the more response I receive. I believe we tend to relax just a bit too much after we have finished a prior task that was difficult. Just because we are a family doesn't mean we will think like-mindedly. We are talking more and more about the problems, big or small, that we have in our lives. Time is a big factor here. Hopefully we will practice a meeting technique called SCRUM, which my dad uses at work. I use a digital voice recorder. There are so many uses I can find for it that I don't know where to start.

14. *How well do members identify criteria?* We do a superior job at identifying criteria. When identifying criteria I will sometimes notice that because we have so many things to do on our lists that we will have a continual re-evaluation of criteria. I think a deep desire to know what the other person's input and ideas are will form an agreement on how to solve problems and what the outcome should be. I have realized that empathy doesn't mean you have to change your happy emotions for the other person. I also think we lead others to believe that being on the same page would compromise our individuality. Just the opposite. When you have a set plan, then you can manipulate it to meet your goals within that. My parents as a group are very supportive of my goals but also expect me to do my part in the family. I think if you can get used to compromising early on, even in small agendas, then your group morale will succeed more often than not.

15. *How well do members generate solutions?* We usually do a superior job at generating solutions. I am learning a lot about myself and my parents know a lot. In order to generate a solution, there has to be a problem. Generating solutions as a group requires creativity. There is a certain implicit energy level in our group that says that we should always bring relevant information to the group table. Knowledge is not just about what you know, but how you can apply it to things you don't know anything about.

16. *How well do members evaluate solutions?* Sometimes we do a satisfactory job at this and sometimes we do a superior job at this. How do you be polite but also time conscientious? I have noticed that sometimes our group mentality is just off because we are overworked, tired, sick or hungry. Sometimes I will have an opinion that I firmly believe in, and then a new fact or idea will be presented by my group; and then I will change my mind. This is the act of evaluating solutions, and it is an important step.

17. *How well do members focus on the task*? We do a superior job of this. We are incredibly focused as a group and individually. Sometimes our habitual natures will make us overwork. I think as a group we tend to be bigger thinkers than most families. I am starting to see how lucky I am that our personalities form together nicely. When we are discussing things, one member may add commentary that on the surface may be off topic and indicate a lack of focus. We don't view it that way; we see it as elaborating.

18. *How well do members manage conflict*? We do a superior job at this. We all seem to get upset at the same types of things. I think that helps. I think we are our strongest at being conflict managers when we are all together. Rare occurrences will test our patience within the group. Raising your voice or being silent isn't necessarily bad things. If you start to perceive people as being positive, you are then more likely to react positively to others' questionable behavior. Group think is something to watch out for here.

19. *How well do members maintain a collaborative environment*? We do a great job at this. I believe as a group we are collaborative, but we also sometimes set our expectations too high for one another. What I mean by that is that we internally praise each other, or come up with tangential ideas, but the true understanding of values and decision making styles is sometimes overlooked. What we perceive is what creates the climate. I think the most important thing for our group is to ask for feedback. Sometimes we don't give each other enough recognition. It is important to not view a tired or hungry person in the group as not engaged. In other words, there are certain things that we have to just let the other person do or solve for themselves. It is important not to over-collaborate.

20. *Do members communicate effectively*? We do a superior job at this. We are all interested in each other's communication styles. It is interesting to see cultural and gender factors play a part in what decision making style we use. My dad took symbolic logic in college. He has tried to explain it, but maybe I could get more familiar with it now that he isn't as stressed by communication at work. Since communication includes effective listening, I notice the different listening styles and roles we each try out. It would be interesting to have the family take not only the Myers-Briggs and personality tests which I have already taken, but also to use heuristics to get more concrete data for our communication styles.

FINAL PAPER: SMALL GROUP ANALYSIS OF MY FAMILY

Introduction to Group Communication

The group I studied is my own family, which consists of my dad, mom, and me. We each have our own personality and learning style and this affects our communication. My dad has a very visual learning and communication style. Since my dad is computer savvy he has me or my mom e-mail an example of a problem to him so he can look at it on his computer. This helps him communicate better. It's not my goal to be smarter than my parents, but I do want to be as smart as they are. Interdependency is a part of my family. Primary groups are defined differently in my two communications textbooks, but for Small Group Communication class, a primary group is what I am in for support and affection. The dialectics between wanting and needing something and happiness and seriousness is what my family deals with a lot.

Groups such as family and friends are good, and some isolation is good, too. To add to this, the book lists potency, meaningfulness, autonomy and impact as characteristics of empowered groups. I think that my family has a need to be "like" each other, but not "become" one another. My Proseminar professor said, "Sometimes on the road to becoming happy, we need to just stop and be happy". Likewise, my parents' generation had to be creative to have fun and be happy. Creativity is a positive attribute of groups, but we need to face the negative attributes. Also, we should be more consistent. What I mean is that we can only help each other if we show our feelings. If you were to say you feel a certain way, but not act that way, it is confusing to the other group members.

Group Development

I found out that the rewards that my mom and I have for good behavior are not thought of as really that big of a deal. We are motivated enough to create our own intrinsic rewards such as free time, relaxing, or watching TV. Since my mom is an opinion seeker and giver, she brings my dad and me together well, and we talk about or day and our work. Both my parents were fascinated by what my studies revealed about our group dynamic. Procedural norms are often a problem for groups today, especially if group members do not buy into the belief system. My family has few procedural norms, but since everyone in the family buys into our belief system, we have few frustrations.

Each role that my parents have is an implicit norm. For example, I notice that when my mom gives me information about college credits or loans she is pumped up about it. I believe that the excitement of father-son or mother-son conversations when I was a little kid was because they wanted to help me be excited since many younger kids have a hard time relating to things that don't explicitly say happy all over them. Now I believe they do it because they are just happy themselves for having knowledge in that area and that is how the happiness is transferred. My group is functioning as an open group. However, it is good to know that we need one on one time with each other sometimes.

Group Membership

At my dad's office they use a project and meeting tool called Scrum, which drastically improves group morale. Now it is easier for them to see when roadblocks and problems occur. It is a helpful tool for keeping people on track and making each team member feel valued. Maslow said that we are not completely aware of ourselves until all the other hierarchical needs are satisfied. We bought my dad a book called *Stress for Success*. The book says to increase self-actualization by performing difficult tasks. To find out how to improve time management in my family will be a challenge, because we are stretched thin to begin with, and we plan things very well. Maslow's theory aligns with Fredrick Herzberg's motivation hygiene theory in that if you correct satisfaction needs in a group or individual, they won't necessarily be satisfied. I think this has a religious element for our family. Our faith never quits, and always asks us to get better and better. It's interesting for our group to look at both a quiet monk and an evangelical charismatic as both correct ways to worship.

Just because my dad happens to be a social member doesn't mean he will participate often in a group. It is important to see that our needs will appear differently even if it is the same shared need. I believe communication apprehension comes from the fear that no one can relate to you. Even if everyone was in your immediate family, there would still be some days when you would be less prone to reveal your heartfelt feelings. Giving effective feedback in our family is not always easy because we are almost martyr-like in our acceptance of praise. In *Working in Small Groups*, Engelberg and Wynn said to give a feeling, then a thought, and then a want when it is hard to give feedback. Just as we are martyr-like in our acceptance of praise, we also take care of each other too much. It is a great experience to take a vacation trip to another family member's house to solve this. We renew our relationships at that time.

In order to be assertive I have begun to reverse the order in which I talk, listen, and give eye contact. At times I find it helpful to not look at the person when I speak, and then look at the person when I listen. This helps me avoid communication apprehension. I have seen teachers use this technique, too.

Group Diversity

My family believes it is important to be open and accepting of diversity in people. To avoid self-serving biases it is important to determine to what extent positive behaviors are related to external factors and to what extent negative behaviors are related to internal factors. I think it is important to see that information is needed when talking with my mom and dad; but the right information.

The family dynamic we have is special. I don't see a lot of close knit family interactions from others when we are out at church, the fitness club, or other places. I used to think there was some special magic that made family members like each other. I found out that that something special is discipline and practice, and being aware of each family member's personality traits. Thus, in public it is a satisfying thing to show that we bond with each other. In contrast, when I was younger, and less emotionally mature, it felt abnormal to act that way in public.

Verbal and Nonverbal Communication in Groups

There was a pollster on the news named Frank Luntz. He explained the power of language. He emphasized that women and men differ in verbal and nonverbal communication. My parents have told me several times that they want me to speak up if I am bothered by their tone of voice, eye contact or gestures. Sometimes I will say words out of order just to see my parents' reactions, but other times I can tell when I have talked too much. I believe my role in the family is vaguer than my parents' roles. In order to avoid missing each others' meanings (bypassing) it is important to ask questions. The act of asking questions not only makes the speaker feel listened to, but it makes the listener more receptive. We live in a dynamic world of change! There is no limit to how good or poor of a job we can do in completing our daily tasks. My dad jokes and is serious by repeating a fortune cookie he read. It said "any day above ground is a good day". Philosophically speaking, if you don't try your best every day, then why wake up in the morning?

My communication skills have improved. The staff at a ranch I worked at said it was easy to detect my feelings. Even though my parents can sense my emotions, I still have to explain why I feel the way I do. Communication is full of emotion. Our family can use Gibb's defensive and supportive group climate behaviors to be more aware of our effect on each other. When we are in conflict it is important that our family focus on issues, not people. Creativity is limitless for solutions, but people and their feelings are not expendable. What I am going to do is record and videotape family discussions and meetings. Then I can analyze how to improve the group's communications. I will also utilize different survey functions on my blog such as zoomerang.com. I tend to keep my textbooks so I can keep my communication skills sharp.

For psychological health, my Spanish professor said that a person should only hold in their head what is important and toss the rest. This involves discernment about what is important. This means to listen to everything a person says and get the main points. My grandma always says that if she forgets something it will come to her "in her sleepies". Yes, rest is also a key part in absorption of knowledge. All these factors are part of my family's communication.

Critical Thinking and Argumentation in Groups

Our family enjoys a good sparring match of words. Sometimes after a long period of study (say several weeks) I might not have been vocal about my opinions and beliefs with my parents. Once I do something that lets them know I am still Josh, they are very happy. We constantly make each other re-evaluate how we perceive the world. Sometimes out of excitement I will come up with a good theory, and my claim, warrant, and evidence are all good, but my parents just don't know the answer. To solve this I will personally write down in a journal every unanswered question so as to research it later. I don't care what the question is or when I get around to researching it; it will be nicely stowed in that journal for later use.

Since my dad is an engineer, he uses qualifiers a lot; even when he is 99% sure that something is truthful and factual. In our group I don't think we do enough gathering of evidence. I think we fall into the trap of giving too many opinions and not enough examples, illustrations, and statistics.

I believe that a person must repeat themselves to be heard these days. How many ways can you deliver the information? This is why it is a good idea to summarize your argument for people, and when you refute an argument to preview your objections. The more you know about your audience or refuters, the better. A general rule of thumb that I see from having a counselor and reading textbooks is to only give the information that people are ready to hear.

Our family can learn communication skills by role playing various speaking positions. You could put people on the spot with limited preparation and let them demonstrate what they can handle. There are times when you just shouldn't argue. We always think that arguments won't happen because we are better than that, but actually at times we are worse off when we don't argue. Arguing has gotten a bad reputation, but as long as people are collaborative, an argument can provide a way to work out solutions to the issues.

Conclusion

In conclusion, I think that some groups think that it is ok to treat someone unfairly because they have been together for a long time, and they are invested. That is not the case with our group. Sometimes two people that care deeply about each other can become bitter towards each other in the midst of that caring. Emotion, love, and respect are all abstract words, so my group needs to find applications for these words on a day to day basis. In order to enjoy life, you have to open yourself up. Sometimes opening yourself up leaves you vulnerable if you are not careful. Small group communication skills in my family are a work in progress. We are becoming more aware of our communication style differences. With this understanding, conflict has been greatly reduced. We can usually count on each other for support, challenges, and new ideas. Through the use of new skills, role playing, and staying focused on appropriate communication, our group will become even more effective.

CHAPTER SUMMARIES

Chapter 3 Summary

Chapter 3 begins with a compare and contrast of Maslow's hierarchy of needs and William Schutz and his theory of Fundamental Interpersonal Relationship Orientation (FIRO). Knowing that people generally fall into these three categories, and using Maslow's hierarchical needs shows us that in groups leaders can deal with each other under or over, or just as social, democratic, or personal members. I see that this has the potential for confusion and stereotypes, which the book discusses. These are models, after all.

Groups will have confidence, which has to do with both competence and confidence. It is easy to see the cultural factors or the high percentages of communication apprehension. The chapter explains that groups have task, maintenance, and self-centered rules. While self-centered roles are fine by themselves, they have the potential to stagnate a group's goals and attitudes. Hyper-personal communication explains why some people are more confident on the computer in communication. People that are polite on the internet are more likely to receive communications. Thus, despite anxiety or discomfort in communication, if people receive positive reinforcement, their anxiety drops. It can be easier to interpret the actual message of an email than the many nonverbal facts that accompany a spoken message.

Both the Belbin team role theory and the Kenneth D. Benne and Paul Sheets essay conclude that there are people who pick roles based on their personal attributes and characteristics. This is evident in dialectics. Randy Paterson stated that people don't say no for several reasons: people won't accept that I will say it; people won't like me if I say it; and I don't have the courage because of our roles in our relationship. This reinforces other concepts from other chapters that explain that people are more likely to accept a person as a leader if they make decisions and talk frequently. This aspect shows why some people do not become leaders. The reason is that they can't put their foot down and say "yes, yes" or "no, no".

Chapter 4 Summary

Our nation expanded from 1990 to 2000 when more than 13 million immigrants came to the United States. It used to be that our doctors, lawyers, and work force was mostly white and male. Stereotyping, ethnocentricism, prejudice, and discrimination are extremes in attitudes. There are external and internal forces taking place in these attitudes. Groups suffer because of these attitudes. Even though groups may succeed in the short term while holding these views, they will cause more harm to themselves and others than they realize. Dialectics from other chapters, and this one, revealed that if a few people in a group of similar people are different from the people in that group, group performance will actually be better.

Sensor-intuitive explains how people perceive the general world. Thinker-feeler theory explains how people make decisions. Judger-perceiver explains how people deal with the world and the problems that arise in it.

With the United States sharing in the 30% of the globe that favors the "I" orientation, they still fall to 16th on the list of low-power-distance cultures. This shows that uncertainty-avoidance, masculine-feminine values, and high context/low context and monochromic and polychromic elements need to be examined to see why our country is made up of co-cultures. It is hard to get away from the media and culture that shows us what are supposed to be masculine and feminine traits. As a result, men and women may accept these media beliefs.

Hofstede's theory means the societal perspective of men and women, not the individual men and women themselves. It is interesting to find that most researchers believe gender is intercultural or learned from your culture, as well as being a hereditary factor.

The field of nonverbal speech is important, as it makes up roughly 75% or all communication. It is shown to be of interest as to why things might get overlooked by different cultures, and has implicit and explicit rules.

Technology is seen in cultural dimensions in addition to generational characteristics. Generation X-ers spend less time at work than Baby boomers, but through technology, often get just as much done. Generation X-ers believe the idea of paying dues should be re-evaluated. On the flip side, older people are better at problem solving, and are more flexible in their life skills and strategies. They also remain calmer in stressful situations than younger people.

Regarding religion, the question is how people's different religions affect their work, environment, and group activities. It is important to keep in mind that religious affiliation and the structure of organizing activities uses the same group techniques that are used in other settings. When trying to categorize individuals and groups it is important not to over-generalize, over-attribute, or use bias of any kind. I firmly believe that discrimination, harassment or any sort of belittling creates more of the same. It is fine to acknowledge differences (and similarities) in people. To use peoples' differences to define them is a mistake.

Chapter 5 Summary

There are differences between a leader and a manager, and a leader and a leadership role. Psychologists Gary Yukl and Cecilia Fable described three extra types of power: information power, persuasive power, and charisma. The majority of power can be summarized by two categories: position power and personal power. Research points out that reward, legitimate, and coercive power are the least effective. Being in the right time at the correct moment, or being the only person that has the guts to take the job is what it sometimes boils down to for those who can become an effective leader or a leader at all.

Sometimes two people can use legitimate power, but the power that the staff or group gives to the designated leader can cause difficulties in adjustment for the outside leader and the group members. Morale is strongest for the emergent leader. To become a leader is not easy. If the person does not use these things (information power, persuasive power, charisma, reward, legitimate power, and coercive power) it makes it more difficult to be effective. By talking early and often, the leader shows motivation to lead and commitment to the group. If the leader shares knowledge it increases the chance for leadership. It is shown that even if the leader presents the same information, but presents it more clearly than another person, chances increase to be considered an effective and ethical leader.

Leaders welcome dialectics and have the tendency to offer their opinions. They realize that listening is an important part of the communication process. Ultimately, the book stated that it is the kind of person the leader is that makes that person an ethical and effective leader, not just the other skills the leader possesses. Four theoretical approaches to leadership are covered. Trait theory states that people can become great leaders if they are born with a knack for being people persons. Styles theory describes autocrat, democrat and laissez-faire leadership models. It is obvious that democratic leaders are good in the most general sense, but there are times when the other two models are needed.

Situational leadership theory says we use different styles for each specific situation. Fiedler's Contingency Model of Leadership Effectiveness stated that effective leadership happens when the leadership style matches the situation. Task motivated and relationship motivated are the two sets of models he described. Once leaders determine their style, they must use three things to judge the situation: the relationship between the leader and the members of the group, the task structure, and power. Task motivation and relationship motivation are completely opposite.

Hersey Blanchard's Situational Leadership model links the style of leadership with member readiness. Being willing and able are two things a ready member has. The telling stage is when followers are unable and unwilling. A leader must be autocratic in this situation. The selling stage is when members are unable but willing. The leader needs to provide lots of explanation, and member input is needed. The participating stage is when group members are able but unwilling. The leader needs to participate and motivate members. The delegating stage is when group members are willing and able. The leader should give trust and independence to the members.

Transformational leadership theory looks at what leaders accomplish rather than what their skills or characteristics are. Charismatic, visionary, supportive, empowering, innovative, and modeling are the six attributes that fit this theory.

The 5m model of leadership of effectiveness has five interdependent functions. Model leadership behavior is only granted by group members. It is often referred to as image management, and is assertive. Motivating members, managing group processes, making decisions and mentoring members are the other points of this model. In *The New Why Teams Don't Work*, Harvey Robbins and Michael Finley stated that it is better to make a bad decision than no decision at all. An important aspect of mentoring is that the leader is trying to encourage group members to become leaders themselves. The very fact that women need to act differently to gain leadership makes the stereotypes and perceptions continue. Research shows that there are really only slight differences between men and women as leaders.

Finally, culture plays a part in how leadership happens. Status and personal achievement are important in the United States, but may be detrimental in collectivist cultures. Femininity and masculinity clash. Spain, for instance, emphasizes spontaneity, while the United States can claim low uncertainty avoidance. Knowing enough about negative stereotypes so that leaders do not portray biased attitudes is one thing, but leaders must be careful not to then assume they are better than others because of this. This is how stereotypes and ethnocentric attitudes began in the first place.

Chapter 6 Summary

The concept of empowerment was introduced to the theory of small group communication theory in 1991. Previously it was a "just follow rules" environment. But as we see in the chapter, motivating and encouraging are tools to see things differently. Blind obedience is not favored over enlightened commitment. Optimal group experience occurs when groups are energized and productive. Motivation is like power if it is done correctly. It creates more of itself. Having one motivator in a group is not enough. What works is motivating that focuses on members' needs, personality types, and culture. Motivators are higher level needs like belonging to a group, self-esteem, and self-actualization.

Collectivist vs individualistic comparisons show that achievement needs can work on both types of groups. They just work differently because of culture. But culture is made up of individuals and vice versa. It is a balance that makes it hard to see the difference sometimes.

Both introverts and extroverts need time to prepare in advance. Introverts collect thoughts and extroverts collect resources. Kenneth Thomas descrives four elements that motivate and energize the entire group: a sense of meaningfulness; a sense of choice; a sense of competence; and a sense of progress.

Assessment is necessary for group success. It's not witholding group rewards, but how that group can improve, and what will happen if they do improve. Finding out if interpersonal or procedural problems are issues is the key here. Goals and feedback are reciprocal in nature. The table on page 149 of the textbook describes where in the book the reader can find applicable ways to assess a group.

In my opinion, controlling feedback can be used, but it doesn't motivate. Sometimes people need to have things said more directly. However, rules and procedures should prevent most mishaps if everyone buys into them. In that case, controlling feedback doesn't even come up. Informational feedback doesn't use "you" statements, it uses "it" statements.

Reprimands seem like positive reinforcements to me. If the person knows they did something "wrong" and the leader uses back channeling cues to make the person feel at ease, then reprimands can work. The key is to provide adequate information and rules that are clear. Sometimes rewards can have little to do with motivation. Extroverts prefer the compliment to be known to the group as a whole, while an introvert may prefer a more subtle reward.

Extrinsic rewards satisfy physiological and safety needs, and come from outside sources such as paychecks and perks. It can be dangerous for workers to have their self esteem rely on just big extrinsic rewards. Then if they don't get a big reward the next time, it may affect how they feel about their competence; then their motivation could decrease, even if it is from a seemingly small problem. Balancing the group needs with the need for personal recognition and praise can result in making someone less likely to quit their job. Workers will catch on if the reward is given just because of status and not ability or performance. The book clearly states that satisfying the group is more important than glorifying someone for a short time privately; or giving them incompetent group members to work with. It is a matter of reality.

Objective rewards should be fair (giving rewards to those that have deliberately earned them), equitable (giving the opportunity to earn rewards to everyone), competitive (people that do the same kind of work should get equal rewards), and appropriate. In my opinion, if you can't offer a good enough reward as a pre-task motivator, then you shouldn't offer one to start with.

What are effective rewards? Giving personal recognition is a prime example. Researchers have found that celebrations are an effective way to build a group up. Material compensation is a type of extrinsic reward. Punishing workers should be reserved for when major laws or rules have been broken. It involves the situation and the person. Furthermore, it is found that using referent and charismatic power can also be used to discipline or demote.

Chapter 7 Summary

Non-verbal communication is usually emotion based, and is said to make up more than two thirds of our communication. Denotation is a definition one would find in the dictionary. Conotation is the feeling that we get about all communication. Abstraction is not preferred over being concrete in meaning.

The use of plural pronouns creates interdependence by creating opportunities for opinion sharing, minimizing power differenciating, using causal and informal language, paraphrasing, and conflict mangament, and asking "what if" questions can all help teams to talk. "Team talk" shows that a group works nicely together. Not only does it help, but it demonstrates that participation is the process for success.

Some pointers that play into all the dimensions of team talk include: refrain from interrupting others; demanding that people use names or nicknames; asking the group to listen to outsiders that don't agree with the group; and always ask questions if you don't understand something a group member said. It is interesting that individuals that use "I" language in a positive way get positive results. However, groups that are successful use "we" and "you" pronounds. In this case, "you" usually implies the whole group.

There are specific aspects that are ineffective in group communication. Bypassing can be detrimental. It can be avoided by focusing on the meanings themselves, not just the words. It is important to avoid using gender focused words and offensive language. Labeling people and discriminatory language is harmful. Jargon should only be used if everyone in the group understands the terminology. Group members would actually gain more self esteem and power by letting others in the group know what the jargon means prior to using it.

Tags (additions to sentences) and qualifiers (such as maybe or perhaps) are often used by an unsure person. Women tend to use these more than men. The use of tags and qualifiers can actually make a group come together, rather than just demonstrate a lack of confidence.

Standard American english is a dialect spoken by about 60% of the United States. Research shows that there are stereotypes that focus on people that don't speak standard American English. Accents are an aspect of language that is noticed when speaking another language. Dialect is what people actually mean when they say, for example, that someone is speaking with a southern accent. It would be a southern accent to someone from a non-English speaking country heard them.

Personal apperance and artifacts, facial expression and eye contact, and vocal expression are all part of nonverbal communication. Word stress, tone, inflection, and speed are all paralanguage types of nonverbal communication.

Corner-to-corner and side by side seating is shown to be popular for group communication, because this type of seating does not emphasize power; even inanimate objects can send messages.

Gibb's defensive and supportive group climate shouldn't be looked at as good or bad. Rather, we should vary our approaches in different situations. The dialectic climates of group include the following aspects:evaluation←→description;control←→problem-orientation;strategy←→spontaneity; neutrality←→empathy, superiority ←→equality, and certainty ←→provisionalism. I can see that personal, democratic, and social members would be great for synergy in Gibb's model.

Nonverbal immediacy shows that positive group interactions happen by:

- More leaning forward

- More physical closeness

- More openness of arms and body

- More direct body orientation (point or face towards the other person)

- More touching (never take, always give)

- More relaxed posture (assertiveness is still optimal)

- Positive facial and vocal expressions (they are supposed to match)

- More laughing and smiling.

Chapter 8 Summary

Listening is the number one tool for communication. As a matter of fact, 60% of a chief executive's day may be devoted to listening. Most of us are not great listeners, because 50% of information is lost in recall for most people. Discriminitive listening is key for any type of the listening styles listed in the chapter.

There are specific aspects for each type of listening. Comprehensive listening focuses on the meaning of what a person says. Empathetic listening focuses on active listening and a person's feelings. Analytical listening focuses on persuasion and evidence. Watch out for the changing of your original attitudes or beliefs. Apprieciative listening is noticing others' good deeds, but we hesitate to follow through with a plan for how that could benefit the group or group members. Good leaders are proactive listers. We think faster than we speak, so to use our extra thinking time effectively we should consciously avoid daydreaming.

Dialectics are used in the Golden Rule. Attitudes such as responsibility, patience, and open-mindedness are all good qualities.

Listening strategies include listening for big ideas, overcoming distractions, listening to non-verbal messages and behaviors, listening before you leap, and helping your group listen. Listening to big ideas might be hard when a poor speaker talks. This needs to be addressed by group members asking for clarity, and also engaging in more active listening. Overcoming distrations is easy in the physical realm as long as you have the power to stop the distractions. However, our own psychological distractions, and the speaker's distractions are what need to be addressed.

A good example of listening to non-verbal behavior would be whether someone is extremely excited and vibrant, or speaking in a monotone. It is best to view their body language in an even more critical light. One example of this would be even though Hispanics tend to often be jovial and exuberant in their speech, they still use gestures like non-Hispanics.

Ralph Nichols said that evaluation isn't complete until we fully comprehend something. I can see the more people do this, the more it will have a contagious effect on the group. Helping a group listen can be done through the use of periodic listening checks. From a practical standpoint, I relate the impact of this to the impact of periodic drug tests in the work place. It is a strong incentive to do the right thing if the tests are done at random times on random people. Thus, if people in the group know that someone will be occasionally checking to see if they paid attention and understood, they are more likely to pay attention and understand.

Chapter 9 Summary

Substantive conflict is over ideas, issues, decisions, actions, or goals. Dean Barnlind and Franklyn Haiman say that significant private motives (either conscious or not) that are beneath the surface will influence discussions in subtle ways. Affective conflict is more difficult to solve than substantive conflict because it is subjective feelings.

The chapter discussed aspects of procedural, constructive, and destructive conflict. Procedural conflict often arises because groups have a hard time resolving substantive or affective conflicts. It is a way to vote or decide to move on to the next discussion. Constructive conflict is balancing the group's dialectics of value and learning. Destructive is the opposite, and can even be conflict avoidance. Although defensiveness and competition can get you far in sports or in the military, it is always best in groups to put these aside, focus on the issues, and for group members to respect each other. Principles for constructive conflict include the following: it is ok to disagree; status should not matter when someone approaches another group member with an honest opinion; and the group has agreed on rules for handling conflict.

Avoidance conflict style isn't a bad style when: you don't find interest on the issue; you need time to control your emotions before you speak; others are addressing the issue well enough without you; and the consequences of conflict are risky. Competitive, compromising, and collaborative are the styles of conflict the book describes.

The "4R" Method includes: reasons, reactions, results, and a resolution. These four R's help decide on what model to use. The AEIOU Model focuses on positive intentionality coined by Jerry Wisinski.

Negotiating in groups is another model that uses bargaining to reach solutions. Principled negotiation focuses on: separating people from problems; focusing on interests, not positions; options that help mutual gain; and criteria which point out the main rules people can agree upon.

Third party intervention is when an outside source that has no ties to the group is called upon. If mediator can proceed with introductions, storytelling, agenda building, negotiation, testing an agreement, and closure and be unbiased, they are good candidates to act as mediators for the group. Arbitration is an even more extreme process than mediation.

Culture is involved with conflict when conformity is involved. Regions can be a factor, such as the difference between Franco-Canadians, and Anglo-Canadians. Gender is significant because the group needs both. The author believes that women tend to be more private about conflict than men and they may react more strongly to acts of perceived betrayal or unfriendly behavior. I think this is slightly stereotypical and interprets men's behavior as being the normal one. To enhance group cohesiveness one can: establish group and social identities for everyone in the group; emphasize teamwork; reward contributions; and respect group members.

It is interesting to note that diverse groups are actually said to have better strategies for marketing and sales than less diverse groups. Group-think focuses on the imbalance of homogeneous and heterogeneous groups. It is possible for group members to think that their group is always right if their group is cohesive enough.

To run the risk of becoming a non-questioning group is not good. Irving Janis identified eight expressions of groupthink: invulnerability, rationalization, morality, stereotyping outsiders, self censorship, pressure on dissent, illusion of unanimity and mind guarding. The first three sound good, but not when groups are using groupthink. Stereotyping outsiders is self explanatory. Self censorship is what people do when they doubt their opinions because the majority of the group thinks one particular way. Pressure on dissent means that group members are pressured to agree. The illusion of unanimity means that the group members believe that everyone agrees. Mind guarding happens when knowledge or information is unfairly kept from or given to group members.

Chapter 10 Summary

Decision making is passing judgment on an issue or consideration, and also the act of making up one's mind. Most groups make decisions, but don't solve problems. I can see that decisions come from core values, beliefs and ideals. Problem solving, however, requires many decisions to be made. Groups do this better than individuals because of the sheer number of differentiation in the ideas.

Problem solving is a functional approach, whereas decision making can be seen as meaning-centered. Voting, consensus seeking, and authority rule are decision making methods. Consensus seeking only works if voting hasn't worked or the status of the group members is roughly the same. Decision making questions include: questions of fact which are true or false types; questions of conjecture which are presumptions that something will or won't happen; questions of value which ask the general favorability of an object, person, or idea; and questions of policy which ask how to address a problem.

Decision making styles are as follows:

- A rational decision maker makes observations and uses facts to make decisions.

- An intuitive decision maker goes with a gut feeling to make decisions.

- A dependent decision maker relies on others opinions to make decisions.

- An avoidance decision maker doesn't like to make decisions.

- Spontaneous decision makers often make fast decisions they often regret later.

The standard agenda was founded by John Dewey. This reflective process happens as described in the following situation. You would clarify a task, and then identify the problem. Group members need to buy into the process of problem identification. Fact finding doesn't exclude common sense, either. The solution-criteria stage asks what the solution should accomplish. The solution-suggestion stage shouldn't be limited by common sense either. Solution evaluation and selection uses criteria to focus on the pros and cons of the suggestions. This might be the hardest but most rewarding step. Finally, the solution implementations stage is when the group decides if they will proceed to acting upon the solution. Great plans can fail if there is no way to implement them in reality.

Another approach is the functional perspective, which is based on a communication behavior process. The first step is the preparation function, in which groups should agree to make the best decision, identify the resources, recognize obstacles, and specify the ground rules. The competency function allows for the up and down movement of the order of procedures, in contrast to the Standard Agenda, which does not. The communication function states that members should be: well-prepared and competent; members agree upon criteria; members base arguments on facts and if necessary refute them; members use the leadership function to advance the group.

A third approach is the single question format which is a question/answer process. This format: identifies the problem with a set of questions; creates a collaborative setting (generating a list of "we will" statements for the group); analyzes the issues (like the other two methods, this helps avoid premature decision making); identifies possible solutions, and answers the single question.

Creativity is amazing if used appropriately. Imagination, incubation, and insight are used in creative problem solving. Brainstorming is used by 70% of business people in organizations. Two things underlie brainstorming techniques: deferring judgment improves the quality of input and the quantity of ideas, and output breeds quality.

The Nominal Group is a type of problem solving and decision making process. Nominal means in name only. Members of this kind of group are individual workers before they are a functioning group. The first phase is a generation of ideas. Listing of ideas continues until no more ideas occur. The second phase is idea evaluation and voting, where voting is private, and the decision reached is based on the collective ideas of the individual members.

Decreasing Options Technique (DOT) helps sort ideas. Generating ideas can happen multiple ways, but should only be one idea per piece of paper. Posting the ideas means to put the ideas up on the walls. Sorting the ideas just means to group similar ideas once they are on the walls. Dotting the ideas means to place colored dots on words or phrases to eliminate ideas and select the final idea.

Enhancing group activity includes these process steps:

- Controlling judgment, which involves avoiding premature closure to ideas that sound bizarre.

- Encouraging innovation, which has four sub-steps: inertia, instruction, imitation, and innovation. The first three pose very common statements, but they get in the way of innovation.

- Ask "what if" questions. Raw knowledge is different from insight.

- Use metaphors.

Other problem solving realities include politics, which states that people have hidden agendas and motives. Special interest groups can become bogged down in their own interests. The concept of pre-existing preferences was made known by psychologist Farhad Manjoo. An example of that is the scientific journal published that 928 studies have been conducted about climate change. In the studies, no one disagreed with man caused climate change. However, only 41% of Americans believe that this is true. Time is a factor for preconceptions to change. Finally, power can cause a group to do very bad things. Power is sometimes needed by just one person mainly, but if that person abuses it, switching to power shared by the group can be beneficial.

Chapter 11 Summary

Christopher Kayes concluded that critical thinking is more important than ever for groups dealing with diversity, goals, and rules. An argument is something that supports a viewpoint and reasons to support it. Argumentation is the way groups should use argument techniques. Cooperative arguers are better than competitive arguers for a group. It is possible for some members of a group to view non-hostility and conflict avoidance as lacking in decision making processes. Argumentative group members create more arguments on both sides of a position. The philosopher Toulmin has a six step Model of Argument. The first three steps include: claim, evidence, and warrant. Types of evidence are facts and opinions, definitions and descriptions, example and illustrations, and statistics. A warrant is how the evidence supports your claim in your position. The final three steps include: backing, reservation, and qualifiers. Backing puts meat on the bones of your warrant. Reservations are exceptions to the rules that need to be taken into account. Qualifiers are important because one can never be sure beyond a shadow of a doubt that a position is true or right. "Maybe" and "probably" are qualifier words.

Testing the evidence includes five steps: is the source identified and credible; is the source unbiased; is the information recent; is the information consistent; and are the statistics valid. Oral citations are used when written documentation is not available. It is important to note how statistics are reported, because bending the truth or interpreting it is not always lying. Then you will want to present your evidence. Stating your claim has four elements: Claims of fact try to prove truth; claims of conjecture suggest something will or won't happen; Claims of value are the desirable qualities in a person, place or thing. A corollary is the persuasive and informative type of presentation; Claims of policy focus on rules and how to change them; and supporting your claim by providing the reasons and the summary of your argument.

To refute an argument, you first listen to an argument. Critical and analytical listening is appropriate only after you have understood the meaning of the argument. Stating the opposing claim involves letting others in the group help you if you misunderstood the claim. Again, from the last chapter, effective conflict strategies make everyone feel comfortable giving their input after they understand the rules, of course.

Previewing reasons gives structure so that people can be prepared for your refute. Assessing the evidence is bringing new and better evidence while pointing out faults in the argument you are refuting.

Assessing the reasoning involves fallacies. Ad hominem, appeal to authority, appeal to popularity (this one could be used by a charismatic leader), appeal to tradition, faulty analogy, faulty cause, and hasty generalization are the types of fallacies. Then a summary of your refutation is helpful for the group. This keeps the discussion going. Both genders have an equal struggle and gift for creating success in the group. Some cultures think that no one is objective and therefore giving your own opinion is useless.

Emotional intelligence is used to curb inappropriate emotions and express appropriate ones. There are several tips to do so, including self-awareness, self regulation (which involves delaying personal gratification to achieve group goals), self-confidence, self-control, and empathy. Some researchers in the field of emotional intelligence have found that when the emotional part of the brain is damaged it affects someone even with a normal IQ level in their business and personal life.

Chapter 12 Summary

There is a correlation between time spent in a meeting at work and the desire to find a new and different job. Employees are in meetings about 15 hours a week. There are more than 11 million meetings that are going on in the U.S. every day. Three fifths of meetings are found to be unsatisfactory according to one study.

The schedule, chairperson, and structure make up the three elements of meetings. In setting up a meeting, the following elements should be addressed:

- ***Why are we meeting?*** A meeting goal is the outcome and the subject of a meeting is the topic being discussed at the meeting.

- ***Who should attend?*** Include room for discussion through varying opinions and special facts. For effective discussion, the number of participants should generally be less than 12.

- ***Where should we meet?*** The more attractive and comfortable a room is, the more valued the employees will feel.

- ***What materials do we need?*** The chairperson's job is let participants know what to bring and to bring his/her own handouts for the meeting as well.

- ***Set the agenda:*** The agenda can be a list of important discussion topics, which is sometimes done in a question format. The length of time estimated for each topic (and the order of discussion) should be provided to attendees ahead of time.

Dealing with disruptive behavior at a meeting is important. Respond positively to members when they respond appropriately. Loudmouths deserve attention, but the chairperson needs to then engage other members. In fact, if someone is a loudmouth it might distract other attendees. Interrupters need to be stopped so that the original speaker can finish his/her thought. Direct eye contact makes whisperers more aware that they are distracting people. The chairperson shouldn't confront latecomers or those who leave early right then, but they should be talked to later. The level of distraction should warrant appropriate reprimands.

Preparing the minutes is an important element of a business meeting. People can learn a lot from reading the minutes. The person recording the minutes should not also be the chairperson. By asking for clarification while taking minutes, this person often clears up confusion for the other meeting attendees as well. Parliamentary procedure is often used at meetings. The Robert's Rules of Order is considered the parliamentary bible by many (it can be found online). There are four subcategories noted for parliamentary procedure:

- Majority will

- Minority rights

- Balanced discussion

- Orderly progress.

To evaluate a meeting, one can use the Post Meeting Reaction (PMR). This is a written reaction from participants. Several interesting points to check into would be chaos theory and complexity theory, as well as how they relate to dialectics.

Chapter 13 Summary

There are three types of group presentations. There are those you would present at group members' meetings, those that non-group members receive from your group, and the more collaborative presentations for combined groups, such as a panel discussion. A panel is an example of a team presentation. The purpose of any presentation is what you want an audience to know, think, or believe. The audience has demographics and individual traits, as well as opinions. When putting together a presentation, presenters should try to predict how the audience will agree or disagree with them. It is important to go more slowly during the presentation if the audience disagrees with you.

There are additional factors in group presentations. Credibility is a key factor and involves competence, character, and caring. Logistics involves when and where you make the presentation. Content and organization are important to presentations. There are many organizational patterns to choose from, such as: cause-and-effect and stories-and example.

Impromptu and extemporaneous are two types of delivery that require quick "thinking on your feet" skill. In general, public speaking is different from team presentations. Team presentations are well coordinated and persuasive in nature, and they try to sway a specific group of listeners. Public speaking involves speaking to a public audience. In either case it is important to be prepared for question and answer sessions after the presentation. This involves being brief, honest, and specific. Restraint in the area of visual aids includes:

- Keeping the summary stated in the heading on the slide;

- Using no more than six lines of text that support the idea;

- Each line of text should have six words or less, in order to be most effective;

- Generally choose a type size of less than 24 points; and

- Keep in mind that Power Point has a bad reputation in some businesses (such as 3M Corporation).

Thorough handouts can signify that you are serious about the information, and that your message has actual consequences attached to it. There are specific strategies that help the presenter use multimedia and presentation aids effectively, including:

- Explain your points;

- Use time effectively: let them see the slide before expecting them to look at you;

- Don't talk to your presentation; and

- Be prepared with a backup plan if the presentation gets botched.

ORGANIZATIONAL COMMUNICATION

In Organizational Communication, we explored various methods of communication and personnel theories. The final project was developing a business proposal for a fictional company of my choosing.

ANALYSIS AND PROPOSAL FOR ABC COMPANY

Background

After meeting with each of the company's employees, it is apparent that our problems fall into three broad categories. Communication issues related to task, value, and mission. In regards to task service people have no geographic territory resulting in added driving time and no guidelines are given to the office staff for assigning service calls to the service people. The team captain's report that they are short staffed in service personnel. As a result captains are getting frustrated because they try to organize with the office staff but fail.

In regards to communication problems in the values area, there are multiple problems. The company is not receptive to new ideas and is a closed system. Management is struggling financially and has a negative perception of most employees. The flow of networks and data is only up and down but not horizontal. When employees try to reach out to customers they are inexperienced in communications styles and or focused on not ruining their profit or salaries therefore making internal to external communication difficult. Employees believe they lack a voice within the company, and they view current management styles to be autocratic. Employees want more financial incentives to improve motivation and to prove that the company values them. In this economy layoffs are imminent, however no one seems to realize that by increasing employee productivity, added profit can flow into the organization.

The problem with communication regarding mission is very straightforward. Communication is only vertical and not horizontal. There is a lack of understanding and communication between departments, and this is hurting everyone's performance. There are no opportunities for the entire group to meet, and thus there is no feeling of team.

Costs

Unfortunately time is money. Fixing the problems within the company can be accomplished with little net cost. To address the value issue, several strategies are recommended. The first is to create ad hoc groups. Employees will join whichever group(s) interests them. Examples of groups include: rewards group, quadrant group, new ideas group, and any other group that employees would like. These groups will initially meet once a week, and later will meet every other week. The purpose of these groups is to give employees a voice, and to help employees make changes. To address the financial incentives problem, I recommend the creation of the Bucks Bucket system. Each month (or week) employees can receive rewards in the form of gift certificates for various services. The money for these rewards comes from the gas savings. Snacks and drinks will set the organization back one hundred dollars a week. To fix the motivation problems I forecast that $625 to $840 will be needed for the bucks bucket.

Benefits

The benefits to solving excess driving time would be a reduction of miles driven. We are trying to be conservative so we are saying that 16 non captains would save 1 hour each day. When multiplied throughout a week 80 extra hours will be added that could be spent trying to increase revenue that was normally spent driving. We could go from 1,200 miles per week per truck to 900 miles per week per truck which brings me to my next point. Gas for a fleet of 16 drivers would roughly be $3,840 per week. With the new system it would be $2,880 per week. Per year that would save $49,880 just from using the grid model. The grid model puts one captain in each corner of the location the organization covers. Captains shift a lot because of customers and new employees so they would still be driving roughly the same amount.

The bucks bucket is going to draw directly from our savings of time using the grid model. We will lose no money at all with this system. Each reward is $25. Also, the bucks bucket is a nice way to give employees an option as to where they want that money to go. Gift cards and special services are what I had in mind.

We will have two meetings per week for starters. Then it will move to one a week. They won't take place on Monday or Friday to save people the extra personal time and family time. The ad hoc meeting will be from 7:30 am to 8:30 am on Tuesdays. The large group meetings will be during the same time slot but on Thursdays. We have also added an employee-of-the-year surprise reward. Every year the secret gift should be bigger and better. If an employee was employee of the month they are eligible to become the employee of the year. Management picks the employee of the year where as employees pick the employee of the month. Also role playing workshops will be fun for employees because it is completely unbiased and has a small enough reward, such as a gift card to keep employees internally driven, but big enough to provide outside incentive.

Risks

Employees must work together or this will fail. Failing because you don't try is worse than failing when you have tried. It is management's job to not give up. Risks are as follows. Management could put forth more money into the bucks bucket earned from the grid system. Secondly, if employees are not trained in communication and ethics then they won't know what to do in emergencies such as looking out for elderly people who rely on our services. Thirdly, knowing which front desk employee needs to be taking calls and which ones collect data in the meetings is crucial. If this doesn't happen not only would we lose customers but possibly make our valued customers call back asking more questions bogging down the phone line. Lastly, and most importantly, management needs to use decision and problem solving to know what actions deserve what rewards. The plus side of having every employee become eligible for incentives and prizes is that they will start to think like a family and a team. The bad side to watch out for is if management or an employee makes a bad move causing the other to react badly. Managers must watch out for employees that are so stressed about the rules of the organization that they look for problems where there are none.

Alternatives

Lastly, a rating system should only be introduced if employees want that. This must be a consensus. New employees could rate captains and vice versa. Also new employees could rate new employees and captains could rate captains. This rating is separate from the employee of the month and year. It is designed to be less formal and bond the group members in a fun way.

To conclude I will say that a football team is more than just the quarterback. If our business continues to leave a negative complacent work climate then customers will pick up on this. I am just as concerned for those in the company that have no real complaints as I am for completely undone employees. Just like school is about more than just school, so it is that work is about more than work. Life trickles into everyone's decision process and affects everything. For those who think being a manager is easy, and for those who think that being an employee is easy; it's time to take a second look. Nobody got to where they are by lacking commitment or ignoring customers or each other. Teams are supposed to act like teams. I advise against the status quo and encourage new ways of thinking. Lastly, this process will take time but when God made time he made enough of it.

BUSINESS COMMUNICATIONS

CONCEPT & APPLICATION PAPER: VERBAL COMMUNICATION

Concept Definition and Explanation

Hamilton stated that "communication is the process of people sharing thoughts, ideas, and feelings with each other in commonly understandable ways (2008, p.5)." Verbal communication simply means to express those thoughts, ideas, and feelings with the spoken or written word. Effective verbal communication requires that the frame of reference (of speaker and listener) be taken into account. When verbal communication is used, for instance in advertising, the frame of reference is assumed to be from the point of view of the average person or buyer. In a classroom situation, the frame of reference is both professor and student.

Emotional intelligence plays a big part in understanding what is verbally expressed, and in effectively expressing oneself verbally. While 65% to 70% of meaning is conveyed by the non-verbal and paralanguage codes (Hamilton, 2008), this fails to look at what people actually understand. Furthermore, although verbal expression is only a small part of communication, it is essential to keep in mind that without verbal expression, communication could deteriorate into just body language, grunts, and visual effects. Verbal communication ties all of communication together.

Verbal messages sometimes conflict with the visual messages. When that happens, people tend to believe what they see, instead of what they hear (Hamilton, 2008). This is a constant challenge to effective verbal communication, and must be kept in mind when choosing the verbal message. No method of communication is effective 100% of the time. There seems to be an emphasis on visual stimulus in our country that ignores the impact of words. Visual communication is non-verbal. Listening is to verbal code as sight is to non-verbal code. True communication of meaning requires verbal expression.

Verbal Language in Communication

DeVito (2008, p. 159) cited studies that found "the facial feedback hypothesis holds that your facial expressions influence physiological arousal." Non-verbal cues and communication do impact verbal language communication because people react first to the visual input, even if it is different from the verbal input. This increases the difficulty of verbal communication; it does not reduce the importance of verbal communication. Instead, it demonstrates that it is essential for the verbal communicator to override this tendency of the listener, whether it is in direct communication or in advertising.

Concept Application

When I consider verbal communication I think about encounters in my everyday life. If I pass someone and they smile at me (nonverbal communication), I may or may not respond with a similar expression. If, however, they stop and give me a fact or some information, I now have been given the opportunity for verbal response. I believe it is much more satisfying to be able to express yourself verbally first (verbal communication), and then follow up with forms of non-verbal communication. Furthermore, the verbal communication provides an excellent foundation for introducing and interpreting the non-verbal expressions.

My life as a college student continually requires verbal communication, most specifically in a classroom situation. Has communication really taken place if the professor lectures, but no one else speaks? My answer is no, because the professor has no way to judge whether or not the verbal message was correctly received until the students interact with the professor.

An analogy will clarify the importance of practicing their verbal communication. Most people do not have to think about or practice their breathing. They just go through each day and breathe well enough. However, a marathon runner must practice a different kind of breathing when they run a marathon in order to have an optimal performance. So, too, must each person (including the professor and the students) be aware of their verbal communication effectiveness in order to improve. This goal of effectiveness must include revising the message if the receiver misunderstands the message. I have found it inspiring to be in classes where professors and students continually try to support each other in improving their verbal communication. It helps reduce people's communication apprehension, which is usually seen in people's shyness and reluctance to share verbally.

Hamilton (2008) described a study by a college professor who taught three separate sessions of the same course. After the first exam each session had averaged the same grades. The professor varied the verbal feedback for each session's students when returning the papers. The first group received very positive feedback and praise. The second group just received their papers back with not much mention of the grades at all. The third group received extremely negative verbal feedback and criticism. When the professor gave the next exams, student achievement matched the verbal feedback from the first exam. Thus, the success or failure of a group has a high relationship and correlation to the verbal communication. Feedback given in the form of verbal communication in this case was much more powerful than any other message received by the students.

In my role as a communications director, verbal communication is used differently than in my role as a student. Specifically, my role as a communications director requires me to analyze the effectiveness of advertisements. Although visual aspects of an advertisement are important, the verbal message can make or break it. As Lindstom and Underhill (2008, p. 141) eloquently stated:

> But what if I told you that much of this visual, in your face advertising is, on the part of the advertisers, a largely wasted effort? That in fact our visual sense is far from our most powerful in seducing our interest and getting us to buy.

Once again, in advertising, just as in the classroom situation, although the visual communication may dominate the receiver's attention, it is the verbal aspect that really is the pinnacle of importance. Whenever I analyze a company's advertisements, I determine whether or not the verbal communication is effective, so that the message is not lost in the visual and other non-verbal aspects. If the verbal communication conflicts with the visual communication, the advertisement generally does not communicate what the company intended. Yes, potential buyers "look with their eyes" but the advertiser must remember they "look with their ears" as well.

Conclusion

The ability to effectively communicate verbally is essential in every setting. It occurs when the person that listens to it clearly understood what was said. Just as the marathon runner improves his breathing (and performance) through constant practice, so too do people become effective communicators through using words in their messages that convey the intended message. Constant practice and use of verbal communication reduces communication apprehension. Fine tuning verbal communication makes people more effective in future communications. A final advantage of effective verbal communication can be discovered in the work of Dr. Daniel Amen (1998). His brain imaging studies indicated the human brain continues to grow much longer than was originally thought. Effective verbal communication enhances brain growth. Through honest and accurate verbal communication, and continual practicing of verbal communication skills, people become better communicators and smarter as well.

References

Amen, D. (1998). *Change your brain, change your life: The breakthrough program for conquering anxiety, depression, obsessiveness, anger, and impulsiveness.* New York, NY: Three Rivers Press.

DeVito, J. (2008). *Interpersonal messages: Communication and Relationship Skills.* Boston, MA: Pearson Education.

Hamilton, C. (2008). *Communicating for results: A guide for business and the professions* (8th ed.). Belmont, CA: Thomson Wadsworth.

Lindstrom, M. and Underhill, P. *Buyology: Truth and lies about what we buy.* New York, NY. Doubleday Publishing Group.

CONCEPT & APPLICATION PAPER: GROUPTHINK

Concept Definition and Explanation

In any group there develops a tendency for group members to take on the viewpoints of each other to a greater or lesser extent. "Groupthink, a term developed by Irving Janis, is an uncritical way of thinking, often characteristic of groups in which the desire to avoid conflict and reach agreement is more important than careful consideration of alternatives" (Janis, 1989, Turner & Prattkanis, 1998) as cited in Hamilton (2008, p. 254). In businesses there is often great emphasis on team building and unity of purpose. While this does reduce conflict, it can lead to the groupthink systems defined by Janis.

Regarding groupthink, the illusions of vulnerability and group morality come strongly into play regarding the ethics, decisions, and strategies of a business. When the group comes to believe that whatever the leader decides is correct, moral, and ethical, they can buy into decisions that are in fact incorrect, immoral, and unethical. They have been conditioned to think this way, because of the culture of the organization. Furthermore, group members on an individual basis can feel pressure to agree with the team/group or not mention a contrasting idea because they fear they will be rejected or ostracized. When this happens, group members do not truly consider the full implication of their decisions (Hamilton, 2008).

If the leader does not sufficiently communicate responsibility for the decisions to each group member, group members may not realize that their silence about a decision or strategy communicates agreement to the leader. If the members do not demand of themselves that they speak their minds, they will be seen as agreeing with each other (DeVito, 2008). If this happens, group members can become more afraid to express contrasting opinions. Each group member has a specific status within the group. This affects members' willingness to communicate for fear of overstepping their perceived boundaries or even losing their status (Hamilton, 2008).

Furthermore, group members each have specific knowledge. When group members fall into a pattern of groupthink, they might hold back their knowledge. They do this because of their strong need to belong. Maslow's hierarchy of needs explained that the need to belong is a need so strong that it guides the actions people take, for fear of being alone or left out (Shockley-Zalabak, 2009). Thus, rather than provide alternative knowledge or information, and risk being rejected or seen as a show-off, they hold back, and by their silence buy into a less desirable strategy. The need to belong is even greater than the need to be right. In today's economy, Maslow's hierarchy comes into play at the most basic level as well. Thus, people may fear to be individualistic for fear that they will both lose their sense of belonging and their jobs, which fulfills their need for shelter.

In groupthink, the need to see each other as right can overrule critical thinking. As Edward DeBono (1990) stated, "the need to be right all the time is the biggest bar there is to new ideas. It is better to have enough ideas for some of them to be wrong than to be always right by having no ideas at all (p.108)." In order to avoid groupthink, the leader must continually guide the members to encourage them to think critically and come up with best solutions. Unless group members are convinced that providing many ideas is the goal, insufficient strategies or ideas will be proposed. Groupthink does not always occur because of the leader. Groupthink can exist outside of the leader's knowledge, which makes it even more problematic, because the leader isn't even aware it is going on. In business situations, as in life, peer group pressure can often override any policies or procedures (Shockley-Zalabak, 2009).

Concept Application

The concept of groupthink has entered many aspects of life. It exists in the political arena, the classroom, and the business world. Lateral thinking is when you consider all possible outcomes so as to have as much data as possible before making a decision or choosing a strategy. This, in theory, results in a choice that has the greatest chance for success. Lateral thinking isn't the *pursuit* of being open-minded, it *is* being open-minded. Groupthink, in contrast, runs the risk of being the opposite of lateral thinking, as it typically results in fewer possibilities being introduced. The possibilities that are mentioned in a meeting tend to be choices that are not that different from each other.

At times, groupthink can be a good thing. For example, in the case of a football team, one wouldn't want various team members to veer off from the game plan in the middle of a play. In this instance, success can only happen when the entire team is on the same page. This is not the time for uncritical thinking. However, in the course of football practice, when strategies are made, the team should avoid groupthink at times, so that the best game plan possible is made.

In a classroom setting, groupthink can take hold. In my own experience, during a math class, groupthink occurred whenever one man in my class asked a question. He was rather unusual and had a strange way of asking questions. The professor would react rather sharply to him whenever he raised questions. As the weeks wore on, more and more of my classmates would give this man a hard time. They would only listen to him in order to gather ways to victimize him. Rude, hurtful behavior became the norm in the group. Furthermore, the man put up no protest to the treatment, because it had become the norm. Class members who did not indulge in this behavior felt powerless to stop it and said nothing.

In the political arena, no more profound example exists than the entire Watergate scandal. In the Nixon White House, and among his staff, they all had fallen into line with whatever Nixon expressed as the strategy that would be taken throughout the cover-up. When questioned later, each of these staff members stated that they went along with the plan because no one else was disagreeing with the plan, and they assumed their superiors would not order them to do something illegal. Each of these staff members ignored their own knowledge and background, although many of them were highly trained lawyers who knew (at least intellectually) what was illegal or legal. The only one to take a major stand was press secretary Elliot Richardson, who refused to do what Nixon ordered him to do. Thus, he was fired. This made the rest of the group fall even stronger into groupthink.

In the business world, my own personal experience was at Pete and Mac's Pet Resort. Although we had staff meetings where input was sought, it was easy for workers to think they were just supposed to agree with the managers, even if they had an idea they thought would work better. The reason they thought this is that they witnessed the firing of co-workers and managers who appeared to be doing a good job. The staff had the impression that it was "the supervisors' way or the highway". This is the exact climate that creates groupthink, and weakens the overall organization as a result. It ultimately made for a stressful environment. The reason for this was that they witnessed inconsistent treatment by supervisors. Groupthink became a pattern of discouragement and overall motivation decreased. Good managers can counteract this by becoming consistent: in rewarding high performance, providing positive outcomes for innovative contributors, and punishing negative performance. Doing this consistently reduces the reliance on groupthink.

The chain of events preceding and during the Challenger disaster show how groupthink inadvertently led to the disaster even though no harm was intended. A sociologist named Diane Vaughan concluded that the Challenger space catastrophe "happened because people at NASA had done exactly what they were supposed to do. No fundamental decision was made at NASA to do evil" (Gladwell, 2009, p. 282). Rather, a series of seemingly harmless decisions were made that incrementally moved the space agency toward a catastrophic outcome (Gladwell, 2009). "Risks are not easily manageable, accidents are not easily preventable, and rituals of disaster have no meaning" (Gladwell, 2009, p. 282). What Gladwell meant is that groupthink can take over the entire process. Although each step seemed to have sufficient safeguards, the overall process emphasized speed rather than caution. This became the groupthink that led to the disaster.

Conclusion

It is essential to avoid groupthink. Thomas Merton famously said that no man is an island. To that I would add we are all like castles, and we have the option of having our drawbridges up or down. In groupthink, the drawbridges are up. The point of competition through differing ideas is to retain your job, not get someone else fired. Groupthink doesn't allow for competing ideas, weakening the company or group. It is hard to change a person's perception of something once that person is convinced that it is a certain way. Thus, once groupthink takes hold, it is difficult for individuals to make new contributions.

I see more and more Ottawa students that are using their education to change their life. Sometimes, just showing up to work is enough to succeed. Through their guidance, each of our professors at Ottawa encourages us to think critically and avoid groupthink. There are many ways to motivate people to do things. One of those ways is to show, as a leader or a teacher, that you can walk the walk. Whether a person is a group member or a group leader, communication can be used to improve the individual and the group (DeVito, 2008. Shockley-Zalabak, 2009). God encourages us as well, "I command you to be strong and courageous! Do not be afraid or discouraged, for the Lord your God is with you wherever you go (Joshua 1:9). When we are afraid to speak our minds as a result of groupthink, it is important to remember this.

Just because we are imperfect, and have bad assumptions from time to time doesn't mean we should ignore the bad assumptions. It means we should figure out why we had those bad assumptions and figure out which concerns can be addressed. Then we can move forward, helping our groups in any way we can. A priest once told me that every person at Mass matters. Each person makes the Mass that much better and more complete by being there. So too, in avoiding groupthink, group members begin to matter and believe they matter, strengthening the group and each member.

References

DeBono, E. (1990). *Lateral thinking: Creativity step by step.* New York, NY: First Perennial Library.

DeVito, J. (2008). *Interpersonal messages: Communication and Relationship Skills.* Boston, MA: Pearson Education.

Gladwell, M. (2009). *What the dog saw: And other adventures.* New York, NY: Little, Brown and Company.

Hamilton, C. (2008). *Communicating for results: A guide for business and the professions* (8th ed.). Belmont, CA: Thomson Wadsworth.

Shockley-Zalabak, P. (2009). *Fundamentals of organizational communication: Knowledge, sensitivity, skills, values (7th ed.).* Boston, MA: Pearson Education Inc.

CONCEPT & APPLICATION PAPER: SITUATIONAL CONTINGENCY THEORY

Concept Definition and Explanation

Situational contingency theory is especially interesting to me because it emphasizes the people without ignoring the realities of the tasks and circumstances facing the group. When considering the idea of leadership and management, it used to be thought there was only one way to lead and manage (Shockley-Zalabak, 2009). This often ended up in a very autocratic way of managing things. The reason it worked that way was because original supervisors were seen mostly in a manufacturing business, on the production line. Decisions were few, and rules and procedures were exact, predictable, and put in place by management (without input from line workers). As American businesses and society have evolved, so have the employees. Employees today often want to have a say in how things are done, and want a say in decisions that affect them and their work. Contingency theory addresses this situation.

Time is a factor in deciding which leadership model to use in contingency leadership theory. "In selecting an appropriate leadership style, you need to consider the time needed to (1) reach a decision, (2) get group commitment, and (3) implement the decision" (Hamilton, 2008, p. 291). It is interesting to me that leader-directed decisions have the most time spent on developing employee commitment to the decision. Although leader-directed decisions are made faster, when you add in the length of time it takes employees to buy into the decision, more time is spent on leader-directed decisions than group plus leader decisions (Hamilton, 2008). The group plus leader decisions typically have the best overall chance for successful implementation because the *process* of the group decision making helps ensure the commitment to the decision they make. Not only that, when you look at the time span between beginning the decision making and having commitment to that decision, group-plus-leader decisions take less time than leader-directed decisions.

When considering using contingency theory, and having the employees participate in the decision making, there is an important factor that must not be overlooked. Stephen Robbins (2008) observed: "The issues in which the employees are asked to get involved in must be relevant to their interests. The employees must have the ability to participate. This includes intelligence, technical knowledge, and communication skills (p.194)". The implication of this is employees should participate in areas they know about when it is related to their own work and lives.

Bill Grace, the founder of W.L. Grace and Associates believed in finding the best way to help his employees succeed. "He created a place with hardly any hierarchy and few ranks and titles. He insisted on direct one-on-one communication. Anyone in the company could speak to anyone else (Shockley-Zalabak, 2009, p.291)". By doing this, he created an atmosphere that helped build the desire to and belief in participatory decision-making. He knew that once you have people communicating with each other you increase the possibility of willing participation in decisions.

This is a huge parallel to Henry Fayol's bridge. Shockley-Zalabak (2009) explained that "Fayol suggested that when the necessity for rapid message exchange occurred, it would be advisable to use a 'gang plank' whereby peers communicated directly without regard to the scalar chain" (p. 69). In other words, the messages should move both up and down the chain of command. "Research by Fidler, Chemers and Mahar (1976) shows that managers can be trained to identify and modify various situations to better fit their own communication and leadership styles" (Shockley-Zalabak, 2009, p.291).

Path-goal theory is similar to contingency theory. With this, "neither directive nor supportive leadership will be effective unless employees perceive the leader as helping them achieve desired goals" (Hamilton, 2008, p. 55). Participation in decision-making does not change everything, but it helps the group in general. This participation can be the key to making or breaking the chance for success a change will have. Stephen Robbins (2008) stated that "having employees participate in decisions that affect them is no panacea. Participation has only a modest influence on factors such as employee productivity, motivation, and job satisfaction. But it is a very potent force for combating resistance to change" (p. 194).

Of course, building consensus is a bit different from agreeing on everything. A group can come to an agreement based on considering the advantages and disadvantages of the choices. When they come to an agreement, the process itself helps them buy into the decision. With contingency theory, autocratic decision making is also part of the model.

There are times when even the most democratic organization or manager must be autocratic in making decisions. Some managers are more autocratic in nature, so this isn't difficult for them. Of course the autocratic manager has a very difficult time with democratic decision-making. The best way for that manager to understand the benefit of democratic decision-making is to prove that the implementation of democratic decisions is more efficient.

Some managers are much more democratic, and really do not like to make an autocratic decision. For instance, a kind-hearted manager may not want to reduce staff even though he has been told he must. It is important for managers to keep in mind that people like having leaders more than they like to be self-governed. "Research has shown that the person who speaks first and most often is more likely to emerge as the group leader. The number of contributors is even more important than the quality of those contributions (Engleberg & Wynn, 2010, p.113)". What does this mean for the manager? That the group *process* proves to the individuals that they are allowed to participate. I believe people accept quantity over the quality because people prefer to avoid conflict. Although people like to be led by a leader, employees must buy into the leader's premise for operating. Even a great manager or leader is still prone to becoming dull after awhile, and then losing his ability to focus his employees.

A great leader is someone that serves as many people as he can. Consider Malcolm Gladwell's perspective: "group's made up of smaller teams work well together as long as the number of group remains below 150" (Hamilton, 2008, p.292).

The most important point to all of this is the time to make a decision and the time to develop commitment to that decision. In business, time is money. The time to make a decision is very short for a leader-directed decision and gets longer when more people are involved in making the decision. As I stated earlier, the opposite is true for commitment to the decision. If only the leader made the decision, it takes a great deal of time to get people committed to the decision. People will accept a decision much more easily if they helped make that decision. At that point it is almost as if they unconsciously say, "So what's to accept? This was my decision"!

Concept Application

The concept of situational contingency theory has been seen to varying degrees in my life and in my father's work life. In my father's work life he has worked at a number of companies. The management style and decision making strategies at these companies have been vastly different. When he worked at Mitel, the company had become very autocratic. His manager did not seek input from the engineers regarding what was a reasonable estimate of time for developing the software for various products. He laid the deadline on them, and micro-managed them throughout each day. This led the engineers to rightly believe that the manager had absolutely zero trust in their abilities and reliability. He spent so much time belittling them and holding meetings to humiliate them that the engineers were completely alienated from him and each other. As a result, there was no sense of teamwork, and the engineers were given negative feedback if they helped each other. This in turn meant that deadlines were missed, and products had errors that might have been corrected if the engineers had been encouraged to work together.

In contrast, at SMART Modular Technologies, where my father now works, they use a number of different strategies and policies for decision-making and project management that are very much based on contingency theory. They have very brief (10 minutes) meetings every morning about the project(s) they are working on. Each engineer just says one or two sentences about how his particular task is progressing. If he has hit any snags or needs input or help, he says so, and they bond together to fix it. The manager is still responsible for "riding herd" and trying to ensure deadlines are met. Through the daily brief meetings, troubles are addressed. The engineers are treated as trustworthy, capable adults. The engineers through the brief meetings get to be on the part of the project they feel most comfortable and competent with. They all have their say as to what is a reasonable deadline. Everyone buys into the decisions and deadlines because they have helped create them. The manager is instantly aware if an engineer is at a point where he needs some overseeing or handholding. It is a system that works well, despite the fact that different supervisors and engineers vary in whether they prefer democratic or autocratic systems. It is a successful compromise.

I wish this approach had been used when I worked at Pete and Mac's. There was a big difference in work ethic and overall trustworthiness within the group of employees. To address this, the manager decided to treat us all alike. She didn't vary the level of trust or autonomy she gave each employee. Thus people who had a high level of trustworthiness and a strong work ethic to boot (like me) were treated as though we were irresponsible, forgetful, and lazy (like many of my co-workers). It was a disincentive to the hard workers, because there was no recognition or even realization that we were accomplishing so much. This treatment was an incentive to the lazy, irresponsible workers because the hard workers automatically picked up the slack. It was especially bothersome to me, because it is very important to me to be trusted and believed in.

Conclusion

It is essential to consider the personality types, skills, and overall work ethic of the workers (and managers) at a company. I believe that contingency theory offers the best chance for success for each person in the group, and the manager. Obviously, not every decision is open to lengthy discussion so that the group can make the best decision. In the midst of a battle during a war is not the time for the whole company of soldiers to discuss what the best plan is for taking the hill. In that situation, the group must immediately do what the officer has decided, or more soldiers could die.

Other than situations like that, though, I believe that contingency theory is one that provides the best chance for success because it respects each person. Improving a business is like improving a team. Great teams need great players and a great coach. The coach conveys a message, vision, and way of thinking to the team. Bill Walsh (2009), former coach of the San Francisco 49's football team was a terrific coach and business leader. He summarized it this way:

Great teams in business, in sports, or elsewhere have a conscience. At its best, an organization – your team – bespeaks values and a way of doing things that emanate from a source; that source is you – the leader. Thus, the dictates of your personal beliefs should ultimately become characteristics of your team. (Walsh, Jamison & Walsh, 2009, p.15)

The use of contingency theory helps managers and their employees believe that their decisions and efforts help the group succeed. When they own the process, they own the outcomes.

References

Engleberg, I. & Wynn, D. (2010). *Working in small groups: Communication principles and strategies.* Boston: Pearson Education Inc.

Hamilton, C. (2008). *Communicating for results: A guide for business and the professions* (8th ed.). Belmont, CA: Thomson Wadsworth.

Robbins, S. (2008). *The truth about managing people (2nd ed.).* Upper Saddle River, NJ: Pearson Education Inc.

Shockley-Zalabak, P. (2009). *Fundamentals of organizational communication: Knowledge, sensitivity, skills, values (7th ed.).* Boston: Pearson Education Inc.

Walsh, B., Jamison, S., & Walsh, C. (2009). *The Score takes care of itself: My philosophy of leadership.* New York: Portfolio Hardcover Publishing.

CONCEPT & APPLICATION PAPER: DRESSING FOR THE INTERVIEW

Concept Definition and Explanation

It has been said that verbal communication is the smallest percentage of communication. Non-verbal communication speaks even louder than the verbal part. What does this non-verbal communication include? The body language of the communicator, the paralanguage, and the overall image the speaker creates are all pieces of the non-verbal communication. During an interview this overall image is defined by how interviewees present themselves. This implies that being well-dressed for an interview is more important than many people realize. Blakeman's study (as cited in Hamilton, 2008, p.227) found that "when a negative impression was created during the first five minutes of the interview, applicants were not hired 90 percent of the time; however, when a positive impression was created in the first five minutes, applicants were hired 75 percent of the time".

In order to have a successful job interview the job seeker must remember that there are three factors for the job seeker to deal with: the interviewer; the other applicants; as well as the interviewee's own strengths and weaknesses. My theory is that we dress nicely and appropriately so that the interviewer forgets about our clothes and focuses on us. Why would the interviewer focus on our qualifications more if we dressed nicely? If the interviewer (consciously or unconsciously) decides the job seeker cares enough about the interview to dress appropriately, there is a good chance the job seeker would fit in with the company's needs.

Since interviewers typically make an initial judgment about the interviewee within the first minute of the meeting, it is essential to dress in business clothes. Dressing in business clothes means women and men should wear a suit, conservative dress shirt, tie, and polished shoes to an interview. This communicates to the company that you are serious about the job. Experts say that you should dress for the job that is at least a couple of levels above the job you are applying for (Criscito, P. and Funkhouser, D., 2006). The reason is that it shows how seriously you take the interview and the job. It communicates that you are someone that already knows how to be a part of their culture.

If your appearance is neat and polished people form an impression about your abilities and decide that you are a polished, organized thinker. In management theory they call this the halo effect. Shapiro (2008, p. 88) explained that "a sloppy dresser will be interpreted as a sloppy, disorganized thinker". Of course, if the interview itself results in you revealing that you are disrespectful or unprofessional then your clothing will not save you. However, being dressed nicely helps you focus better and behave in a classy way.

Job applicants should even dress in professional business attire if they are applying for a job at a company that is known to dress casually. This will communicate to the company how seriously they take the interview and the job. It is essential to use professional body language and words during the interview so there isn't a mismatch between how you look and how you speak. This means sit up straight, be pleasant, have a good handshake, and speak like a professional (avoiding slang).

Unemployment is very high right now. It is more important than ever to dress nice for an interview. It is difficult for interviewers and companies to reach what they believe to be the best person to hire for a job. If two people have the same qualifications and experience, then the person that will be hired will be the one that made the best overall impression. That person will almost always be the one that was dressed and acted like a conservative business person and looked neat and polished. Looking that way reinforces everything the interviewee says and does. Job applicants must keep in mind that everything that they say and do will be seen through the lens that was created by the initial impression created by their appearance.

My theory is that many businesses have gotten so lax that they are beginning to see that employees could improve and dress better. Thus, businesses will be more selective about dress in the future, which can actually increase the number of current employees that are willing to dress better. Interviewers will make their first impression and then judge and measure everything during the interview to reinforce their first impression.

Concept Application

When I interviewed for my job at Pete and Mac's Pet Resort I dressed conservatively. I wore a shirt and tie, nice shoes, and a pair of Dockers. Although everyone at the business wore jeans and a uniform T-shirt, I still created a good impression in the mind of the manager (Mike). He was impressed by how I presented myself. I stood up straight, shook his hand, looked him in the eye, and looked and behaved like a gentleman. It is because of all of these aspects that Mike hired me on the spot, although he technically had no openings. Mike believed I was serious about getting the job and would be serious about performing well on the job. My clothing and attitude impressed him. Other people had come in applying for jobs dressed in what people would consider "play clothes".

In addition to getting hired, my appearance continued to benefit me. Although we all wore jeans and a uniform T-shirt, many of my fellow employees looked like slobs. They had piercings, wild hair colors or hairstyles, and just didn't look professional. I always looked neat and professional. As a result, my managers believed in me and knew I was trustworthy. I had a good work ethic, and it wasn't contradicted by my appearance. Pet owners talked differently to me than many of the other employees, because I looked nice. My appearance helped them believe I was responsible with their pets. The result of all of this was that my manager told me when I left that I was always welcome back there, and that I would be an excellent manager. To reinforce this point, one of my supervisors (Michelle) even took note of the difference in my appearance and body language compared to my co-workers. Michelle commented that it appeared that I had been in the military, because I was so neat and polished. This increased her respect for me, although she really treated almost everyone with disrespect.

An important distinction needs to be made. Although experts often say to dress for the job you want to have, or to dress for a job a few levels up, this does have some limits. In the acting industry it doesn't mean that actors should show up wearing their costumes. Perhaps for these people they should dress the way the executive producer or the studio executives dress. This communicates the level of professionalism they plan to bring to the project.

Conclusion

It is essential to consider the impression you make when applying for a job. People often spend lots of hours rehearsing and answering interview questions in order to prepare for an interview. It doesn't matter how impressively applicants answer questions if they create an unprofessional impression. The casual Friday mentality has overtaken much of our culture to the extent that every day is casual dress day. Proof of this statement is seen in how some recruiters are beginning to view the process. "An increasing number of recruiters say that a business suit is too formal for an interview at their company" (Kennedy, J. 2008, p. 134). Does this mean that people shouldn't wear a suit? No, it means that it has become less typical. There is a difference between wanting a job and being serious enough about the job to get it. In order to be taken seriously, people need to dress in conservative clothes and be neat and polished. Casual dress can lead to people lowering their own standards when it comes to work ethic. I saw it all the time in my workplace. If people dropping off their pets at a kennel believed that my work ethic and level of responsibility are better at least partially based on my appearance, then this belief is also present throughout the business world.

Dressing professionally for an interview is just the beginning. Perhaps our nation can improve through dressing nicer as well. We must start treating everything with a new perspective and respect. Through dressing more professionally in our work lives we can begin to subconsciously raise our own standards about our work. President Kennedy said, "Ask not what your country can do for you; ask what you can do for your country". This can be applied to our business lives as well. Through dressing professionally and conservatively for an interview, and dressing professionally in the workplace, we are demonstrating dedication and responsibility through our dress. This then can become part of our work thought processes and raise our own standards.

References

Criscito, P. and Funkhouser, D. (2006). *Interview questions in a flash*. New York: Barron's Educational Series, Inc.

Hamilton, C. (2008). *Communicating for results: A guide for business and the professions (8ᵗʰ ed.)*. Belmont, CA: Thomson Wadsworth.

Kennedy, J. (2008). *Job Interviews for Dummies (3ʳᵈ ed.)*. Hoboken, NJ: Wiley Publishing Inc.

Shapiro, C. (2008). *What does somebody have to do to get a job around here? 44 Insider secrets that will get you hired*. New York: St. Martin's Griffin.

14

PERSUASIVE COMMUNICATION: PAPERS AND SPEECHES

RESEARCH PAPER: REDUCING SPEAKER NERVOUSNESS

Introduction

Literally thousands of books and articles have been written about dealing with speaker anxiety and nervousness during a speech. This information, combined with classes in public speaking, and organizations like Toastmasters International all serve a purpose. That purpose is to help people improve their speaking and reduce nervousness. In this paper, these facts and techniques will be presented and explored. This paper will first describe the factors that contribute to speaker nervousness/anxiety. Then techniques for solving these factors will be presented. By learning about and applying these strategies and techniques, speakers improve the likelihood of delivering effective speeches.

Statement of Purpose

The goal of this research paper is discover and describe the various theories, techniques, and strategies that experts have used to reduce nervousness during the delivery of a speech.

Research Question

Will acquiring knowledge about speaker anxiety and learning strategies for dealing with be helpful in reducing nervousness?

Thesis

This knowledge will help speakers reduce or even eliminate their nervousness during a speech because speakers will have information and a new roadmap to help them avoid paralyzing nervousness.

Significance

The ability to deliver a speech effectively without being nervous is something each person should be able to do. The fact that this ability has not been emphasized enough is evident in this country, as fewer people than ever are able to deliver a speech effectively.

Method

I conducted a literature search through libraries as well as an internet search on the World Wide Web to gather my research information.

Findings

Physiological Component to Speaker Anxiety/Nervousness

Contrary to what many people believe, it is not just a psychological fear that speakers experience when they are nervous. There is a definite physiological factor behind that fear. In other words, you are not just imagining that your body feels fear. It can be seen in the actual brain imaging. This is a surprise to many people, as their fears and anxieties are often minimized by others. According to Berkin (2010) there is physical proof of anxiety in brain imaging:

> The design of the brain's wiring – given its long operational history, which is hundreds of thousands of years older than the history of public speaking – makes it impossible to stop fearing what it knows is the worst tactical situation for a person to be in. (p. 15)

This physiological component cannot be ignored. It is similar to the stress the body feels whenever it is in a fight or flight situation. This is the reason for the quivering voice, shaking hands, dizziness, or sweating that many speakers experience. Thus, the speaker cannot overlook the fact that his brain is wired to feel fear, which translates into speaker anxiety. To overlook this fact invites disaster. Why? According to Berkin (2010), "fear gives us the energy to proactively prevent failures from happening" (p. 17). Being in denial about the fear prevents speakers from using that fear to their benefit. "If you pretend to have no fears of public speaking, you deny yourself the natural energy your body is giving you. An important point is that "anxiety creates a kind of energy you can use, just as excitement does" (Berkin, 2010, p. 18). Through proper preparation, a large part of the physiological aspects will be overcome.

Situational vs. Trait Anxiety

An important distinction for speakers to keep in mind is that there is a difference between situational and trait anxiety. Situational anxiety is related to the situation. Sometimes it is appropriate to feel anxiety, such as if you are in great danger. When delivering a speech many people feel anxiety. The situation is often one they have created themselves, through their negative thoughts or through not being well prepared. Trait anxiety, on the other hand would be a natural tendency that some people have to be anxious or shy. This can be overcome through seeking help (in addition to practicing the speech). The distinction is important.

Although both types of anxiety can be reduced through the strategies I discuss, trait anxiety may very well need the help of an understanding counselor as well.

Speakers' Thought Patterns

Speakers' own thought patterns greatly contribute to speaker nervousness. How does this happen? I believe that speakers sometimes feel nervous because when it is their turn to listen to someone else's speech they continually compare how the speaker is doing and judge how we would be doing it instead. Thus, when speakers speak they very correctly know they are being continually evaluated. This feeling of being under the gun creates a huge amount of anxiety which in turn causes the speaker to do poorly.

If speakers continually give themselves the image that they are terrified, they will be terrified. It becomes a self-fulfilling prophecy. If instead of focusing on their anticipated fear they focus on preparation their fear is reduced. In order to become an effective public speaker, you must accept that the secret lies in letting go of the 'public' part and focusing on the speaking part (Zeoli, 2008).

Self-defeating Preparation Techniques

Speakers with high speech anxiety often have several similar habits that end up causing them to be nervous while delivering a speech. The most common tendency is that speakers do not practice their speech out loud enough. They greatly underestimate the amount of time it takes to deliver their speech effectively. As a result, they do not know their material well enough, they rely on notes too much, they do not have sufficient eye contact, their hand gestures and voices do not do enough to draw the listener in, and they are just plain ineffective.

Besides insufficient practice, speakers often make the mistake of choosing too broad of a topic or having too many major talking points in the speech. In general, it is considered the most effective too have three major points within your speech. If you provide too much information in a speech, the audience will not be able to absorb all of the material. Having to remember too much information increases the nervousness of the speaker as well (Gallo 2010, Zeoli 2008).

An overlooked technique is that speakers do not put enough time into defining who the audience is. They must consider this factor when preparing their speeches or the speech might not engage the audience. It is far better to dig too deeply into figuring out who will be in the audience and how they think than to lose most of the audience because they don't care about your speech (Zeoli, 2008).

Physical Strategies to Counteract Nervousness

It is critical for speakers to know that the presence of anxiety or nervousness provides a benefit. If they focus on it as only a bad thing, they can block the benefits that come from the nervousness. "Some anxiety is a good thing. It makes you perform better. Think of athletes; before a race they are anxious but they are able to control the anxiety and they channel it in a positive way" (Provan, 2009, p.126). If speakers think about their anxiety in this way, then when they feel an attack of the jitters they can go through self-talk. They can say, "Oh, I am getting psyched up to speak. This is great. I will have the energy I need to do well".

There are definite physical strategies that speakers can use that reduce nervousness and anxiety. Taking deep, slow breaths or a walk outdoors can reduce nervousness while giving energy. Another strategy is to get some intense physical exercise.

> I want to make my body as relaxed as possible and exhaust as much physical energy early in the day. As a rule, I go to the gym in the morning before a talk, with the goal of releasing any extra nervous energy before I get on stage (Berkin, 2010, p. 21).

Preparation Techniques That Reduce Nervousness

Just as with any performance or skill, the more speakers practice the better they get. Steve Jobs is widely recognized in the business world as an excellent public speaker. There are many aspects that separate him from the others, but the most significant is his preparation before a speech. In an analysis of how Steve Jobs succeeds, Carmine Gallo (2010) stated:

> Relentless preparation is the single best way to overcome stage fright; know what you're going to say, when you're going to say it, and how you're going to say it. Shift the focus to what your product or service means to the lives of your listeners, and be confident in your preparation (p.193).

Speakers must plan on spending hours rehearsing. They should rehearse with their script, "writing arrows for pitch, and underlines that indicate emphasis" (Bartlett, 2008, p. 87). This technique, in turn, helps speakers work with varying their voices. "If you practice changing your voice to engross each listener it will actually take away from the nervousness a person might feel. Don't think how you sound, feel how you sound" (Bartlett, 2008, p. 87). Speakers must vary their voices (both volume and pitch) so that they do not speak in a monotone. Practicing in front of people, using a tape recorder, or filming themselves all are ways the speaker can improve and perfect their delivery. Practicing the speech in the actual room it will be given in before the day of the speech helps speakers feel more comfortable when the day of the speech arrives.

Besides working with their voices, speakers must work with their visual aids. Visual aids should be simple, effective, and memorable. "Always standing on the right of a slide presentation is helpful because people will always return their focus to the left side to see where you are standing" (Bartlett, 2008, p.86). The slides used during the speech should, of course, emphasize the important points of the speech. Gallo (2010) explained that "the speech should have a headline and a passion statement. Then you should write out the three messages you want your audience to receive. The messages should be easy to recall" (p. 7).

Another area that must be practiced is movement. This means to practice when and where to walk during the presentation, and when to use gestures as well as which gestures to use. "Body language and verbal delivery account for 63 to 90 percent of the impression you leave on your audience" (Gallo, 2010, p. 165). The use of gestures also helps speakers improve their own focus.

Techniques to Use during the Speech to Reduce Nervousness

There are numerous techniques that experts mention as effective for reducing nervousness while delivering the actual speech. These include physical things like deep breathing, tightening and loosening muscles, and focusing on not rushing. When a speaker first stands in front of the audience Bartlett (2008) advised, "Keep your mouth closed until you have reached out silently with your eyes to an individual member of the audience" (p. 87). Throughout the speech, the speaker should continually have eye contact with various parts of the audience.

Throughout the speech, speakers can greatly reduce nervousness by keeping their true passion for the subject material in mind. They must let this passion come through in their voice, gestures, movements, and facial expression. "Passion stirs the emotions of your listeners when you use it to paint a picture of a more meaningful world, a world that your customers or employees can play a part in creating (Gallo, 2010, p. 32)".

It is essential for speakers to adjust their speech while delivering it. They should do this if it appears that some of the listeners look confused, detached, disinterested or upset. They must make adjustments to draw the audience in.

In every speech I focused my attention on the audience and read reactions in real time. If I saw or sensed skepticism or confusion, I altered what I said on the spot. I managed hundreds of people at a time in a real exchange because I made the impact of what I said matter more than the content or perfection of my delivery (Cramer & Wasiak, 2006, p.99).

Conclusion

In history, some of the greatest speakers were politicians and philosophers. Abraham Lincoln comes to mind when considering politicians. He always connected with his audience, and spoke in understandable language. His words conveyed passion, and are remembered to this day. "When Aristotle wrote his communication handbook he was not indulging in idle philosophical speculation. He was offering his students advice about how to make an audience listen, believe, remember, and act" (Cramer & Wasiak, 2006, p.29). We rarely think about what makes us react the way we do. The present moment passes into the past, and the future comes either too quickly or slowly. Speakers must keep in mind that the audience is in the present moment. Speakers must keep them in that moment. Focusing the speech on a few points helps the speaker avoid nervousness and helps the audience stay involved with the speech as well.

Through proper preparation and adjusting the speech while delivering it, speakers have the strongest chance to eliminate their nervousness and be effective speakers. Insisting on developing a passionate, compelling speech is important. Aristotle favored emotional appeals, as did Benjamin Franklin. We must always know that speaking is supposed to rivet the audience. Focusing on the passion while preparing, rehearsing, and delivering the speech is the key to reducing overall nervousness. If well-prepared speakers are passionate enough, they completely forget to be nervous.

References

Bartlett, D. (2008). *Making your point: Communicating effectively with audiences of one to one million.* New York: St. Martin's Press.

Berkin, S. (2010). *Confessions of a public speaker.* Sebatopol, California: O'Reilly Media Inc.

Cramer, K. & Wasiak, H. (2006). *Change the way you see everything through asset based thinking.* Beijing, China: Running Press Inc.

Gallo, C. (2010). *The presentation secrets of Steve Jobs: How to be insanely great in front of any audience.* New York: McGraw Hill.

Provan, D. (2009). *Giving great presentations.* Southam Warwickshire, United Kingdom: In Easy Steps Limited.

Zeoli, R. (2008). *The 7 principles of public speaking: Proven methods from a PR professional.* New York: Skyhorse Publishing, Inc.

PERSUASIVE SPEECH: DRINK GREEN TEA

What drink do you reach for the most? One thing we can't refuse to look at in this desert is hydration. Isn't the reason why we stay hydrated so we can feel the benefits of our healthy supplements and daily activity? I am here to convince you to choose green tea. Green tea is a great healthful supplement. Sure it's expensive to a one dollar cheeseburger or the seductively marketed frenzy of a so called health drink from Sobe, but it's worth your money.

There are specific benefits for Good Earth decaf green tea and green tea in general.

First, there is a CO_2 process that leaves all the good stuff in that most processes take out. Not only that but caffeinated black teas natural process to make it black takes out some of the good stuff found in green tea.

Did you know that there are only 4 milligrams of caffeine per serving in this brand of tea as opposed to the 5 milligrams of caffeine in Lipton tea? The problem with caffeine in tea is that it takes away from the healthful effects of the tea.

Now that we have taken care of the caffeine problem, I can say that there are not concentrated amounts of serotonin and dopamine altering substances known as L- theanine in green tea. There is just enough so that people with certain psychotropic medications can still drink up at tea time.

Another health benefit that can be used in foods is Soy Lecithin. Soy lecithin is found in green tea in trace amounts. This helps the liver, brain, and reduces cholesterol.

Finally, Good Earth's website goodearth.com actually lets people vote on which charitable organization will receive part of the profits from the tea.

If you don't like to drink green tea there are many food and supplements at vitamin shops that harness the power of green tea as well. Plus it is as versatile as coffee because it can be served cool or hot.

I have explained the reasons for drinking decaffeinated green tea: there are health benefits, it doesn't interfere with most medications, and you can participate in charitable donations. Besides that, each Good Earth teabag comes with a philosophical quote.

To quote an actual teabag quote from this brand of tea "The free thinking of one age is the common sense of the next". Mathew Arnold said that.

Whether the reasons are physical, mental, social, medicinal, traditional, or scientific, I encourage you to run, not walk to get some decaffeinated Good Earth green tea today, and tell your friends about it. Join the green tea drinkers.

PERSUASIVE SPEECH: USE MSM

The effective treatment of chronic pain is a significant and ongoing medical issue in this country. According to *The Management of Pain*, a 2 volume reference book for physicians, published in 1990, more than 1/3 of the American population has chronic painful conditions. Of those, half or more are affected by pain for days, weeks, months, years, or even permanently. Headache pain is the most common form of pain, and affects over 40 million Americans each year.

There are many medicines for pain that physicians prescribe plus over the counter medications like ibuprofen, Tylenol, and aspirin. *(Show medicine bottles to class)*. These all have side effects. You know the drill: liver damage, stroke, heart attack, serious addiction, and other lovely side effects.

I'm here today to convince you to try something new. I hope you will feel lucky to have heard my words today. It's MSM and it's not new to two renowned experts. Surgeon Dr. Stanley Jacob and neurologist Dr. Ronald Lawrence have conducted extensive research on the use of MSM for treating and managing pain. *(Show MSM to class)*. MSM stands for methylsulfonylmethane. It is a natural substance present in food and in the human body. MSM is a nutritional supplement, and according to these experts, is safe for children and adults.

These experts say most people know that calcium is good for the bones and iron is important for the blood but don't know the importance of sulfur. MSM controls pain symptoms, just as insulin controls the symptoms of diabetes. Be aware that false claims can arise about MSM, just as any product. Stay informed.

Besides treating pain, which I have spoken about, MSM provides other benefits: antioxidants, improved immune system, softer skin, thicker hair, stronger nails, decreased scar tissue, and amazingly, constipation relief.

If you are not intrigued to try MSM, it is probably because I need to mention how much MSM is required. There is no recommended daily allowance for it. MSM comes in a powder, capsule, and as a topical treatment. I should tell you that side effects of MSM include pain relief which is often better than traditional medicines, improved immune system, and lack of organ damage.

Conclusion

Saying no to traditional pain medications might be difficult. However, MSM is becoming more main stream because of the customers who buy it. If I were you, I would get it while the prices are still low. Don't just take my word for it, buy this book as well as MSM, and get the facts.

PERSUASIVE SPEECH: WE SHOULD BAN GAMBLING ADS ON TV AND RADIO

I.   Introduction

A. Did you know there are only two states in the country where all gambling is illegal? I will tell you later which they are if you just stay with me.

B. Gambling has invaded our culture. According to the Louisiana Association of Compulsive Gambling, 87% of adult Americans have participated in legalized gambling in the past year.

C. Can we eliminate casinos, lotteries, and racetracks? No, we cannot; and that is NOT what I am here to talk about.

D. [show the homeless man slide]Look at this man. He is homeless. Why? It is a result of his gambling addiction. How did it begin? It began with advertising on television and radio.

E. There is something especially wrong with TV and radio ads that promote gambling.

F. I want to persuade you that we should ban gambling ads on TV and radio.

II.   Body:

A. Some of you may think that we cannot ban specific types of ads on TV and radio.

    1. In 1973 the federal government banned cigarette ads from radio and TV.

    2. They banned them not just because of the health risk but because tobacco companies were changing nicotine levels to create addiction.

    3. [Show slide showing decline in smokers]. The lack of mass media ads for cigarettes made smoking less desirable and mainstream.

B. Advertising theory says companies make their product desirable by creating an emotional image or culture surrounding the product and repeat exposure to make the objectionable acceptable.

    1. The gambling industry manipulated the viewers through this message:

  a. "G"-gambling is glamorous

  b. "A"-gambling brings acceptance (makes you part of a special group) and is accepted (by society)

  c. "M"-gambling gets you LOTS of money and a rich lifestyle

2. Gambling ads do not show the real risks or low odds. The odds of winning big in the lottery are 14 Million to 1. According to the National Council on Gambling you are more likely to get hit by lightning while standing in line to buy the ticket than to have a winning ticket. [Lightning and lottery ticket slide].

C. According to clinical psychologist William McCowan, Americans now spend more on legal gambling than on movie tickets plus recorded music, plus theme parks, plus spectator sports, plus video games. Obviously the ads have worked. Right?

D. How did the industry do it? A.C. Neilson reports that in the U.S. the TV is on for the average household almost 7 hours a day.

E. There are almost 2,000 broadcast TV stations and 14,000 radio stations nationwide. That is a lot of access to the consumer.

F. Proof of how mainstream gambling is: Complete this statement: "What happens in Vegas...." [Yep...Stays in Vegas].

G. The biggest reason to ban these ads is because the gambling industry must constantly create new addicts to survive. Why?

1. 80% of casinos money comes from 20% of their customers. That group is made up almost entirely of compulsive or addicted gamblers.

2. Thus: manipulating the consumer to become compulsive could emerge as the industry's albatross, the same way the public got a clearer understanding of how the tobacco industry operates.

3. We are waking up to the fact that casinos use flash, and lotteries use convenience, to attract and keep customers (like malls do). That 80% 20% thing is common in business; however the industry is trying to create addicts not just customers. That is why these effective ads must be banned.

4. Harvard Medical School says 15 to 20 million adults and adolescents are addicts.

III. Conclusion

A. I have been trying to persuade you that gambling ads on TV and radio should be banned because:

1. Addiction is a growing problem. Those 15 to 20 million addicts I mentioned would fill 214 NFL stadiums.

2. Casinos vary the flash, payouts, and ads to addict.

3. These ads are so powerful that truthful information about risks and dangers is overpowered and rejected.

5. Remember! The graph I showed you proved banning ads decreased smoking.

6. I hope you see we cannot begin to address the addiction until we eliminate the powerful ads.

B. Last, but not least, the two states where gambling is illegal are Utah and Hawaii.

C. Please take these next words to heart and listen to your conscience. Let's do what we can to stop people from ending up like this. [Show Homeless slide].

1. Urge your congressman and Senators to ban gambling ads on TV and radio.

2.   Start a petition and tell friends and family out of state to do the same thing.

3. Progress may be slow, but worth it to save one woman, man or child from becoming addicted.

15

INTERCULTURAL/INTERNATIONAL COMMUNICATIONS

In this course, we explored the cultural dimensions that make up each country's culture. To reinforce these concepts, the cultural dimensions of the country I chose are included in this section.

RESEARCH PAPER PROPOSAL/ANNOTATED BIBLIOGRAPHY: GERMAN CULTURE

Although I am interested in the culture of many different countries, I have chosen to study the culture of Germany. Since one of the parameters of this project includes interviewing someone from the country, I narrowed my choice to Germany. This is because I actually know someone who grew up in Germany and now lives in the United States. Besides knowing her, some of my dad's ancestors lived in Germany. These two factors motivated me to research the country and culture.

I do have a few preconceived ideas and biases about Germany. Obviously, I know about Germany in regards to World War II. The destruction and Holocaust brought about by Germany is well known. When people think of Germany they often think of this. This dark history affects their culture, as some Germans have a sense of shame about the country's past. There is less of a sense of nationalistic pride in Germany because of this. I also think of the Alps, the German beers and wines, castles, and German engineering in cars. Travel and tourism bring a lot of money into the country. Germany is known for its excellence in auto manufacturing. People tend to think that German cars are examples of superior engineering.

I want to know more about the culture of Germany: how the people think and act; how they communicate; and how they conduct their business. It is important to know about this, as they are one of the largest economies in the world. Germany is an economic leader in Europe, just as the United States is in North America.

I have a preconception about German people. I think of the men as loud, boisterous, and jovial, often wearing lederhosen, at least in a social setting. The women (at least in the movies) are big, strong, and friendly. I think of Germans as having blond-hair and blue eyes. My notion is that if they speak English at all, they speak it with a heavy accent. Despite this image of their friendliness, I also think of them as very blunt and cold in their dealings. Some of this comes from the movies, and some just in comparison to cultures such as the French, Italian, Spanish, and Irish people.

Overall, I believe that communication between cultures can always be improved by understanding the history of the culture, and the current situation in that culture. I believe the research that I will conduct will help me to more fully understand the culture of Germany, and the problems that they face.

Annotated Bibliography

Romanowskiej, J. & Omilanowska, M. (2008). *Germany: Eyewitness travel guide*. London: DK Books. Egert. The authors provide information and advice about some of the customs and laws that are of particular interest to visitors to the country.

Fodor (2009). *Fodor's see it Germany, (3rd ed.)*. New York: Fodor's Publishing. This book provides valuable insights into the current cultural trends in Germany and the challenges of a re-united country. In even has information about foods and social customs.

Ivory, M., Gray, J. & Grever, J. (2010). *National Geographic traveler: Germany*. Washington, D.C.: National Geographic Publishing. This book provides detailed information about the current culture and customs in Germany. Although the emphasis is on various sightseeing highlights of the country, it interweaves current cultural information that etc.

Kempe, F. (1999). *Father/Land: A personal search for the new Germany*. New York: G. P Putnam's Sons. This book explores the current culture in Germany and looks at it through the lens of Germany's history, which is often dark. The author examines the current trends within the culture as well.

Olson, D. (2007). *Germany for dummies (3rd ed.)*.Hoboken, NJ: Wiley Publishing Inc. This book contains some specific details about the architecture in Germany and information about the availability of the arts throughout Germany. It provides details about the history of more famous sites in the country, and the differences between the smaller towns and the large cities.

Porter, D. & Prince, D. (2010). *Frommer's Germany*. Hoboken, NJ: Wiley Publishing, Inc. This book provides recent information about the cultural and economic situation in Germany and the impact of past history on German culture today. There is excellent information about the current immigration situation in Germany, and how that changed Germany from a homogeneous to a heterogeneous society.

World business culture: business communication styles in Germany. Retrieved March 12, 2010, from http://www.worldbusinessculture.clm/German-Business-Communication-Style.html This website provided some very useful information about conducting business in Germany, and gives advice about business etiquette for communications and conducting meetings.

MEDIA PAPER: GERMAN CULTURE

When considering how the media treats the culture in the country of Germany, one must look at many different aspects. The issue of Germany is complex because of the major role they have played in history and in today's world as well. There is often bias against Germans and Germany (in the media and in society) because of the role they played in World War II and the concentration camps. This is completely understandable from the standpoint of much of the world. Any trace of nationalism or any hints of neo-Nazi groups forming in Germany are causes for great alarm. The reason for this is obvious; most of the world believes that the actions leading up to and including the Holocaust should never be repeated.

There are even hints of this conviction in popular entertainment. The Broadway show and movie "The Producers" go to great lengths to heap derision on the Germans. This is made clear in the play they want to produce, which they believe will be disastrous. The production number "Springtime for Hitler" exemplifies their derision and distrust for the Germans, but in a roundabout way. The producers believe a show that supposedly celebrates the Nazis, yet makes fun of them, will be a disaster and help them lose money. Instead, the audiences "love the joke". I believe that the writers of the script could only have gotten away with this level of derision because of the audience's bias against Germans. For example, I don't believe that anyone would have been able to make a successful show or movie with a song and dance called "Springtime for Lynchings". Obviously, it is still politically correct to vilify the Germans for what they did during World War II. In defense of the media, I believe most of the world feels that this is an appropriate strategy to help make sure that the Holocaust never happens again.

A similar sort of climate has arisen because of sexual abuse by Catholic priests. These, too, are evils that people want to ensure are never repeated. As a result, the media currently has a new cause for bias against Germany. That reason is the recent scandal involving sexual abuse by priests in Germany, and for how the current pope, Pope Benedict XVI handled those cases. According to The Week Magazine (3/26/2010, p. 7). "But a new wave of allegations of sexual misconduct by Catholic priests continues to spread across Europe with more than 300 people coming forward in Germany alone".

There was only a brief mention of the other countries' abuses since those stories are older. The focus here is squarely on the Pope, who is originally from Germany. The article points out that the Pope has not been forthcoming with apologies, explanations or suggestions for change. In fact, according to The Week Magazine:

Christopher Hitchens in Slate.com stated in 2001, that when the Pope was a Vatican official, he warned bishops that sexual abuse charges should be conducted 'in the most secretive way' and those involved should be 'restrained by perpetual silence' or face excommunication (p.7).

This brick wall between the Vatican and the people has created a perception of a lack of compassion. Germans know that although it is part of their culture to be hush-hush, that this was not the correct way to handle this problem. Even they want more openness about this. The main reason they want more openness is because German culture is relatively high on uncertainty avoidance. They want ways to control behavior. They want everyone to stick to what they believe to be correct social behavior.

For at least the last 20 years the media has written stories about the sexual abuse of children by priests. Although the stories in general report some of the facts, they are also typically full of bias. A current example includes Time magazine's article "Sins of the fathers". In this article like in most articles, celibacy is called into question. This is a common bias, and implies that a person's marital status is the cause of pedophilia. If celibacy caused pedophilia there would be no married or sexually active pedophiles. Nothing could be further from the truth. The bias against the Catholic Church and the reason for it is explained as a bias against its teachings. Time Magazine reporter Bobby Ghosh stated:

Another senior official goes further. 'They want to involve the Pope at all costs', (he tells Time). 'It's a desire to destroy the Church. And this is an operation that has been well planned. They don't like the Church's teachings on moral questions and sexuality, and this is how they think they can strike'. 3/29/10 p. 36).

German culture, and its high uncertainty avoidance, has a severe problem with the Church's sexual abuse issue and the way the Church has handled it so far. Germans assume and demand that members of society (including the priests) will not deviate from what society deems appropriate behavior. This would obviously include the fact that society does not accept the sexual abuse of children. In Europe, in general, and in Germany, the authority of the Church (and authority in general) is not questioned.

Stories did not come out about sexual abuse in Europe as early as they did in the U.S. Pope Benedict biographer David Gibson explained "the church was always more tightly controlled in Europe. There's not the same kind of legal and journalistic advocacy as in the U.S." The interpretation here should be that the reason we haven't heard as much about sexual abuse by priests in Europe is because the Vatican controls the discussion much more in Europe than it possibly can in the U.S.

The Week Magazine provided an additional voice for open examination "Cardinal Christoff Schonborn of Vienna, Austria, believes that the Church should conduct an "unflinching examination" into the abuse crisis, including studying whether the celibacy requirements were a factor. (3/26/10 p.7). Although this is a quote by a Catholic authority, rather than an arbitrary reporter, it is still biased. It gives too much sway to the argument that celibacy caused the sexual abuse. German culture doesn't tolerate deviant behavior. If the writer and some other authorities lay the blame for the deviant behavior on celibacy, they group both things together as cause and effect. The *implication* is that this would eliminate pedophilia on the part of priests. This recurring bias and belief in the press and the public at large does not help the discussion and leaves the focus for solution in the wrong place.

Priests are often in a position of trust. The Catholic Church is very much in the public eye, and rightly expected to be a guidepost and example of moral behavior. Obviously, pedophilia is a violation of that position of trust. It is the climate of being unaware of how to protect children from the opportunity for abusers to act that allows the abuser to act. Therefore, sexual misconduct is committed at least largely in part because of the desire to be sexually deviant with a child, not just because of the need for sex. Ghost stated, "the Vatican argues that there's no connection between vows of celibacy and sexual deviance" (3/29/10 p.37). In other words, some people claim that if priests that sexually abuse could get married, they wouldn't sexually abuse. A valid parallel can be drawn in this situation. Just as experts now realize that rape is about power and not about sex so pedophilia is not really about sex or marital status.

What is reported can be even more dangerous than what actually happened. The entire story that is in each magazine only tells a small part of the story. It does not say, for instance, that back when the Church was moving supposed pedophiles around that psychiatrists felt they could be cured. The lack of this information and data make it look as though the Church was incompetent, rather than relying on expert advice. Furthermore, saying that ending celibacy would fix the problem would create new potential opportunities for abusers.

A lot of the victims in the 1950s and 1960s, and even as late as the early 1980s, felt there was nowhere to go for help if they were being abused. This was true throughout society, not just in the church. Now there is greater awareness of resources for people to turn to. Some countries (like apparently Germany) do not necessarily have these resources. The article does not address this fact. Nor does it mention whether they have sex registries for people to track dangerous pedophiles.

German culture has a high need for non-variation from society's values and morals. Since they have this need, they falsely assumed that all were complying with this, since they have a code of rules of behavior. This false assumption is what created the opportunity for abuse, just as it did in the United States. The Catholic Church in Germany will now develop codes, policies and procedures. The article does not mention that either. People in Germany would be less fearful if the Pope explained that in-depth. Ghosh's article leaves the impression that the Pope is doing nothing about the crisis.

Touching on the celibacy issue again, a less biased article would have quoted statistics outlining the percentage of priests that are pedophiles, as well as the percentage of married and single men who are not priests and yet are pedophiles. Articles about priests and sexual abuse never mention that.

Lastly, there is no comparison with how Catholic bishops and the Pope handle sexual wounds in the church, and let's say Protestant ministers that have also gotten public attention for sexual deviance. The difference is that when a Protestant minister engages in deviant behavior, media articles do not generally then try to lead the reader to come to the conclusion that all ministers in that faith are evil. They reserve that bias for the Catholic Church.

It's one thing to want to help move the Church along and protect yourself or children. That may be the intent of the articles' authors. However, continually blaming celibacy and the past mistakes of reassigning priests ignores the truth. An unbiased article would have discussed at length the history of psychiatry and its influence on the Church's treatment of pedophiles. It would have also mentioned the fact that some of the "alleged cover-ups and reassignments" were requested by victims desiring privacy. Finally Ghosh's parting shot, "The Pope remained silent" (3/29/10 p. 37) leaves the reader with the impression that the Pope does not care and is doing nothing. An unbiased article would have explained that he is a scholar who believes in conducting thorough research, and then designing an effective policy. Unfortunately, this may indeed not satisfy the German people. The lack of immediate, huge apologies is especially difficult for them to handle because of the high uncertainty avoidance in their culture. If the author had explained that the delay is because they are trying to uncover everything and fix the problem, it would have reduced the peoples' fears.

Bibliography

Ghosh, B. (2010, March 29). Sins of the fathers. *Time Magazine*, pp. 34 – 37.

(2010, March 26). The Pope under fire. *The Week Magazine*, p.7.

SPEECH ON GERMAN CULTURE

Introduction:

Germany: World War II; Beer; Wine; Fancy cars; Singing men in lederhosen; I am here to tell you Germany is so much more than any of these.

Let's look at Germanys past and then I will compare it with Tanya the woman I interviewed. She grew up near Munich and moved several times. She lives right next door to me.

Hitler capitalized on Germans' fears about unemployment, blamed the Jewish people for their troubles, and told them he would solve everything. Many youth joined the movement and or the 3rd Reich. You may recall the young man in The Sound of Music.

Youth played a big role in defining their culture. As a result, Germany's cultural dimensions became highly collectivistic and high power distance in nature during the War.

I want to persuade you that Germany's culture today has changed across multiple cultural dimensions and is seen in many customs today.

Body:

Do you know why Germans wanted to change its culture after World War II? The world didn't trust Germany. Even now we have military bases in Germany. They did not want to make the same mistakes again.

After World War II, Germany changed from a highly collectivistic culture to a more individualistic culture.

Germans are on guard against blind obedience. They value uniqueness rather than conforming, but not to the extent we do in the U.S. Obviously the government during WWII failed. Was that the people's fault?

They are much more open to new ideas than they were. They have their first female chancellor, and many people have become strong environmentalists.

Germany remains high on the Masculine Dimension. Achievement, education, and work are valued far more than softer values like nurturing, which is highly valued in Sweden. An example of this is seen in their powerful German-made cars. The first thing Tanya mentioned was cars, when I asked her about technology in Germany.

194

Uncertainty Avoidance is still somewhat important to Germans. They only accept a limited amount of "deviant" behavior. However, neither country tolerates odd behavior in a business setting.

Greetings are with a firm handshake, people are addressed as "Herr" or "Frau" followed by the last name.

Plus businesses are run by technical experts and engineers, not management gurus and accountants. The brother of the woman I interviewed is now a top engineer at Intel, although in the German schools they wouldn't let him go to college.

Meetings are formal. Business cards are exchanged. Men enter the room before women. At the end of negotiations, Germans often rap their knuckles on the table to show they approve of the deal. This is similar to some American behavior.

Managers' offices are put on the top level or in the corners of the building to signify their importance. By contrast, in France they are located in the middle.

Here are some social customs.

1. If you are invited to someone's home, you must bring a gift.

2. Interestingly, in a bar, after Germans make a toast, they rap their mug on the table before drinking the beer.

3. You may not know that German's celebrated Unify Germany day each year on October 3, well before the wall came down in 1989.

4. Germans love coffee, Beer, sausage, wine, cooking, and also, there are more smokers than here.

5. They love the arts, hiking, and skiing. My neighbor, however, said she has never gone skiing.

6. German's put the date first, then the month, and year. (27 April, 2010).

7. My neighbor's husband said when they went to visit Germany recently, he used a rest room in a restaurant. There wasn't a door on the rest room, and you could see right in. He found this shocking, but the Germans thought nothing of it.

8. When they visited Germany recently they drove 140 miles per hour on the Autobahn. (although they did have to translate from kilometers per hour to miles per hour)!

Education is highly valued in Germany. But college education is not widely available to every person. By the time students are 10 years old, tests are done on each student that decide which students will be directed to go to college, trade school, or told to drop out early. Imagine your choices in life are decided by the time you are 10! This is very much like Japan.

1. However over 30% of students do attend college. In 1960 only 3% did, as reported by German culture expert Frank Kempe.

2. My neighbor and her family moved to the U.S. because her brother had dyslexia and wouldn't get to go to college in Germany. Here he had education opportunities that ensured his success.

Conclusion:

I have been trying to persuade you that German culture has been transformed and become a world leader for some very specific reasons.

They have become more individualistic while hanging on to many of their traditions.

Even though they have a highly masculine culture, women have opportunities too. Their business excellence is world-famous.

Frank Kemp states that Germany is the 3rd largest economy in the world. They have successfully gone from being a villain to a world leader by considering future consequences and gaining real allies.

Please take these next words to heart. A country's culture changes based on pressures from within and outside the country. That is what Germany did.

Knowledge about German culture helps you communicate with them.

Finally, I offer a caution about over-reliance on the Globe dimensions. The data are limited in their usefulness. Globe dimensions don't allow for differences based on age. Age plays a role in how people behave and believe.

Our goal should be cultural excellence, not just cultural competence. Go beyond the Globe dimensions. We often judge others by what they are not and not by who they are. We can change that. Germany has.

RESEARCH PAPER ON GERMAN CULTURE: GOOSESTEPS TO NEW STEPS

Abstract

Germany is a member of the European Union, and is a leader among nations. Their history and cultural changes from the early 1930s to the present day have all helped to define and redefine their culture, communications, and position in the world. This paper explores specific cultural dimensions of German culture, including: power-distance; individualism; masculinity/femininity; and uncertainty avoidance. Information and analysis of specific parts of social and business settings in Germany today are presented as well.

German Culture: Goosesteps to New Steps

Introduction

Today, Germany is a transformed culture. They are respected, almost revered for their business leadership, automotive engineering talent, and political influence. This change from a feared and despised nation after World War II, to a country divided into two countries, to a reunited country and finally to the influential position they hold today has both affected the country's culture and been caused by its cultural changes.

Statement of Purpose

The goal of this research is to discover the characteristics of German culture and communication through the lens of their history. Using this lens, the direction of this research is to determine how the cultural characteristics affect the country, its communication, and its ability to address problems.

Research Question

How have changes and cultural characteristics within German culture helped the country overcome the prejudice the Western world had towards it and become a respected world leader?

Thesis

Knowledge of the dimensions of German culture can help explain their people, culture, communication styles, and their problems. Understanding their culture can help improve communication between their culture and the United States.

Significance

Every country is more than just its history. However, to examine the cultural characteristics of a country separate from its history makes it impossible to fully understand the rationale behind the characteristics. Effective communication requires understanding not only what is transmitted, but why. In order to avoid communication problems and errors, it is essential to understand both. Full understanding of German culture can lead to not only intercultural competence, but intercultural excellence. The goal should never be to be merely competent.

Method

The sources of research information for this report include: an internet search, books, periodicals, and an interview with a former German native.

Pre-research Knowledge and Beliefs

My knowledge, beliefs, and biases influenced my prior understanding of German culture. I pictured German culture as a merry, boisterous beer hall with strong men and jolly women. I saw it also as a place filled with castles, mountains, and forests. My knowledge of history formed a strong bias against German culture, largely because of its role in World War II.

Findings

Germany's Historical Background

From the end of World War I through a few years after World War II, German culture became highly collectivistic. This occurred in response to the economic crisis facing Germany. The fear that people felt due to the high unemployment and inflation caused them to bond together against the Jewish people.

Their chancellor (Hitler) convinced the people and the government to eliminate the Jews because he said they were the cause of the crisis. He then planned to take over the world one country at a time. The people followed him and didn't try to stop him. This institutional collectivism defined the culture of Germany at that time. Hitler closed many of the universities and any other organization that was opposed to his goals. The possibility of being sent to the concentration camps kept people from questioning authority.

Although they now feel freer to question, they still prefer order and security. Ivory, Gray and Grever (2009) stated: "A liking for order and security in personal and working life can perhaps be explained by the traumas of history, when the country's very shape seemed uncertain and there was an unthinkable burden of guilt" (p.15). Thus, when they do question government or other authorities, they generally tend to do so in an orderly fashion, and preserve the institutions.

Power Distance Dimension

Germany's response to post World War II was to re-examine how they felt about power distance. They had trusted the higher ups and put up with fascism (even embraced it). The results of this devastated the country and destroyed people (Kempe, 1999). The citizens of Germany were rejected by the world. The result was that the German people wanted to be able to question decisions, and no longer accepted the high power distance. Today they demand more responsiveness from their government. They are open to new solutions. They insist on sharing in the decision making. Fascism is no longer welcome. New ideas and solutions are sought. Proof of this is seen in the fact that they now have their first female chancellor.

Individualism/Collectivism Dimension

During World War II, Germany had become a completely collectivistic culture. This cultural shift is what made it possible for fascism to take hold and the Holocaust to occur. People completely trusted and went along with the Third Reich; although there were some who resisted. In general, the German people believed that Hitler and the Third Reich would solve their problems (Kempe, 1999). This motivated them to follow their authority unquestioningly. Since World War II, each generation has moved more towards being individualistic. This shift was seen as a way to ensure that the country would not make those same mistakes again. This is seen in the reluctance that Germans have to demonstrate any large national pride. According to Ivory, et al. (2009), "with traditional ideas of nationhood debased and disgraced by the Nazis, many Germans have been inhibited about putting too much enthusiasm into anything that smacks of nationalism" (p. 14). They know it is essential to consider and question decisions; but they also still have strong allegiance to their institutions.

The crisis in the Catholic Church in Germany is a strong example of this mismatch. They want to be able to trust and follow their institutions, but they expect those institutions to follow specific moral guidelines. Thus, they are shocked by the pedophilia that has come to light. This is showing them once again the problem that can occur if they blindly trust a leader or an institution. Ghosh pointed out "Catholics in mainland Europe rarely challenge the priesthood" (3/29/10, p.36). With the new calls for investigation and reform by Germans, it is obvious that they have learned that they must question.

Ivory et al. (2009) further explained "Germans study for their careers, often at great length, and plan them down to the final pension contribution. Correct procedures govern many aspects of life. Timekeeping is meticulous; jobs are done properly and standards are defined and adhered to (p.15)". Although they have become more individualistic, planning is still highly valued.

This is all a sharp contrast to the individualistic nature of culture in the United States. The motivation in the U.S. to be individualistic is truly the basis of our entire country. We are a country founded on freedom, and we take the role of questioning our government, laws, and regulations as our birthright and our responsibility. This makes it difficult for leaders and institutions to infringe on our rights for very long.

The difference in the historical reasons behind the individualistic dimension is extremely important in how it is practiced. Although Germans now do want lower power distance, they do so out of reaction to the fascism they experienced. This determination to not experience national humiliation is a different motivator than our individualistic dimension. In our country, every step of the way at least some group is questioning whether or not "our freedoms and rights" are being taken away.

Masculinity-Femininity Dimension

The emphasis placed on achievement, work, and education is a hallmark of German culture. This emphasis is called the masculinity dimension. Their culture is even more masculine than the U.S. culture. Porter and Prince (2010) stated:

> Germany is one of the most modern and at the same time, the most traditional of countries. Its advanced technology and industries are the envy of the rest of the world. Here you'll likely meet people of learning and sophistication, boasting a long cultural heritage and devotion to music and the arts (p. 13).

In the past, women were expected to be home raising the children while the men worked. As in the U.S., this has changed. The emphasis on achievement and education has made German cars, for instance, highly admired and respected. Germany's economy is the third largest in the world. Education has become much more important in Germany. Kempe (1999) reported "One of postwar Germany's achievements is that by 1995, some 30 percent of all youth between nineteen and twenty-six years of age were enrolled in higher education. That compared to less than 5 percent in 1960 (p. 143)". This all fits with the emphasis on the masculinity dimension. Achievement, work, and success are very highly valued in German society.

Uncertainty Avoidance Dimension

Germany is measured low, a 7 on the uncertainty avoidance scale. Although they value predictability, reliability, and prefer to not have any acceptance for deviant behavior or attitudes, they are somewhat adaptable to change and unpredictability. If this aspect had been studied during World War II, they would have been measured even higher than they are now. As each new generation has come along, things loosen somewhat. In contrast, the U.S. measures -87 on the same scale. This aspect is one of the reasons the Germans perceive that Americans are wild and deviant.

Social and Business Settings

The arts and availability of symphonies and museums are important to Germany. Olson explained (2007) "Every midsize—to—large German city has at least one art museum, a symphony orchestra, and an opera house, making a visit to Germany a feast for those who enjoy world-class art and music" (p.9). Germans see these cultural places as proof that they are a modern, educated society that has achieved high status.

Social gatherings are important aspects of German culture as well. German people love to be out and about in restaurants and beer halls. Despite this, the social and business settings are relatively formal. This is not a culture that will instantly befriend you. If the person introduces himself as "Herr" something (which means Mr.) or herself as "Frau" something (which means Mrs.) you must always refer to the person that way. It is important not to refer to this person using only their first name. Regarding business meetings customs, German culture, customs, and business etiquette (3/15/10) reported:

> There is rigid protocol. Business meetings are very formal and have little small talk. Business
> cards are always exchanged, titles respected, and Germans expect guests at the meeting to
> present their credentials. The early meetings are meant to establish trust, as Germans will not
> automatically trust an outsider. Generally speaking, in a German business meeting, men enter
> the room before the women. At the end of negotiations, some Germans signal their approval
> by rapping their knuckles on the tabletop.

Germany did not follow the path that England and the U.S. did regarding who would manage their companies. Germans highly value engineering skill and technical skill. Thus, these are the people running German companies (German business culture 3/15/2010). In contrast, American companies are often run by business or legal experts. This can pose a problem when an American comes to a meeting, especially if that

American is not a technical or engineering expert. Americans need to be aware of this, and know that in that case, they must openly give the German experts more respect because of the Germans' technical or engineering expertise.

Formality and rule emphasis is even seen out on the street. Travelers should be aware of this and follow traffic rules very strictly. Egert-Romanowskiej and Omilanowska (2008) warned "it is a violation, for example, to cross the road when there is a red light showing, even when the road is clear, and can result in an official reprimand" (p. 14). While this shouldn't be a surprise to Americans, these kinds of rules are enforced more loosely at times in the U.S. than in Germany.

Germans have become big believers in volunteering. Pacheco (2008) explained "Germany's volunteering opportunities often involve environmental preservation—working on farms or in forests and educating people on conservation---though civil service and community building prospects still exist, especially in eastern Germany" (p. 389). Their citizen's environmental awareness and activism of their youth is bringing emphasis to humanitarian dimensions. Porter and Prince (2010) emphasized that "Many younger Germans are likely to be guided by a sense of idealism, even zeal, for ecological and other causes" (p.14). Being green has become highly valued by the Germans. Fodor (2008) cited an example of a green home "triple glazing prevents overheating in the summer and electricity is generated by 48 solar modules in the family home named House R. 128 on a hillside overlooking Stuttgart. It was designed by the engineer Werner Sobek in 2000" (p. 17). Despite the environmental enthusiasm, however, the overall German society still places far more emphasis on achievement (masculine dimension) than on humanitarian dimensions.

Conclusion

Kempe (1999) stated "the Germans created a stable state, where there is order and no enemies. Germany is a postwar miracle; a creation of Western values, freedoms and resolve" (p. 151). This deliberate recreation of itself is how Germany has come to be a strong ally of the United States and in many ways resembles significant parts of our culture. While this has made Germany strong and more acceptable to the world, ultimately its people may begin to question whether they have traded away their individuality as a nation in order to become acceptable to the world. They may then shift some of their cultural dimensions. Proof of this tendency to change is seen in the fact that from World War II to now they have shifted their cultural dimensions.

By comparison, the United States underwent a similar transformation after 9/11. The fear that people felt after the attacks made them more willing to accept losses of freedoms. They were willing to trade freedom for certainty and safety. Thus, even a nation built on freedom can come to the point where they are less willing to accept uncertainty. This means that the cultural dimensions in any culture are not set in stone and are subject to change (by the people, by the government, or by outside forces). As a matter of fact, due to the economy, change is happening in Germany once again. Unger (2010) reported, "If you let me govern with the liberals, promised the chancellor, Angela Merkel, Germany will recover faster from recession. Voters granted her wish" (p. 90). He further stated "the main task will be to redeem Ms. Merkel's pledge and to launch a programme for Germany that is distinctive but still unthreatening to an electorate wary of radical reform" (p.90).

Despite the possibilities of change, and the future influence of other countries, Germany today is a culture that is greatly similar to the United States. They place an even higher emphasis on the arts and are an even more masculine-dimensioned society than ours. Their overall transformation as a culture has been very successful. Those who choose to communicate with or do business with German people should keep in mind the dimensions of its culture, and the expected formality.

References

Egert-Romanowskiej, J. & Omilanowska, M. (2008). *Germany: Eyewitness travel guide*. London: DK Books.

Fodor (2009). *Fodor's see it Germany, (3ʳᵈ ed.)*. New York: Fodor's Publishing.

Germany -- German culture, customs and business etiquette. Retrieved March 15, 2010, from http://www.kwintessential.co.uk/resources/global-etiquette/germany-country-profile.html

Ghosh, B. (2010, March 29). Sins of the fathers. *Time Magazine*, pp. 34 – 37.

Ivory, M., Gray, J. & Grever, J. (2010). *National Geographic traveler: Germany*.

Washington, D.C.: National Geographic Publishing.

Kempe, F. (1999). *Father/Land: A personal search for the new Germany*. New York: G. P Putnam's Sons.

Olson, D. (2007). *Germany for dummies (3ʳᵈ ed.)*.Hoboken, NJ: Wiley Publishing Inc.

Pacheco, I. (Ed.). (2008). *Let's go Europe 2008*. New York: St. Martin's Press.

Porter, D. & Prince, D. (2010). *Frommer's Germany*. Hoboken, NJ: Wiley Publishing, Inc.

Unger, Brooke "Changing the colours" *The Economist: The World in 2010*, p.90.

World business culture: business communication styles in Germany. Retrieved March 12, 2010, from http://www.worldbusinessculture.clm/German-Business-Communication-Style.html

16

STRESS MANAGEMENT

This course taught theories and techniques for understanding and managing stress. This knowledge helps in deciding how to take in communication and in making personal communication more effective. The course involved projects and reading analyses. Of course, every student should learn about healthy stress management techniques – either from me, a course, or both!

BOOK REVIEW: POSITIVE ADDICTION BY WILLIAM GLASSER M.D.

This book explores addictions both positive and negative. He provides a framework for replacing negative addictions with positive addictions. Besides the actual framework, he describes how negative addictions impede people and positive addictions help people. He specifically recommends the use of either running or meditation to form positive addictions. I chose this book because my counselor had recommended it to me. My counselor was very excited to have me read it. I chose it because it is written concisely, it is full of ideas, and written in straightforward language. The title intrigued me, because when you hear the term "positive addiction" it makes you re-examine your understanding of what addiction is. Negative addiction is what we all usually think of when we hear the term addiction such as drug abuse and alcohol abuse.

Positive Addiction to Reduce Stress: How it Works

When Dr. Glasser writes about positive addiction, he is talking about engaging in running or meditating every day. He says that to form a positive addiction requires that you do the activity every day for an hour and that you not worry about how well you do it. His theory is that you pick an activity that you aren't going to obsess about how well you do it. Running and meditating are powerful ideas. The point of these activities is to empty yourself to the process.

Being positively addicted is a subtle thing. Dr. Glasser says that running is one of the most natural things you can do to your body. Positive addiction must revolve around engaging the body in natural activities. If you were to set a goal that you had to be a marathon runner or you wouldn't be happy, it wouldn't work as a way to positive addiction. The way to positive addiction is to slowly build up through commitment to the process and see it as self-care.

Positive Addiction happens through self-focus, but for the sake of others. You become a complete instrument whose purpose is helping others. Professional athletes improve for the benefit of the entire team. The addiction to the running affects a change within the person. For this reason, I believe we need to spread the word about running and meditations. Meditation teachers typically don't want their students to talk about meditation. Meditation isn't a spectator sport, but we should hold it in reverence because of its origin in religion.

Why I Recommend This Book

I would recommend this book to everyone. Dr. Glasser writes of the importance of positive addiction and cites numerous examples of people's experience with running. He doesn't try to nag them to run. He demonstrates how much becoming positively addicted to running helps. People generally won't do things that they do not want to do. Positive addiction provides a framework without taking over your life. It's amazing how you lose track of time when you run. I don't even look at my time when I run with my caloric heart rate monitor on. You would be surprised how good you feel after even 10 minutes of running.

We shoot ourselves in the foot when we don't accomplish something and use that as an excuse to stop trying. Having a positive addiction to running creates a new pathway. This commitment to purpose will spread to other areas of your life. This spreading to other areas helps the positive addiction take hold. Society is a direct reflection of how we treat ourselves because every person has good days and bad days. We get so hung up on the things that we can't do (or that we have failed at) that we forget about the things that we can do. Then we strive less and less. If we reverse this we experience the exhilaration that comes from continuing to work at it.

Glasser discusses stages of the weak: giving up, picking a symptom, negative addiction. I think people get confused in the second stage and believe it to be realistic self-acceptance rather than picking symptoms. It makes it easy to deceive ourselves into not trying; this spreads eventually to all areas of their lives. This is where the need for negative addiction comes from. They are no longer comfortable in their own skin. Rather than use that discomfort as a catalyst for change, they suffocate it with negative addiction.

Although you spend time each day running, the result is the rest of your life becomes more focused and efficient. PA provides a way to release many of the negative thought patterns from the mind. Glasser measured 3 types of people: a baseball player, a monk, and meditators. They each became addicted to running or meditating. This is a different experience from drug addiction, which typically comes from peer pressure.

How I Have Changed After Reading This Book

In others is where you find love. In yourself is where you find motivation to love. Both are needed. Positive addiction (through running) has the power to turn your whole life around. It has changed mine. The internal motivation to continue to run and or meditate is what makes the positive addiction to it so completely life changing. It takes a long time to get into the rhythm. PA is more than increase in oxygen, lung activity, breathing, and euphoria. Until you run long enough to regularly experience the PA state you are becoming addicted to commitment to the process. Commitment spreads, just as success builds upon success.

This book is very revolutionary because it is a relatively new field of study. Long ago, people just went for a run, came back, and that was it. People have always been running. This book looks specifically at the activity as more than just a series of rapid footsteps. It demonstrates that the brain and mood actually change through the running commitment. It becomes positively addicting after you have practiced it for so long. You become addicted to commitment. That is what builds the PA. PA is certainly the physical state of being so motivated that you literally say, with great joy "oh, yeah, I HAVE to run"! PA runners would go for a run even if they could feel the same benefits in other ways. Exercise makes everything go better: you think better, sleep better, eat better, work better, and pray better. These are broken up into many different facets as well. You move from I like to eat healthy food to I like to shop for and prepare healthy food. Again, you become part of the process. It regulates your body clock so that you can then get up earlier and be productive earlier.

Another thing that I have noticed with my running is that I run easier. I look very serious when I run, as do most runners. You really can reach that point within yourself through PA running; then you can then master it in the rest of your life. My own life has changed through commitment to running and working towards Positive Addiction. The heat, my stamina, and physical pain prevent me from longer runs at this point, but that doesn't reduce my commitment to the process. PA helps me deal with stress. I have done so well with my physical training that the focus has shifted to a higher step. Some people get intimidated by that. They say "as soon as I accomplish something, someone will turn around and ask me to do something else". Actions speak louder than words. Accomplishment proves that you are capable. Becoming one with your life, or integrating your life is the ultimate benefit. Positivity has no limits. You can't change human nature. We are all meant to move. How much each person chooses is up to them.

Although a master meditator might not be able to run a marathon, he still might be able to conceive a way to run that distance; then he still might be able to do it. Blending meditation and running together would be the perfect path to PA; this combination brings mind and body together.

RESEARCH PAPER: MEDITATION TO REDUCE STRESS

Introduction

The study of meditation as a way of reducing stress was of particular interest to me. We often mistake misplaced energy with lack of energy. Meditation takes misplaced energy, focuses it, and redirects it. Most people associate meditation with some of the eastern religions, but it is much more widespread than that, and is not exclusively a religious practice. However, God, who is the source of all that is good, created meditation. On the seventh day, He rested.

Dr. Diane Powell reported (2009) "meditation synchronizes the activity of the two hemispheres such that the left brain is no longer dominant" (p. 160). This is significant because we often have 'self-talk' that jabbers away at us; this distracts us from our ability to establish inner peace. It is easy to become confused and believe that our thoughts are us. There is a conundrum. The harder we try not to think about things and worry excessively, the more we think and worry. Our minds have become very busy places to be. If people are worried about the past and the future, there is no time left for them to dwell in and deal with the present. This creates stress. The best way to deal with that stress is to find a way to change this pattern. Meditation provides that way.

How to Meditate

Meditation is one of the easiest ways to reach a higher state of reality. It is different from hypnosis because it doesn't use cues like hypnosis does. There are many ways to meditate, and there really isn't one best way to do it. Some general guidelines include:

- Find a place that helps you be more likely to relax. I would recommend meditating in the same place each time, at least until you have perfected your methods.

- Breathe slowly and regularly using your diaphragm.

- Sit or lie down, in whichever position works best for you.

- Some people who meditate sit for so long a period of time that they get stiff. They can use this pain and stiffness to help them focus and meditate.

- You should pick a specific thing to focus on. It doesn't matter what it is. Some people use meditation balls to help them focus. These balls can be used almost anywhere.

- You can use a phrase or mantra while meditating, but it isn't essential.

- If your mind wanders during meditation, bring yourself back to your focal point slowly and gently. It is ok to ask yourself "why am I thinking about this" if ideas cross your mind while you are meditating. Be aware these ideas may be helpful to you.

- It can be beneficial to have a meditation teacher.

Setting time aside on a daily basis helps perfect your meditation skills and re-centers your life, just as having a daily exercise and prayer routine do.

Benefits of Meditation

Some people claim that meditation has the same effect as being out in nature. Davis, Eshelman & McKay (2008) stated "with regular meditation, a person feels more focused and calm in her life, more capable of making new choices in the moment, and less prone to engage in struggle and reactivate responses (p.49)". Meditation reduces stress because you aren't fighting against your current reality. It helps people stay in the present. Furthermore, Davis said. "The benefits of meditation increase with practice: Levels of relaxation deepen. Attention becomes steadier. You become more adept at living in the present moment (p.49)".

Accessing your higher self is possible through meditation. Some people reach a positive addiction (P.A.) state while meditating. This is when your mind is allowed to spin totally free. People describe an overwhelming "out of body sensation". Glasser (1985) explained "the meditator quickly gains more access to his brain, an access not usually achieved by most of us who never take this regular time off to be non-self critical" (p.128). An interesting thing happens to brain waves when people meditate. Kabat-Zinn, (2010) discovered "meditators showed a pronounced shift in activity to the left frontal lobe. In other words, they were calmer and happier than before (p.1)".

Meditation is not a way to control your mind. The point of meditation is not perfection, but enlightenment. People are often private about what they think about during their meditation time because revealing too much about it can then interfere with the spontaneity of their meditation. Meditation helps you seek out and discover your weaknesses rather than hiding from them. This helps you embrace life. By being in the moment during meditation you learn to stop living in a reactive state. Meditation helps you tap into your subconscious; this can help you resolve problems and issues.

Tips and Pointers

It is helpful to experiment with multiple types of meditation, adapt them, and make up individualized techniques. This helps you fit your meditation method to you. I find that I don't feel tired or asleep when I meditate. Yet when I finish meditating, I feel both a little groggy and yet refreshed, as though I have awakened from a nap. There is a stream of energy consciousness that always exists; you tap into this during your 20 minutes of meditation.

I like to focus on a point. When my eyes are closed during meditation, I roll my eyes back slightly; this helps block out light. There is still a dot of light, though, and I let that dot of light morph into whatever it wants to be. Even if you are in a dark room, when you close your eyes you can see some light. When I was little, that dot of light acted like a kaleidoscope. This came easily to me and the colors were vivid. This ability changes over time, and requires practice. The point of meditation is not to shut your mind off. If you are feeling anxious or twitchy during meditation, you can try to imagine moving that part of your body, but don't actually move it. When you finish meditating, actually move that part of your body, and see how it feels, to see if it is better or worse than you thought.

Once, when I had finished a day's work at the ranch, I felt that I had tapped very deeply into my subconscious. This created an inner peace that was extraordinary. This is the same inner peace I receive from meditation. I prefer my meditation to remain spontaneous. If it becomes overly predictable, the meditation can become artificial.

Conclusion

In order to feel good about something, we need a challenge to drive and animate us. Meditation can be that constant animating activity. After a meditation session you have an overwhelming sense of peace, renewal, and a sense that you are on fire and doing the right thing. But you shouldn't take that feeling and focus on it. If you think about how awesome it was and give it too much focus, you make the *feeling* the goal rather than make the *process* the goal. The true benefit of meditation is the *participation in the process*. Whether or not a specific emotion results, the meditation benefit is still there. Kabat-Zinn (1990) explained, "When your whole life is driven by doing, formal meditation practice can provide a refuge of sanity and stability that can be used to restore some balance and perspective" (p. 60).

In getting rid of the mental clutter through meditation, we find that the clutter was just a pattern or a habit. You had been letting the matter control you, but now you control the matter. If you do not control yourself the world will control you. Meditation helps you attempt to control your passions, desires, pains, sorrows, and the stress these cause. The *attempt* is the point. Here is why. If we were to actually control those things perfectly, we might be tempted to say "I'm done; I don't have to do it anymore, because I already did it". So it is the process and the attempt that reduce stress.

Even those at higher state of consciousness have only begun to tap into their potential. Sometimes the smallest thought or feeling upsets us. Feelings are just how we interpret things. Meditation helps us to re-interpret and re-assess what is really going on. We are not really under siege. It isn't the fear of change that keeps people from admitting or facing their problems. It is that even if they do change, it will be insufficient. It is essential to remember that we are never done perfecting the process.

We shouldn't associate anything with that inner peace that we get from meditation. We should become the peace. It is like when basketball coaches tell you to use "soft hands". They don't say that because the ball will break. They say that to enable you to re-focus and catch it. Each person has to meet the demands that life has placed before him. Meditation gives us "soft hands". This "soft hands" state reduces stress. Beauty begets beauty. Mathematicians and engineers tell us "a = a". In the same way, meditation creates the meditative peaceful core within you. That is the power we need so we can reduce stress. Trulock (2006) explained "A master meditator doesn't flinch at the sound of a gunshot--something that even an experienced marksman does" (p.41).

Once people have been enlightened they are transformed and love what has happened within them. When this transformation occurs, people shift from saying "I have to meditate" to "I get to meditate". Meditation is one of the most fundamental and strengthening things that you can do to improve your life because it moves you into the present. As Trulock (2006) concluded, "A strong mind and body will automatically help you live a less stressed life because you will be more consistently healthy and in shape" (p.86).

References

Glasser, W. (1985). *Positive addiction*. New York: Harper Perennial.

Powell, D. (2009). *The ESP enigma: The scientific case for psychic phenomena*. New York: Walker & Company.

Davis, M., Eshelman, E. & McKay, M.(2008). *The relaxation and stress workbook (6th ed.)*. Oakland, CA: New Harbinger Publications, Inc.

Kabat-Zinn, J. (2009). *Full catastrophe living: Using the wisdom of your body and mind to face stress, pain, and illness*. New York: Bantam Dell.

Kabat-Zinn, J. (2010) The benefits of meditation; Psychology Today: http://www/psychologytoday.com/articles/200304/the-benefits-meditation .

Trulock, A. (2006). Zen meditation balls. Philadelphia, PA: Running Press.

17

CAPSTONE COURSE

The purpose of a capstone course is similar to a thesis course and project at the graduate school level. It requires the student to synthesize all of the learning and coursework in a number of ways. In my case there were numerous analysis papers required and the development of a personal philosophy and professional plan. Beyond that, there was, of course, the case study project. This required the development of an entire plan for an actual business facing a problem.

LEARNING ANALYSIS 1: ACQUIRE/SYNTHESIZE/APPLY KNOWLEDGE IN THE MAJOR

Introduction

Students select their majors for a host of reasons. Potential income is a deciding factor for many. Others choose a major because their friends or family have encouraged or insisted that they major in a specific area. Finally, others choose a major because they love the subject and want to learn everything they can about it; that is the case with me.

As is the case in any major, my initial goal has been to learn and understand communication theories so that I can later analyze the information, apply those theories, and integrate my knowledge about communications. When I began my coursework, I knew that communication was the central part of every interaction. I quickly learned that communication is truly the hidden gem. It deals with all things and is central to every field of work or study. In a sense it is like philosophy, which leads to religion, which leads to science, which leads to other fields. Effective communication is a catalyst that in turn supports other areas; ineffective communication is an impediment to progress.

Although I found every concept and theory of communication interesting and important, I intend to focus on only some of those theories. Even though I investigated many areas, read through mountains of research material, and wrote numerous papers, I am only going to include some of them with this paper.

Communication Theory

Communication theory was obviously covered to a great extent in each of the six Ottawa University communications major courses I took. In Interpersonal Communications, Small Group Communications, and Business Communications, a great deal of time and effort went into defining, analyzing, and exploring the facets of communication. These facets include discussing verbal and non-verbal communication, listening, and the speaker's responsibility. This responsibility includes anticipating and determining how the listener(s) receive the message. Besides these concepts, I have read and explored the impact gender differences and role differences have on communication. These all affect the speaker(s) and the listener(s). Understanding the potential receiver of the message should determine how the speaker sends the message. Furthermore, non-verbal communication and paralanguage comprises a significant percentage of communication and must be fine-tuned as well.

Along with these concepts, my coursework covered the aspects and dialectics of listening. Listening skills and other group concepts such as leadership and understanding the dimensions of groups, including the concepts of collectivist vs. individualistic groups or cultures, and being intrinsically or extrinsically motivated have been explored in multiple courses. Specific explanations, definitions, and explorations of these concepts are provided in the examples listed in the next section.

Analysis of In-class Work

My Organizational Communications class gave me an understanding of personality types (in myself and others) and helped me to understand the importance of using that knowledge to understand an organization and effectively communicate with the organization and in the organization. Working in small groups during class and discussing various topics helped me to become more adept at confidently communicating with various types of people. The more I have learned about verbal and non-verbal communication, and personality types, the less intimidating it is for me to communicate with people.

In Interpersonal Communication we spent time discussing the effect gender difference has on communications. Yes, we are only men and women, but we are so different. In reading the book *Men are from Mars and Women are from Venus,* I was able to learn about and explore the impact gender difference has on communication. In researching gender differences, I learned about the concept of role switching. This is the term for men acting more like women and women acting more like men. My Interpersonal Communications course taught me that gender differences are a learned behavior and a belief that is culturally defined. This fact was a significant factor in assigning us the task of researching communication in another culture.

An interesting aspect of my Interpersonal Communications course and my Business Communications course was that they were online. This posed a particular challenge from a communications standpoint. It brought home the fact that I relied on visual and verbal cues in all of my communication. With these online courses, all I had to go on for cues was the electronic words. This was more than a little nerve-racking at first. However, I quickly assumed a bit of a leadership role. It seemed to me that many classmates were hesitant to post very much in their weekly posts. I encouraged them to post more by posting very in-depth responses to the discussion questions. In addition, I posted in-depth responses to their responses. Eventually many of the students did follow my lead and go much deeper with their postings. This really thrilled me, because it demonstrated to me that they were actually integrating the information at a deeper level, just as I was.

Group communication came alive for me in my Small Group Communication course. I had an outstanding professor for this course named Jerry Malizia, PhD. This class was a wonderful in-depth exploration of small group communication. It was special to me because there were only two students in the class (including me). I included some of my chapter summaries for the course in the work attached to this paper. As you can see in my reading summaries, I truly loved learning about Situational Leadership and Contingency Theory. These two theories convinced me that effective communication is the cornerstone for everything. In the next Learning Outcomes paper, of course, I include even more.

Managing the communication in a group setting is essential since message receivers may be dispersed throughout the organization and will not be receiving the message at the same time, or in the same way. I have examined the impact that group size, management style, cultural dimensions and personality types have on group success and motivation. Some of these aspects of communication will be further explored in Learning Outcome Report Two. For this report, it is important to note that since group communication involves more people, it must be managed in different ways. During Organizational Communication we examined and analyzed case studies to determine whether or not specific organizations had effectively managed their communication. Discussing this in class and small groups sharpened all of our skills, and helped me to analyze the communication from a business and professional standpoint. This was similar to a speech class I had as an underclassman. In that course we analyzed speeches to determine whether the speeches communicated the message ethically and without error.

Conclusion

During my course of study I have interviewed people about their experience and knowledge of other cultures, and followed other communication while observing the news, commercials, billboards and conversations. Now that I have acquired knowledge of communication theory, I have a lens and system to organize my observations, judgments, and strategies. I can see that my knowledge of communication theory, practices, cultural dimensions, and strategies will help me to much more fully understand and excel in any endeavor. Communication underlies every aspect of life, and every field. Effective communication involves sending, receiving, analyzing and integrating information and messages. This reaches beyond just the study of communication itself. For example, the study of psychology, sociology, management, and philosophy all involve communication. I have reached this conclusion because communication theory has taught me that communication and its cultural dimensions can impact and touch every single part of our lives.

My coursework and projects have taught me to think in a more orderly way. Orderly thinking after acquiring knowledge is the prerequisite for analyzing and applying my knowledge. One of my favorite communication theories involves dialectics. This comes from philosophy and involves the examination of viable alternatives. Effective communication is what allows differing points of view to discuss an issue and leaving their egos out of the process. This is the key to advancing society.

LEARNING ANALYSIS 2: EVALUATE KNOWLEDGE WITHIN THE MAJOR

Introduction

I have always believed that merely acquiring knowledge is insufficient. The mark of a professional is to be skilled and knowledgeable enough to not only gather the information and understand it, but to analyze, evaluate, and apply the information and theories. My Persuasive Communication course is where I spent the most time studying and analyzing audiences. This seems essential, when you consider the implication. It is impossible to be persuasive if you do not consider the perceptions and learning styles of an audience. That would be like speaking French to a non-French speaking audience. The message would be lost.

Analysis

The Persuasive Communication course made me aware of the audience from the speaker's perspective and the listener's perspective. With each speech I became more aware of the necessity of solid preparation and connection with the audience. I learned it was extremely important not to overwhelm them with too much information, because listeners only retain about 20% of what they hear. It is essential to deliver only a limited amount of information, but to do it persuasively using words, data, and imagery.

All of my communications courses have made me aware of how to be a better message receiver. Now I know that an essential part of the message is more than just the words. The key to true understanding, according to communication theory, is to also get inflection and meaning behind the verbal message.

Communication theory has taught me about audience receptivity in a group. In order to really apply theories about group settings, I use myself as an example. If someone tells me something and my ears are too tired, I won't receive the message properly. If I didn't listen right as they spoke the message, then the message was at best only partly received. If I believe I know the context of the message, let's say, then I may believe that the actual words in my feedback are not that critical. In each of these cases I may be judging the message without really knowing completely what I just heard. Awareness of how individuals could be receiving messages is really important. The words I choose in a presentation must always persuade, even if it is an informative speech. It is my responsibility as a speaker to persuade and grab the attention of my audience (whether that audience is an individual or a group).

The differences in people must be taken into consideration when delivering a message and receiving a message. For example, performers and painters differ in how they present their art. Audiences and individuals interpret and react to their art in differing ways. This can be compared to the differences in learning styles. I studied these differences in my Proseminar class, and I am including a copy of that paper. Auditory and verbal learners generally learn best from what they hear. As a result, if a speaker is speaking to a group that is primarily auditory learners, the spoken message can heavily sway them or turn them off. Having to sort through a lot of data and word-laden slides will distract them, and will make the message less effective and meaningful. However, if there are visual learners in the audience, these word-laden slides will help them. Since most audiences have people from many learning styles, effective and persuasive speakers will use find ways to appeal to each learning style in their presentation.

The best example (in my coursework) of me persuading and moving an audience was in my speech about eliminating gambling advertisements. My communication was effective and persuasive because it was concise and grabbed the attention of my audience. I have attached the speech and the slides. It took me all semester to really hone my skills, but my entire class and the professor were persuaded. I did this by remembering that since people in an audience each have a personality and learning style, they may have to learn ways to make it easier for them to receive the message. I led the audience (my class) by using multiple styles of persuasion: visual, verbal and even kinesthetic. The kinesthetic way included giving audience members ways to participate in the presentation by allowing them to participate.

I learned that motivation is different from stimulation. You must first stimulate someone's intellect or emotions before you can motivate them. Many people live in a state of doing rather than thinking or being; they are reactive instead of proactive. It can be hard to know what motivates some people. Although there are multiple theories on motivation, the theorist who really led the way in discussing motivation is Maslow. His hierarchy is related to what motivates people internally, even though some of the inputs themselves are external. According to Engleberg & Wynn (2010), this hierarchy includes "a specific sequence of needs (physiological, safety, belongingness, esteem, and self actualization) that can explain why people are attracted to particular groups" (p. 371). It also explains that motivation happens after basic needs are satisfied, and that the needs progress in stages as each previous stage is satisfied.

The more I compared Social Information Processing Theory with Maslow's hierarchy of needs, the more I liked it. Information Processing Theory says that the best behaviors of a person coupled with the information in the present will shape the future needs of that person (Shockley-Zalabak, 2009). Granted, those are perceptions of past behaviors, and Maslow's needs are based on actual realities of the internal nature. The reason I like Information Processing Theory is that it makes you think about how what you do in the present will affect how you view the past, which affects the future.

I believe people are also motivated by five elements described by Davis and Eshelman: intellectual, emotional, spiritual, physical, and social are the five areas that can affect and motivate people (2009). These aspects are actually another way of looking at Maslow's hierarchy. Although this is not a communications course, the stress management concepts are tied to communication.

Leaders have the toughest jobs because they must make people improve by raising the bar. Effective leaders do this through persuasive communication. If they do, their people see the new standard as a challenge instead of a criticism. Good leaders step back and trust in their workers. When their people receive this message of trust, they tend to rise to the occasion. This message of trust is one of the most important and overlooked ways to persuade the people in a group or organization.

One aspect that can interfere with or propel motivation is groupthink. This is the tendency for the group to want to always be right. Leaders can motivate their people to avoid groupthink by rewarding them for coming up with the best solutions. Groupthink fits with Maslow's hierarchy of needs; it is related to the need to belong (Shockley-Zalabak, 2009). I discussed this in-depth in my Groupthink paper, which I have attached to this report. The important aspect is that leaders must always consider that groupthink may be lurking in the shadows, and their strategies must be geared toward overriding this tendency.

I have discovered that it is possible for me to help classmates improve their performance in small group discussions by asking probing questions and letting the discussion evolve, rather that completely taking over and dominating the discussion. I have seen classmates improve dramatically after I have shown them ways to engage in the discussion by discussing the communication theories and applications. They have followed my example over and over again.

Conclusion

"It is not about how many times you get hit. It is about how many times you can get hit and keep getting up". Rocky Balboa said this to his son in the movie *Rocky Balboa*. This is the essence of continuing to strive for excellence in communication (or anywhere else in life); whether it is sending or receiving the message. Each communication is another opportunity for each side to improve and get it right.

Every professor at Ottawa has been a constant inspiration regarding communication. From the moment they enter the classroom, they continually try to draw the best out of each student by their communications with them. They make great efforts to be receptive to what is said by students in the classroom. This creates an environment of respect that is critical for effective communication. This in turn creates a truly motivational environment for students, because we get to learn about how our teachers have applied what they have learned or the problems they face. In an organizational environment, LMX, or Leader-member exchange theory is similar to the observation I have made about our professors. Shockley-Zalabak (2009) explained "supportive communication from supervisors perceived to have high upward influence was more satisfying to employees than supportive communication from supervisors perceived to be low on the ability to influence their own supervisors"(p. 153).

Dr. Glaser (1976) discussed the fact that we only have very simple thoughts hopes, and wants, during the day. He claims that positive motivation must be formed from positive addictions, which can come from something noncompetitive that you can choose to do. You can devote an hour (approximately) a day to do it. It should be something that is possible for you to do easily, and it doesn't take a great deal of effort to do it well. You must believe that it has some value (physical, mental, or spiritual) for you. In order for this to help you change, you must believe that if you persist at it you will improve. This positive addiction theory can, in turn, help to motivate people toward effective communication.

References

Davis, M., Eshelman, E. & McKay, M. (2008). *The relaxation and stress reduction workbook (6th ed.).* Oakland, CA. New Harbinger Publications, Inc.

Englebert, I. and Wynn, D. (2010). *Working in groups: Communication principles and strategies (5th ed.).* Allyn & Bacon. Boston, MA. Allyn & Bacon.

Glasser, W. (1985). *Positive addiction.* New York, NY: Harper & Row, Inc.

Shockley-Zalabak, P. *Fundamentals of organizational communication: Knowledge, sensitivity, skills, values (7th ed.).* Boston, MA: Pearson Education, Inc.

LEARNING ANALYSIS 3: SOLVE PROBLEMS PRESENTED BY THE MAJOR FIELD

Introduction

Trust is the cornerstone to solid, effective communication. Conversely, a breakdown of trust or lack of trust is an impediment to trust and creates serious communication problems. These problems are often demonstrated in one way by managers and another by their staff. Trust is an outward sign of healthy relationships and communication.

Identifying Communication Problems Caused by Lack of Trust

Lack of trust by management in their employees can create specific communication problems. They micro-manage them and yet have not focused enough time and attention on clear instructions. They don't believe that their employees are motivated enough to succeed on their own. These managers may even be openly hostile to their employees and belittle or demean them when they make errors. Brainstorming sessions and meetings that are run by managers that lack trust in their staff extinguish participation by employees. In turn, this further convinces managers that the employees are unwilling to participate and are untrustworthy. It becomes a self-fulfilling prophecy. Some managers that demonstrate a lack of trust in their employees do so because they have come to believe that is what good, effective managers do.

Employees that do not trust their managers have communication problems as well. The key to it all is how the employees perceive the communication with their managers. Workers place their trust in managers they believe can be trusted (Shockley-Zalabak, 2009). If they are living in constant fear of losing their jobs, their communications will be terse and closed off. They may be afraid that their managers do not believe they can handle the job or task. Shockley-Zalabak (2009) emphasized that "Donald Pelz found that supportive communication from supervisors perceived to have high upward influence was more satisfying to employees than supportive communication from supervisors perceived to be low in the ability to influence their own supervisors" (p 153).

If employees think their manager doesn't have upward influence, they have less reason to follow that manager as a leader. They will be less willing to risk their own status or reputation as employees. Employees that don't trust their supervisor also don't really trust themselves or each other. Negative behaviors include gossiping and backstabbing. These employees actually lack confidence in their own competence. They are afraid to ask for help or explanations for fear that their manager will trust them even less. In a meeting situation, they don't participate or offer ideas for fear they would be ostracized, ridiculed or even worse.

They have reason to believe that this *will* happen, because in an organization that lacks trust, this already *has been* happening.

Contributing Factors in Addition to Work-Role in the Organization

In any organization, the most obvious way to categorize people is based on their job, such as employees and managers. The way that people learn to trust and learn to be trustworthy can be based on many other dimensions. Current and previous work experience and education will play a strong role in how they trust and communicate. If they have worked in a closed off or hostile workplace in the past, they very often bring those fears to the next workplace. This fear can spread through the organization from these individuals, despite attempts by management to build trust.

The generation an employee belongs to influences how and whom that person trusts. People gravitate towards those they have most in common with. Thus, when working for or with people from various generations, it can be difficult to communicate appropriately. Proof that these trust issues exist is seen when it seems that an organization has become extremely cliquey.

Determining Solutions to Communication Problems from Trust Issues

When trust has broken down throughout the organizations, solutions are difficult. Initially, employees and managers are busy protecting themselves from hurt that either has occurred or they believe will occur. It is essential for management to receive regular training so that they are continually reminded of the necessity to build trust and in turn manage by identity. Both sides are so busy weighing risk management and being safe that they miss the solution.

I recommend training the managers in ways to become more effective leaders. Effective leadership is more than ensuring task completion. Sessions must be made available to managers that teach them how to convey trust. Role-playing sessions for the managers can get this message across to managers. These development sessions for managers must teach behaviors and attitudes that create a positive environment. Team building through cooperative learning, cross-trained work groups, and brainstorming sessions should be modeled in these sessions. They must also be taught how to demonstrate respect to employees from various generations, backgrounds, and any other particular factor impacting each employee. There is no one size fits all.

Employees must be taught effective efficient task completion to ensure that they are on the same page as the company regarding their responsibilities. Beyond this, they must be taught how to recognize the need within themselves for respect. If they are taught how to respect their own ideas and contributions, they can then learn how to respect their co-workers as well. When they are taught how to do this, they can then learn how to recognize the respect from their managers and respect them in return.

These training programs for managers and employees must *not* be a onetime effort. They must become an integral part of the workplace. Rewards and recognition for team building and respect demonstrated will reinforce the importance of respect. The managers will be able to take on the role of much more than a departmental overseer. They can become transformational leaders.

Measuring Results and Outcomes

Restoring trust is an inexact science. Measuring results of these efforts is more complex than, for instance, measuring employee turnover. The outcomes of these efforts can be measured and analyzed by examining the behaviors of employees and managers after the institution of these training programs. Proof of success will be when people are now open to hearing and sharing new ideas on the job and in meetings. Employees will be searching for commonalities and coming together as a group rather than continuing to be divided into cliques. Managers will have re-tooled their training efforts and be clearer in defining tasks and procedures. Employees will understand how their managers want them to approach their jobs, and managers will understand how best to train and treat their people.

If change has not occurred in the organization as a result of these programs, the training methodology can be changed. One method would be to train employees in mixed groups. An example of this would be to train some managers and employees from a variety of departments rather than the manager's own employees. Through discussions and role-playing in a mixed group, new understanding can develop. Once again, through life-affirming training, trust can be renewed. After a few weeks of making changes through training, behaviors and attitudes can be analyzed again. Improvement may be slow, but by proving that the company is committed to the attitude change, transformation can take hold.

Group Leadership and Cooperative Problem Solving

It is critical to realize that conflicts will continually arise no matter what solutions are used to solve previous problems. As a leader I have seen (in the workplace and classroom situations) that conflicts are never going to be precisely the same every time. The reason conflict management is so crucial is that there is no guaranteed right or wrong way to do it every time for every person. Communication theory has taught me that no communication is repeatable and nothing is retractable. What does this mean? It means that communication is a dynamic effort. Successful communication involves placing top priority on each and every communication.

As a leader, I attempt to always be aware that each communication must move the group closer to accomplishing goals and meeting the mission. Thus, if a group is swamped with work, it is essential for the group to come together and help each other. This mentality reduces stress and builds trust. When leading a group towards cooperative problem solving it is important to keep in mind that people are motivated by a variety of methods. Some people use a central route and some people use a peripheral route.

The theory of Situational Leadership tells us that a truly effective leader or manager varies the management style to fit the events and people. If trust has been restored within the organization, then leaders will be able to do precisely that. If they do not trust their people, they will believe they need to hold a whip over employees in order to motivate them. They wouldn't change their style to fit the situation or the individual. Creating a team committed to a mission is a long-term goal that can only be accomplished through trust and effective communication. Effective leaders model the behavior that they want their people to exhibit. Effective employees can motivate their managers by exhibiting trustworthy behavior and demonstrating their newfound trust in their managers. My ability to do that in a classroom setting has made me aware that it is true that one person can transform many.

References

Shockley-Zalabak, P. (2009). *Fundamentals of organizational communication: Knowledge, sensitivity, skills, values (7th ed.)*. Boston: Pearson Education Inc.

LEARNING ANALYSIS 4: HOW THE MAJOR MEETS THE GLOBAL COMMUNITY'S NEEDS

Introduction

In today's world, truly, no man or nation is an island. The global community is here to stay. Courses in the communications major have taught me cultural dimensions that help to describe and define cultures, and these provide a lens to both view and plan communication. The Intercultural and International Communications course obviously explored this in depth. My course in Business Communications also had a significant global focus to it.

This report will discuss my philosophy for ethical/moral/lawful treatment of organizational stakeholders. It will also explain how to develop communication processes suited to the structure and culture of an organization. This will include a discussion of some of Hofstede's cultural dimensions.

Ethical/Lawful/Moral Treatment of Stakeholders

A stakeholder of an organization has an interest in how that organization behaves. We usually lump them together into groups. These groups, in turn, can be classified into two types: internal stakeholders and external stakeholders. Internal stakeholders work within the organization: owners, managers, and employees. External stakeholders are outside the organization: customers, stockholders, suppliers, governmental entities, and even the world at large.

Each stakeholder group has an interest in how an organization conducts its business, and attempts to influence the business in various ways. For example, employees want to perform their jobs to help the business survive and succeed. Each group wishes to be treated ethically, morally, and lawfully. In this country, for example, employees expect to be free from discrimination and sexual harassment.

External stakeholders also want a voice in how the business conducts itself. It is now widely believed that companies have a social responsibility in addition to its responsibility to be profitable. External stakeholders would define ethical, moral, and lawful actions by a company to include honest financial records, proper environmental behavior, and honest dealings with the governmental authorities.

Knowing who these stakeholder groups are and what is important to each of them helps define a framework and philosophy for ethical/moral/lawful treatment of these stakeholders. Different cultures will use varying decision making processes and weigh things differently within their cultures' ethical, moral, and legal standards. Companies and individuals must decide which standards to use. Just because something is lawful in a particular country does not make it moral and ethical. For example, in some countries in the

Middle East, theft is punishable by amputation of a hand. While their culture may accept that, an American company would never make it their policy to punish an embezzler by amputation. Our culture would consider this unethical and immoral, even if we were doing business in the Middle East. In addition to cultural norms, my philosophy also includes consideration of my religious faith and my knowledge of right and wrong.

My philosophy for ethical behavior considers many aspects and attempts to balance them. Is the decision fair to all of the stakeholders? Does it treat them with respect and due consideration? Is the decision legal in all of the cultures to be impacted? Has the overall impact on each stakeholder group been considered? Has the decision-making process included input from all those who will be affected by the decision? All of these are essential factors to help ensure that ethical/moral/lawful strategies are used.

An example of an organization that exemplifies my philosophy for ethical behavior is the maker of Tylenol, Johnson & Johnson (J & J). When the safety of Tylenol was questioned due to poisonings in 1982, J & J looked at the ethics that were required to balance all of the stakeholders' desires, and came to the conclusion that it was best to recall all products immediately, despite the fact that it wasn't required and came at a large expense. As history later showed, however, by taking this dramatic step, J & J demonstrated very clearly to a major stakeholder group, their customers, the company's dedication to ethical behavior despite the cost involved. In turn, ultimately, J & J was rewarded for their ethical behavior by their customers' purchase of Tylenol when it returned to the market.

The Communication Process Must Suit the Structure and Culture of an Organization

Communication processes cannot be developed to suit an organization until you understand what the culture of an organization is. The culture of an organization is defined by its locale and the cultural background of the people in the organization. Hofstede discovered that there are cultural dimensions that in turn explain how communication processes are shaped. These dimensions are seen throughout the culture and in its messages, institutions, business practices, and values. The cultural dimensions include: power distance; uncertainty avoidance; individualism versus collectivism; masculinity versus femininity; and time orientation.

Power distance relates to how much questioning a culture believes is appropriate. In a high power distance culture, decision-making is autocratic; people are expected to follow decisions without challenging them or questioning them. The opposite is true in a low power distance culture.

Uncertainty avoidance describes how a culture deals with changes and unpredictability. Cultures high on uncertainty avoidance prefer things to be predictable and structured. Cultures that are low on uncertainty avoidance are not threatened by change or dissent, and see it as necessary. Individualism versus collectivism covers where a culture's loyalties lie. In an individualist culture, individual opinions and debate are encouraged. In a collectivistic culture, communication processes are geared toward emphasizing, encouraging, and rewarding agreement and consensus.

Masculinity-femininity dimensions in a culture examine the emphasis placed on either achievement, on one hand, or nurturing, on the other. Assertiveness is rewarded in a masculine culture, and cooperation in a feminine culture.

Time orientation is the final Hofstede cultural dimension. Organizations and cultures that have a long-term orientation expect deference to the more senior people in the culture. This would place great emphasis on strategic planning, persistence, and lengthy decision making. In contrast, in an organization with a short-term orientation, youth is king, and communication processes would include snap decisions.

Besides the cultural dimensions, the actual structure of an organization further defines its communication processes. If a company only has a dozen people all working in a single location, they can meet regularly to discuss problems and decisions; a multi-national company with thousands of employees cannot do that. Management must find ways to spread the message throughout the organization, both vertically (up and down layers of management) and horizontally (across a layer of management).

The formality and language of communication must take into consideration the culture of an organization. A major reorganization within a company would be handled almost by edict in a high power distance, collectivistic culture. In contrast, in a low power distance individualistic culture, meetings would be held with care taken to explain the situation and take questions from the people.

Effective communication must take into consideration the culture of the country, organization, and individual. The message must be sent in a way that the receiver can understand it, know what is expected, and can then appropriately act upon it. Knowledge of the culture and the organization's structure must define the communication process. Any communication process requires specific building blocks. These blocks include: verbal, vocal, and non-verbal processes. Omitting any of these blocks will diminish the effectiveness of communications in an organization.

The managers of a company can make or break the communication process. They are the ones who give meaning to any communication. They must use the verbal, vocal, and non-verbal modes to give the receivers everything they need in order to accomplish the organization's mission, goals, or tasks. Planning communication messages can be difficult. The reason is that sometimes the sender of the message doesn't know what the receiver really wants to know. For example, sometimes a boss or a subordinate makes it difficult for you to know what they want to know from you.

Resolving conflict, sending messages, resolving ambiguity are all part of the communication process. They are all defined and limited by the culture. That means that it is difficult to change one component of a communication process; you must address the entire system. We do not have the luxury of poor communication.

LEARNING ANALYSIS 5: THE NEED FOR PERSONAL/PROFESSIONAL DEVELOPMENT

Throughout my coursework I have become aware of the changing nature of the field of communications. During both my Organizational Communications course and my Intercultural and International Communications course it became clear that competence in these areas requires constant pursuit of knowledge. My fascination with these particular courses revolves around me recognizing that communication and the management of it is a dynamic pursuit. People are constantly changing and so are their needs. The methods and styles of communication must change as they change. Professional development has everything to do with effective management. We learned it is the speaker's responsibility to get the message across. Some leaders get bogged down by employees because they can't see the problem is their own stubbornness, which turns into wasted energy.

The concepts of Situational Leadership and Contingency Management are defined as processes that use adaptation to match the culture of the organization, what is going on at the time, what the task and desired outcome are, and the personalities and cultural background of the employee(s). All of these facets are changing as a result of factors inside and outside the organization. My own education, development, and training will teach me how to recognize, analyze, and adapt to these factors. Being observant will always pay off. Since technology is such a significant factor in life today, education and training is necessary to stay current on the latest trends and tools.

My plan is to attend workshops, seminars, and take courses in advertising, management, human resources training and development, and internet communications. Each of these areas is continually changing, and to stay ahead of the curve I will need to become an expert. Many people are stressed in trying to balance their social, work, and private lives. They can get the impression that all that matters is if they can put on a happy face and effectively use their computer, as many of us do to manage life. However, what should be looked at are the roadblocks to their personal awareness and an analysis of their communications. Communication needs constant practice and training in order for it to become excellent. This is similar to how professional athletes strive for excellence: constant practice and learning. Just as my cousin feels left out of a soccer game when there are too many players on the team, I need to find a way to be heard. Active participation in trade associations such as American Marketing Association and Arizona Interactive Marketing Association will give me the opportunity to learn and grow as a professional. Becoming a part of the Toastmasters will provide a venue to practice and perfect my public speaking and presentation skills.

The need for professional development applies to all in the communications field. Whether communication efforts are geared toward conflict management, training, personnel development, recruiting, public relations, advertising or just generally communicating with people, communications in an organization will be problematic if managers are not highly skilled. Thus, there is constant need for updated training and development. Those with the expertise can, in turn, conduct workshops for the rest of the people. Through the knowledge I already have and the expertise I plan to acquire I will, in turn, seek to educate my fellow employees or others in the industry. In the real world it is not just about what you know, but how you apply that knowledge that makes a team of people cohesive.

Life moves fast. We live in a condensed novel, or short story, so to speak. We must be concise but still have meaning and give others the time of day. This is why it is important for people to learn by teaching. Proof of knowledge is the key to teaching the knowledge to someone else. Every communication has meaning or purpose. We may not agree with a viewpoint, but each chunk of information gives us more power. Not only does the statement "if you can read you can do anything" apply; but also if you are nice, you can go anywhere or be anything you want to be.

In particular, within my own company and through my professional organizations, I would conduct workshops to teach people through role playing. These role playing exercises would encompass how to work out disagreements, how to ask for help, how to manage time, how to clear up confusion with your manager or your employees. My education thus far has taught me that professional development in communications should include how to effectively communicate with people with varying personalities, cultural backgrounds, generations, educational backgrounds, and work backgrounds. These people each have specific mindsets, and communications of all forms must take these into account. This concept does not come automatically to anyone, and particular employees or social contacts change over time. The methods of communicating must change, too. I do believe most people don't even recognize our efforts in the communications field. It is harder than most people realize. I like to think about the conference I attended that was put on by the Online Marketing Institute. It inspired me to believe that if they can do that, then so can I.

The passion and drive for learning everything you can about a field and continuing to develop does not come automatically to some people. It exists in me, though. Beyond my association memberships and ongoing coursework, I plan to continue to learn through business and trade journals which include: *Forbes Magazine, Forbes Small Business Magazine, Entrepreneur Magazine, Essential Website Creator Magazine,* and *the Writer Magazine.* I already read these magazines and devour their ideas and advice. Besides these, I will start to receive *Marketing News, the Journal of Marketing, and Marketing Management Magazine.* I mentioned many of these publications in my professional development plan as well.

How can I demonstrate my ability and willingness to change as a professional? We don't wait around for our work to get done, we just do it. The same is true for employers who need people to perform. I could create a side business and use more of my talents there than I can with my current employer. This is one way to change as a professional.

Being able to handle change involves many things, but I will discuss three of them: knowing who you are, planning ahead, and brainstorming. Some people get work done very differently from others. We tend to let our minds wander in life. Semantics barriers and cultural differences get in the way of communication competence. We can only live one day at a time. To let go of the past and yet apply the lessons of the past to the present takes skill. When I was little, I wanted to be every profession under the sun. Then I grew up (although I don't know how I managed that)! Now I know each choice doesn't necessarily eliminate the others. It changes their sequence. With more maturity comes more responsibility. With more responsibility comes better decisions, and less of them, too (if you make the decisions correctly). This means that when you take care of your responsibilities correctly, the decisions become more automatic.

We must acquire knowledge faster these days, which means we must plan more. Eventually, time spent planning causes a delay in your work. We can say that each generation doesn't create problems for the next generation on purpose. Each generation's focus is on achieving their dreams while fixing problems. Each generation gets a chance to shine or hide their light under a bushel.

My mom's dad was unique in his generation, as most people stayed with the same company for life. He was more flexible and moved from company to company. These days, information and solutions are more conceptual than ever before. Businesses get bought and sold. People have more opportunities to start their own businesses, even if one didn't work out before. The opportunities exist for those willing to adapt, grow, and change. We all want a piece of the pie, but it isn't as simple as first come, first serve.

The problem with our results-driven society is that we don't take enough time to acknowledge the progress we have made. Historians will even tell you that history is how we choose to view the past. True flexibility is created by being inflexible with oneself through self-discipline and setting high standards. Glory only comes after you have done an immense amount of work on something. Some people think that flexibility means ignoring the past and creating a new model. I disagree. Flexibility must use the past, examine the present, and develop solutions that address it all. You cannot build a bridge to a new land without attaching it to the previous land and having it span the canyon.

In these busy times when we don't have enough time to pat ourselves on the back, we must remember that God will do it for us. Faith is the key. Faith inspired people in concentration camps to survive and get out alive; it inspired people who were persecuted to endure for God's sake. We still live in a decent, moral society with 85% of people belonging to a religious organization.

How can I (or anyone) be flexible? By taking each opportunity to grow; taking each little thing in life and making something marvelous out of it. An analogy would be that we are like cups, and God's graces are the water. While our cups are small, God's graces have to trickle in. If our cups grow bigger through change, God's graces can flood in. Each time we grow and change, our ability to change gets bigger. Kindness and forgiveness that we give to others creates more possibilities for our own selves as well. We become the change. When we help others, we realize that we are not as helpless as we thought. Through our efforts to help others, we become strong and powerful in the best sense of the word.

MY PROFESSIONAL DEVELOPMENT PLAN

Introduction

After completing almost all of my coursework I can now see that my learning is just beginning. Throughout my future academic and professional life it is important to have goals and strategies for myself. The adage is "those who fail to plan, plan to fail". This, of course is true. I have already begun to map out my future, and I know that I cannot achieve excellence unless I make learning and achievement my lifelong goal. I recognize that as I continue on throughout my life, my plan must change based on new events in my life.

Future Academic Plans

After I finish my B.A. in Business Communications I plan to continue my academic pursuits. I will either pursue an M.B.A. degree here at Ottawa University, a M.S. in Marketing Communication or a M.A. in Applied Communications. I am unsure whether I will pursue this part time or full time. That will depend on what sort of professional position I am able to obtain, and when! The extra credentials and knowledge I gain from obtaining my master's degree (whether I do it immediately or over a longer period of time) will help me to make more of a contribution to an organization and convince future employers that I am serious about my field.

Professional Development Plans

Professional development is an ongoing process. My bachelor's degree is merely the first step. I chose communications, because in the business world it is essential. I love the field of communications, analyzing how human behavior and culture impact it, and determining how to make it better. I must continue to stay informed about the field, the latest techniques and tools, and current challenges. No business will continue to invest in someone that has become a dinosaur. Communications and electronic media are changing so rapidly that constant training and development is essential.

Throughout my career I want to use my talents to help businesses grow. I would like to be able to be an entrepreneur and provide business to business communication services. These services would include web site development and management, newsletters, training, brand management, advertising, and public relations. In order to do this well, ongoing professional development and training is essential. I will continue to seek out courses, journals, and books that help me learn any new communications or marketing information, strategies, and skills there are. In addition, part of my professional development must include work experience in a variety of settings. In order to gain credibility with organizations I must gain experience working for a business to business organization or an advertising organization. Obviously, this is an essential goal in the very near future.

Associations

I joined an organization called AZIMA, which stands for Arizona Interactive Marketing Association. Thus far I have been unable to attend their monthly Tuesday evening meetings, because I am in class. Once I am no longer in class, I will attend these meetings. Each month their meetings address specific marketing and communications concerns: how to maximize your website, how to ethically conduct public relations efforts, effective newsletter concepts, and the use of social media have been recent topics. A couple of weeks ago I attended an all day conference that AZIMA's members were invited to. The conference was conducted by the Online Marketing Institute (OMI). There were online marketing professionals attending the workshops and conducting the workshops. Online marketing professionals create, manage, and consult in many areas: web site creation, search engine optimization, advertising, brand management, public relations, newsletters, and various social media. Workshops were conducted on these same subject areas, and there were many ideas presented that I found to be immediately useful.

Not only did I learn a great deal at this conference, I discovered that they offer certification courses, so that attendees can become officially certified in these areas. These courses are also affiliated with Wharton Interactive Media Initiative. I plan to take some of these as well. The first level of certification courses will help me to gain expertise in search engine optimization, web site development, the use of social media, email campaigns, advertising, demand management, and brand management. Having this knowledge and certification in my pocket, so to speak, will convince potential clients or employers that I am knowledgeable as well. I am currently planning and designing multiple websites and blogs, and will continue to fine tune them to make them more effective.

In addition to AZIMA and OMI, I plan to join the American Marketing Association (AMA) and the Search Engine Marketing Professionals Organization (SEMPO). As a member of these organizations, I will attend the local chapter meetings in Phoenix. These chapter meetings will continue to provide me with learning opportunities and networking opportunities as well. Communication has taught me that it is imperative to continually connect with others. After attending chapter meetings of each of these organizations, I may discover that at least one of these organizations is completely redundant, but I doubt that will be the case. Even though they may cover the same topics, the slant on it may be different, and the speakers and members will be different. Besides these professional organizations, I intend to join a chapter of Toastmasters that is located right in my neighborhood. This will keep me challenged to continue to improve my public speaking and presentation skills.

Personal Development

Beyond all of these plans, I do plan to continue to develop myself in other ways. My Stress Management course has taught me the importance of taking care of the whole person. Having interests beyond all of the areas that define my future vocation is essential. Getting plenty of exercise and taking time to meditate and be creative are core requirements for me.

In addition, I am compelled to make a difference in the lives of others in a special way. As a result, I have and will continue to volunteer at my church's food pantry. This is so very rewarding, and helps people that are struggling in this economy. Being a part of this group has put me in touch with very special people who understand the importance of giving of their time. It is one way of giving back to my community. My communications major drew me to volunteer to be a member of my church's communications committee. It gave me the opportunity to examine how different groups and information about them can most effectively be communicated to the church membership. Our church's Boy Scout troop is looking for Merit Badge Advisors, and I plan to volunteer for that as well. This will give me the chance to mentor these young men and be a positive role model for them by sharing my knowledge of communications with them, and to also share my love of chess with them.

Literature

I have become addicted to acquiring knowledge. I search the internet regularly for new methods and theories regarding both communications and marketing. I already am a regular reader of *Entrepreneur Magazine*, *Essential Website Creator Magazine*, and *the Writer Magazine*. These magazines are chock-full of ideas about effective writing, written and verbal communication, and effective business strategies. Through my memberships in the AMA and SEMPRO I will begin to receive *Marketing News*, the *Journal of Marketing,* and *Marketing Management* magazine. Each of these magazines will provide me with research, as well as actual communications and marketing strategies that today's professionals are using. I look forward to reading the latest articles and issues of these magazines and journals the way a hungry man relishes a meal.

Adaptable and Flexible

Staying abreast of all of the news and developments will help me to know what changes are coming and what I will need to do to adapt to those challenges and changes. Conflict and change are constants in this world. Effective communication skills will help me to remember to meet the person where he lives. This means there are things I must do. Match my communication style to the other person. Be aware of the structure of the organization and characteristics of the other person's culture. Never forget to respect the other person's comfort level when it comes to communication styles, decision making expectations and sharing of knowledge. Flexible behavior on my part involves my willingness to adapt to these cultural characteristics. This is not to say that I become like the other person; it means that I communicate in a way that the other person can understand.

Membership in professional organizations and reading journals and magazines will become my sources of ongoing continuing education. This ongoing education will continue to help me communicate effectively and teach me how to help my employer (or clients) communicate effectively and be socially responsible as well. Remembering to attend to my personal development in addition to all of this professional development will help me to take a holistic approach to life and that is what will truly keep me flexible and adaptable.

MY PROFESSIONAL PHILOSOPHY

I have pursued communications as a major because it gave me so many options. Communications is vital to every profession. What I do well is relate one task to another and people to each other. I have grown and changed; my memory is improving from being dedicated to my studies. I used to be shy and a bit rebellious. I turned from an emotional wreck to an inspired intellect as a result of my studies. Thinking about thinking is what communications majors must do. Philosophy taught me how to do that, and I would have majored in philosophy if I hadn't chosen communications.

I am a very religious person, and I see a religious context in communications as well. God expects me to use my gifts to communicate. The ability to see past your house's walls and the everyday occurrences that pass unnoticed is a skill developed through the study of communications. I learned to motivate myself internally, used my listening skills to analyze and interpret media messages, and my values to ensure that my communications are ethical.

My dad and his brothers have been professors and are great communicators. My extended family is full of people who love to communicate about every subject. I have loved discussing issues and writing ever since I was a child. This, too, motivated me to major in communications. My faith and morals drive my life. For example, my faith gives me strong views about marriage. Even though I enjoy listening now more than any other point in my life, I still need to be able to proclaim my beliefs and teach others what I know. My communications courses have given me the tools and skills to do this. It is essential for me to use my communications talents because what I know and who I am is unrepeatable and unique.

I am fit for this profession because my life experiences and my coursework have shown me that through effective communication, solutions are possible. I love to find ways to relate to and with others in order to find solutions, without dominating the discussion. I would call this going from content to process. I wear my heart on my sleeve, am very easy to get along with, and my grandma even says I am great at talking to old people. I am research oriented and dedicated. I am a wordsmith and have always loved to write. I have worked very hard for the past four years. I didn't come this far for nothing.

My experiences at Ottawa University have fit my personality and values like a hand in a glove. When I finish my degree, I will have had three courses with Karen Bryson, PhD. It is amazing to be in her classes because she helps us understand our feelings. She creates an accepting environment for learning and communicating. I have formed great relationships with my communications teachers, too. Perseverance is a huge part of what I value. This makes me ideal for the communications field, because communications is a field of constant change. Quitting in any area of life makes it that much harder to go back and just do it.

I will be able to advance my career because of the knowledge gained in college. My academic career has been blessed by excellent professors at Franciscan University in Ohio, Chandler-Gilbert Community College, and Ottawa University. Every course I complete gives me more tools and expertise. I am now capable of conducting workshops to help employees relate to each other in more positive ways. Besides that, I can help develop web and advertising content for businesses to inform and persuade consumers.

Five Principles and Beliefs that Guide My Personal and Professional Life

1. God is in charge of my life. I am determined to make my life a gift back to God. It is important to pray, but also to give time and attention to planning and work. I want my life to be a prayer.

2. Treat everyone fairly and with respect without engaging in anything that compromises my ethics. Every endeavor that I undertake must pass my test of it being something I believe in and that also fits my values. For example, I could not take on a public relations campaign for an abortion clinic. Nor could I support those who want abortion doctors dead.

3. Always give back and be humble. I try to always put the other person first, and understand things from their viewpoint. I want to be more observant and less judgmental. I will be involved with causes outside of my work that are beneficial to everyone at large. This is difficult as every cause needs 100% effort.

4. Find the weaknesses and fix what isn't working. Be prepared to re-design my business and change my business plan, work style or my approach to problem-solving. Forgetting this concept limits success and even survival. Success is an internal process and requires adaptability.

5. Remember the "60:40 rule". This means that about 60% of my time will be spent doing the things I was meant to do in this life. This would include creative things that play to my natural talent and using the skills and knowledge I have acquired. The other 40% of the time will be spent doing all of the day-to-day things that must be done to stay in business!

High moral and ethical principles exist in communications, but not all communications are ethical. My definition of high moral and ethical behavior in communication hinges upon the message and the motivation for the message. Ethical communication in advertising should have content and persuasion that is honest and informative without hidden messages that manipulate the audience. Ethical advertising describes the benefits of the product without creating an idealized culture around that product. I believe ads for gambling create an idealized culture and are therefore unethical. I have included my speech on that topic with this paper. Public relations communications should be honest and informative. At times it has been known to be nothing more than spin. To participate in a public relations effort that attempts to not admit guilt and only make the company look good is dishonest and unethical.

There are many highly ethical professionals in the field of communications. Tom Peterson of Virtue Media is an outstanding example. He spent years in the advertising industry putting together ad campaigns for major corporations. He decided that it was beginning to compromise his ethics. He didn't feel right using his talents to create demand for products people didn't truly need. He started his own advertising company that develops advertising and media campaigns to educate people and persuade them to choose life over abortion. He wove his faith and talents together to communicate.

Michael Manson (founder of Pets Mart) is another example of high moral character. He puts his money and time where his mouth is. He is part of the 100 club in Phoenix, which helps the families of fallen policemen and fire fighters. He is involved with the Boy Scouts and his church. He believes that his community involvement is an important part of his position as a business leader. He leads a life of integrity.

Two of my professors at Ottawa University are especially outstanding in their fields: Mr. Malizia and Dr. Bryson. Both of these professors are inspiring in their high standards for themselves and their students. They lead by example and are faithful stewards of their talents. You get a new fact or idea from them every time you enter their classrooms. They work very hard to inspire and affirm their students. They not only teach the subject, they are teachers of life. I strongly believe that affirmation of other people, and encouraging them to grow and participate, are the cornerstones of ethical and effective communication. The more knowledge people have of communication, the more it helps them. It turns out that every person needs every other person and is needed by every other person.

In the field of motivational speakers, Rudy Ruttiger (from the movie *Rudy*) is a stellar example of staying unwaveringly committed to your dreams while maintaining your ethics. He regularly speaks about commitment to your dreams and being steadfast in maintaining both your work ethic and your moral standards.

I will address the moral and ethical shortcomings in my profession in a few specific ways. The first way will be to refuse to be immoral or unethical. If asked to compromise my ethics for the sake of my business or my job, I will not do it. Nor will I ask people who work for me to compromise their ethics. This small step will influence those I come in contact with. Beyond this small step, I plan to further address shortcomings through my involvement in professional organizations (American Marketing Association, Arizona Interactive Marketing Association, Toastmasters, and others). Through my participation in these activities I can continue to keep the concept of ethical success at the forefront of discussions, workshops, and other activities. If possible, I will conduct some of the workshops. Through writing newsletters and blogs I can continue to express my views about being ethical. I know that even though I might provide information from another source, I still must be aware there is opinion in it. A good communicator is one who can meld opinions, fact, and raw data.

Some people have used the drive for success as an excuse for unethical behavior for too long. Success should be about giving people the chance to succeed. We must be journalists for God. This means discerning "*who* we should be and be with", "*what* we should do", "*how* we should do it", "*when* we should do it", and "*why* (what our motivation should be) should we do it". Persuading those who fall short of this ideal that they need to change is difficult. The most successful way to do that is to persuade those in the middle to shift to my side. Finally, once the people who are unethical see that the tide has turned, perhaps they will shift as well.

CASE STUDY ANALYSIS: PET RESORT

Introduction

I studied a multi-purpose pet resort. They board both cats and dogs. In addition, they provide daycare, training classes, grooming, and parties for the dogs. Their stated mission is to place your "family member" in an environment that provides clean, controlled, secure fun, and loving care; they state that they are an activity center, not a containment center. The organization's goal is to go above and beyond what any other boarding facility does. The pet resort is privately owned and thus has no shareholders. They have 132 separate rooms for dogs and room for 36 cats as well. This location is ten years old, and at the time was on the cutting edge of new pet care trends. Haight (2010) reported "Ten to 15 years ago, there started to be a dramatic change in how people viewed their pets, says Joan Saunders, CEO of the Colorado-based trade group Pet Care Services Association. Pets became members of the family, she says, rather than animals that stayed mostly outdoors" (p. D1).

I selected this company for my case study because as a former employee I have seen the operation from the inside. I have boarded my dog and cat at this facility. I believe improvements can and should be made to make the company even better. This case study will lay out specific problem areas and make recommendations for improvements.

Research Method and Study Approach

In order to compile information on this organization, I met with members of the management team and some of the staff as well. I observed the employees on their jobs. I discovered how and where they recruit, how they train their employees, how they handle their ongoing employee training, and how they manage their employees. I conducted online research about the organization and investigated complaints and recommendations found on the internet. I examined their website and analyzed web content to determine its potential to drive traffic to the site and the business.

Beyond the information specific to the organization, I studied specific training and development theories, motivational strategies, and management theories. I researched trends regarding web site content, driving and building web traffic, and managing customer feedback. I then used this information to help me determine reasonable solutions to the problems this organization faces.

Problem Identification

The company faces some very significant challenges, both internal and external in nature. Even though the stated company mission is that they go above and beyond the typical boarding and pet day care facility, the location I studied is missing that mark. There are internal and external problems:

- Training and development programs only address the typical pet care tasks and cleanliness standards. They do not teach the pet guardians about animal behavior or obedience training, nor do they sufficiently explain how or why the standards and procedures are important. As a result, many employees believe the procedures are arbitrary and they do not adhere to them. This has resulted in multiple complaints against the location through the Better Business Bureau and other feedback sites.

- External communications via the website do not provide the information and interactivity that is truly important to the pet owners.

- There is no opportunity for customers to provide helpful feedback (or complaints) directly to the organization so that the company can adjust its programs or procedures.

Problem Analysis

The pet resort is facing problems in their communications within the organization and from the organization to the public. The problems need to be examined and analyzed separately and sequentially. Solving all three problems will, in turn, create an integrated approach that is currently lacking.

Training and Development Programs

Although they do provide specific instructions to new employees during orientation, these instructions are really just "to do lists" consisting of when the animals are fed and given water and medications, when and how the rooms are cleaned, and when the animals are moved from their rooms to the play areas. While all of these instructions are necessary, the instructions do not make Pete and Mac's any different from other typical (and cheaper) kennels.

Management does not teach employees how and why these instructions matter. As a result, employees see the instructions and standards as arbitrary guidelines, and do not always follow the guidelines. Complaints have been posted to the internet by customers (and even actual employees) stating that the supposed standards for cleanliness and scheduling are not met. Examples are cited of employees standing around and talking instead of taking care of the animals. Ongoing development programs to attempt to address this and train employees about commitment to company goals are non-existent, because there just isn't time. Beyond nagging the employees, managers are often unsure as to how to change the situation. More troubling than the cleanliness issue, there have been complaints that some of the employees are rough with the animals and lose their tempers with them.

Part of the problem (as is often the case with lower wage jobs), is that many of the pet guardians are relatively inexperienced before they arrive at Pete and Mac's and they do not receive formal training in the area of animal behavior or obedience training. This lack of training makes it extremely difficult for employees to figure out the most effective ways to deal with the dogs.

Managers frequently use a scattershot approach and jump from problem to problem because the facility is quite busy. Some of the rushing about by employees comes from a lack of cohesiveness of purpose here. There is more of a sense of "get the dogs in the rooms", "get them fed", "get them in" or "get them out" than asking each day "how are we going to build a family with the dogs and staff today"? Managers have not been properly trained in management theory and procedures. They are doing what they can, but without more training they cannot improve their techniques, and their employees will continue to be relatively directionless and clueless.

There are many times throughout the year that the facility is filled to capacity. This creates a lot of stress for the employees and management because it is difficult to accomplish all of the tasks on time. There is no training provided to the employees and managers regarding how to handle the stress and increased work load. As a result, some of the stress and frustration gets directed towards the animals and between the employees.

Website Deficiencies

The website is acting as a static electronic brochure. The content is virtually the same for each of the locations. Current and potential customers are looking for more in the way of content and interactivity in today's internet world. There are no photos or videos showing the actual facility, managers, trainers, groomers, or employees. Pet owners who are willing to pay the high prices charged by the company would love to see a video tour of the facility rather than just a few photographs. Being able to see a video of some of the workers and managers would make them more comfortable with choosing to board their pet there.

On the website, there is no attempt to address or respond to complaints easily found on the internet. The reality of the complaints and the potential impact of these complaints on their reputation are completely ignored. This site is the company's chance to shine, respond, and prove that they are taking steps to be ethical professionals. The company has done none of that. They take no steps to provide the customers with even a sample of their newsletter. The company claims to be on the leading edge of pet care. It confuses and frustrates both current and potential customers that the web site provides no dynamic sense of being fresh, new, innovative or interactive.

Lack of Customer Feedback Opportunities

There is a lack of opportunity for the customers to communicate anything back to the company. Other than complaining to someone at the desk, there is really no interactive electronic method to share their compliments or complaints. There is a question/suggestion box for customers to put in questions for the animal trainer, but that lacks immediacy. This keeps customers at a distance and prevents improvement that could occur as a result of them sharing their feedback with the company.

There are no blogging or social media opportunities for interaction between the customers and the company, or for the customers with each other. Although the company states that they treat customers (the pet owners and pets) like family, the lack of feedback opportunities treats them like estranged family members, despite the fact that they provide pet owners with a "report card" when they pick up their pets. Although the report card is a nice feature, in today's electronic world, it has the feel of a token gesture.

Recommendations

Just as the problems are spread across three areas, my solutions are spread across three areas as well. However, the combination of these solutions will provide in turn an integrated systematic solution.

Training and Development Programs

Training and development programs must be upgraded and continually refined. Managers need to clarify on a regular basis how each and every procedure and standard helps the animals and the company. An example of this would be to explain that dogs are creatures of routine. Predictable and regular feeding and exercise schedule make the dogs feel safe and loved.

Small group communication and management theory both continually focus on the role of managers in providing clarity of purpose and task. Managers need to be trained in the 5M Model of Leadership Effectiveness. Engleberg (2010) "divides leadership tasks into five interdependent leadership functions: (1) model leadership behavior, (2) motivate members, (3) manage the group process, (4) make decisions, and (5) mentor members" (p. 123). The managers need to lead the employees toward the company goals. Through this model of leadership effectiveness, the managers are affecting the dynamic of the whole group. Shockley –Zalaback (2009) "leaders affect how the task is accomplished, how people are supported within the group, and what processes and procedures the group uses to achieve its objectives. Group members also share these responsibilities, but the leader remains influential in guiding task, procedural, and interpersonal contributions (p.247)". Leadership and motivation by the managers will involve being an encourager, coach, and teacher. Each task and standard must be broken down into incremental steps so that each employee knows exactly what to do. Although each employee has gone through orientation training, the fact that there are differences in how tasks are performed shows that the communication was unclear.

There are signs of poor listening within the organization. According to Hamilton (2008) business communication theory tells us that "if a manager is always putting out fires or having to handle problems after they have reached crisis proportions, this too could be a sign of poor listening (p. 109)". The managers need training in good listening skills, and so do the employees. The lack of follow-through on tasks by some employees means that a lot of repetition is needed. Hamilton stated (2008) "As an employee, if you find that your supervisor or coworker has to repeat information to you constantly, it is probably a sign of poor listening. Every time information must be repeated, time is wasted (p.109)". Ongoing staff meetings with role playing situations demonstrating listening (or lack of it) can be very beneficial to teach good listening skills. Staff members can suggest various situations for role playing that are examples when they felt they weren't being understood or respected.

Beyond the listening skills, refocusing the staff on the company mission, and explaining how policies and procedures help reach the mission, the overall leadership style should be changed. Hamilton stated (2008) "Most experts believe that good leaders are not born, they are trained. (p.285)". In the case of this pet resort location, the leadership style that I recommend is called Situational Leadership. Hamilton (2008) found "This will be the most flexible leadership style because the style used with any particular employee completely depends on the expertise and willingness of subordinates to carry out the task" (p. 285). As some employees become more knowledgeable and more in tune with the company mission, they earn some autonomy. At that point they will also be able to mentor and guide some of the other employees.

In addition to the managers, leadership needs to come from the animal trainer because of her expertise. She should provide training to all employees and managers. This strategy is designed to help every employee become more skilled and adept at handling the dogs appropriately. For example, the staff needs to be taught how to establish themselves as pack leader, take the dogs in and out of their rooms, and handle them in their playgroups. This training needs to be hands-on; that way the animal trainer can correct their mistakes and help them improve. It is essential that this training not be viewed as one-time event occurring only during new employee orientation. The dogs and situations constantly change. It is imperative for employees to know that they must keep refining their skills. This training can be scheduled at the same time the trainer conducts animal training throughout the day with the daycare dogs. The animal trainer can continue to monitor and spot check how the staff is interacting with the dogs.

Besides these training and development programs, the company needs to re-consider how they recruit and fill positions. It would be far better to consider recruiting students from the veterinary tech program at

Mesa Community College and the business department at Chandler-Gilbert Community College. In both cases, these students will have had some specific course work that is important to this business. Although the pet guardians make just barely above minimum wage, Pete and Mac's can offer these students something more. They can institute an internship program which will benefit the students and provide some staff members with more training.

Beyond the general training and development of managers, it would be very helpful to have additional meetings throughout the year to help employees deal with stress. When the facility is full and there is a constant flow of customers in and out of the business, things get stressful. Teaching the employees some deep breathing exercises, and having the company provide healthy, nutritious snacks during these times will go a long way toward reducing stress (Davis, Eshelman & McKay 2008).

Website Content

I recommend that the company hire a consultant to improve the website content for its location: respond to complaints and provide a location-specific list of FAQs (frequently asked questions) with the answers. I further recommend that some very specific videos be made and linked to the website so that all customers and potential customers can click on them:

- A tour of the facility conducted by the manager and animal trainer discussing the kennel procedures and pointing out all of the ways the facility helps the dogs feel comfortable and how well they behave.

- A tour of the facility from the point of view of a dog (videographer crawls along at a dog height) with perhaps a script written about how happy the dog is to be there and what the dog is noticing.

- Interview with some of the pet guardians showing them taking care of the dogs and detailing their education and experience.

- Interview with the manager and dog trainer explaining how internal training has changed and how the level of professionalism has improved. The interview will also contain their education and experience.

- Candid video of a dog being groomed. This could be done in a way similar to the *Undercover Boss* television show, so that customers know it wasn't just staged (with the requisite consent forms, of course).

- Video of doggy day care.

- Sample of a dog obedience class.

- Video of the cats at play and watching the birds. Interview one of the cat care employees and show the employee taking care of the cats and being loving towards them.

- Group of employees and managers explaining how they handle high stress days without stressing the animals.

- Interview with the manager addressing past complaints and issues and providing information that shows that these problems have been fixed.

The availability of these videos will put the facility miles ahead of almost all pet care facilities. This is the kind of information and openness that discerning pet owners really appreciate. Besides posting the videos, it would be a good idea to add a short article about each of the videos to the website.

I would put the need for this type of website content on a par with how parents choose a day care facility for their infants. In that case, they would want to: see the facility, ask questions, and know the education and background of the daycare workers. They wouldn't accept an expensive daycare facility employing a dozen teenagers with no childcare certification. Pet care owners think much the same way. Furthermore, having this information in video form gives the company a double impact from their upgraded training programs. Jason Ankeny (2010) reported "people are craving a story. They want to know something about who they're buying from and they feel like they need to like and trust you. You've got to shout what it is that makes you special and what makes you different" (p.50). Remember, marketing theory tells us: emphasize your unique selling/business proposition.

In addition to these videos, there should be additional ongoing videos that are available internally to use in the training and development programs:

- There should be multiple videos made by the animal trainer demonstrating various obedience training and other troubleshooting strategies. These videos should be used as part of the training and development program

- Videos can also be made to show specific conceptual skills such as dealing with high stress times at work; how to be cohesive and cooperative; role playing situations and any other problem that needs to be addressed.

A new level of values must become integrated into the company culture. Integrating these values must also be added to the website content. Oster and Hamel (2001) reported that James Amos, CEO of Mailboxes Etc. found "When values and beliefs become embodied in the workplace, they intensify employees' commitment, enthusiasm, and drive. Once they are embedded in the warp and woof of a business, communication improves (p.105)". What better place to embed in the warp and woof of a business than a pet resort? Again, this instilling of values will begin to occur when the retraining convinces one and all that every single moment they must do what is the best for the animals and the company. This value shift and training improvement must be represented in the website, or the complete impact of the change will not be felt by the customers.

The website, then, should show in an integrated way through words and video that the overall goal is to have this new sense of purpose. It should describe the structure and content of the training program. Successful orientation, training and development programs do define what the company considers good performance and how to achieve it; and understand the company mission and how to achieve that (Human Resource Store, 2010). The reason to make this a major focus of the website, as well as the internal communications, is to prove to the outside world that this company means what it says by having a higher purpose.

Customer Feedback Opportunities

I recommend that the company use social media by setting up a Facebook account and a Twitter account. Ankeny (2010) reported that "social media outreach also lets businesses keep tabs on their online reputations and interact directly with fans and foes alike" (p.51). Having a presence in social media will give the company another way to interact with their customers. Yes, complaints may crop up as a result of the company's new level of availability. However, the company will be able to address and resolve the issues. The company should post its newsletter online, and also start a blog. This would create another interactive opportunity for the company and the customers. Ankeny (2010) emphasized "with each new post, photo, video, and tweet, the company builds and nurtures its brand at no cost while fostering the hip, forward-thinking image its target demographic finds irresistible" (p. 50).

Although customer feedback and complaints are often one-to-one communication, the organization is a small group. The interchange between customer and employee (whether verbally or electronically) must be integrated with the new level of values. Small group communication theory addresses the function of groups in this case, too. Engleberg and Wynn (2010) stated that "a group will not function well, or at all, if members focus entirely on their individual goals rather than on the group's common goal" (p.18). If the company mission (at every moment making each animal and owner a special family member) is the focus of every task, every response to complaints, and every attitude, the customer feedback will become more positive. Their frustration will be reduced if they know that any complaint will be investigated and fixed.

Setting up procedures for handling verbal customer feedback must involve teaching listening skills. Interpersonal communication theory addresses the listening process. Joseph DeVito (2008) determined that "listening is a five-stage process of receiving, understanding, remembering, evaluation, and responding to oral messages" (p.105). Through role playing sessions at staff meetings, employees can practice ways to handle every stage of the listening process. If "understanding" is where the breakdown is, for example, the staff member must find ways to discover what the customer actually means.

The company can try to improve how customers feel about the company (whether or not they have a complaint. This can be done by being more proactive on the Facebook, Twitter, and blog sites that they create. For example, they can provide links to guidelines that the pet guardians are now using. Most useful in this situation would be links to a known expert such as Cesar Milan, the Dog Whisperer. He stated (2010) "training is about communication; conditioning your dog to respect you as you set rules, boundaries, and limitations. If you start to get frustrated or nervous, the dog will sense your energy and the work could be counterproductive". By providing links and educational tools such as this in their customer feedback, the company grabs an opportunity to educate the very customers they care about. As Brondmo (2000) stated that companies "must get their organizations ready to use the Internet to speak personally with each and every customer in order to maximize the long-term value of the organization's relationship capital" (p.209). Pete and Mac can use their customer feedback strategy to help build positive relationships with their customers. This, in turn, can increase customer loyalty.

Conclusion

It doesn't matter how nice the facility looks or smells if the company does not have an overarching and integrated team mission. What good are the good things a company does, if the company cannot resolve one customer's complaints effectively? We know that you are either helping or hindering your brand and company as a whole at every moment. There is no neutral area. Every nice photo or picture of a dog, or box set up for questions to the trainer will be meaningless if one complaint reaches the internet crowd and the company does not respond and resolve it.

The solutions that I have proposed will provide an integrated way for the company to improve the way they do business. It is essential. When I went in to talk to the manager, I witnessed a pet guardian delivering a dog to a pet owner; the guardian didn't even smile. It shouldn't be that way. Problems and complaints from customers give the company the best opportunity to resolve the problem, make changes, and build customer loyalty. Making excuses for problems just ensures that the problems continue. While there are some customers that don't care about how their dogs are treated (there really are some like that), there is no excuse to avoid problem solving.

It is essential to improve the training programs, website content, and customer feedback procedures, in order to become the premiere place they profess to be. When you drive by the building, you cannot tell that it is a pet care facility. I have asked people about it that drive by the building regularly, and they have said they thought it was either a storage facility or a sports bar! It is a nice looking building, but it definitely doesn't look like a pet care place. I mention this because if the company can successfully resolve the problems I identified, it doesn't matter what their building looks like. The company mission overrides the appearance of the building's exterior. Often, people want people that can fix problems; yet at the same time, they don't want anyone pointing fingers at the problem. How then can management fix those problems? The company needs someone like me (and my solutions), who has worked there and cares about the company image. It is essential for the people, website, and programs to demonstrate commitment to the mission of top-notch pet care and safety.

References

Ankeny, J. (May 2010). Building a brand on a budget. *Entrepreneur Magazine* 49-51.

Brondmo, H. (2000). *The eng@ged customer: the new rules of Internet direct marketing.* New York: HarperCollins Publishers, Inc.

Davis, M. & Eshelman, E., & McKay, M. (2008). *The relaxation and stress reduction workbook (6ʰᵗ ed.).* Oakland, CA: New Harbinger Publications, Inc.

DeVito, J. (2008). *Interpersonal messages: Communication and relationship skills.* Boston, MA: Pearson Education, Inc.

Engleberg, I. & Wynn, D. (2010). *Working in groups: Communication principles and strategies.* Boston, MA: Pearson Education, Inc.

Haight, K. (2010. June 14). It's a dog's life: Ritzy pet resorts replace kennels of yesterday. *The Arizona Republic, pp. D1, D2.*

Hamilton, C. (2008). *Communicating for results: A guide for business and the professions (8ᵗʰ ed.).* Belmont, CA: Thomson Wadsworth.

Human Resource Store (2010). The life cycle of the employee. Retrieved from http://www.hrstore.com/free/freeZ06.html

Milan, Cesar (2010). Cesar's way: Take training in small steps. Retrieved from http://www.cesarsway.com/tips/thebasics/training-small-steps.

Oster, M. & Hamel, M. (2001). *The entrepreneur's creed: the principles and passions of 20 successful entrepreneurs.* Nashville, TN: Broadman & Holman Publishers.

Shockley-Zalabak, P. (2009). *Fundamentals of organizational communication: Knowledge, sensitivity, skills, values (7ᵗʰ ed.).* Boston: Pearson Education Inc.

18

HUMANITIES CAPSTONE: GLOBAL PERSPECTIVE

Just as seniors are expected to pull together a final research project in their major, they are often expected to pull together and revisit theories and understanding of the humanities. It is then expected that as seniors, students are expected to apply these concepts to topics of global concern. In my case this included writing a series of essays and conducting a final research project in a subject within the humanities. Although students tend to think of this endeavor as having no purpose, the opposite is true. It is essential to be able to apply, use, and demonstrate this knowledge. As potential graduates, students must be able to prove they have learned across a broad spectrum of subjects.

ARTS/EXPRESSION ESSAY: FRIDA

Frida and her husband, artist Diego Rivera, seem very different from each other in the movie Frida. It seemed as if she got taken advantage of. It appeared that her physical ailments from her injuries masked the real pain she felt from marrying her husband. From a global perspective perhaps the only thing special about art is that other people just don't have the time to create or re-create what Frida and other great artists have done in their lifetimes. Therefore, skill wouldn't be the sole factor in my speculation.

Rivera couldn't just sell his work so he worked on a commission basis. He wouldn't make enough money otherwise. Although politics did poke its head out in this film it may be unclear to the viewer, but seemed to be clear to me that what drove people to do what they did was money and the lifestyles they were accustomed to. A man has needs just as much as a woman does. But they are different needs.

Frida was the most incapacitated, yet she tried to find the balance in her life (despite her husband's disloyalty) to love others and love her life. As an artist she took compliments with grace but she felt she didn't deserve them. From a global perspective I think artists might feel that if not everyone likes their work then no one does. It seems as if they are looking for a person that is compatible or similar to them in every way. Yet I believe once an artist finds that person it could distract the artist. To some artists the work is an expression and thus compliments don't even make sense. From a global perspective artists face such horrible odds that their work will be seen as significant.

Frida didn't try to make a big deal about selling the work. She only sold one piece in her lifetime. The real artwork was Frida's life. Possibly more accurately, it was Frida the person. Just because her father liked her the best didn't mean that after Frida's accident that any of her relationships would remain strong. It is ironic that most artists don't see their work as becoming famous. Frida's paintings sold for five million dollars. I guess that is a reflection of how much people are willing to pay. But as we know, if someone doesn't build a reputation or image for themselves, no one will take notice, especially in the arts and media.

It is ironic that Frida celebrated the art as a pure form. The art came from her heart. She also kept a cool head when the most horrible things happened to her. Her method of painting was to create a message through her paintings in the fashion of a story. She told people that to do art you have to be very good at it and dedicated to it. I believe that all her paintings are like one big mural or chapter of a book if you will. I can observe that what drives certain artists is certainly not the paycheck they receive. The gifts that true artists have go beyond skill level or simply being in the right place at the right time. Frida started to learn art from her father who was a photographer. Society helps artists become who they are. That's why it was important to Frida to give back to the people in her life. American society always looks for the best products or services. Who wouldn't? However some people don't know something good when they see it. This could be for financial or other various restricted circumstances. That is why it so great when people respect or uplift an artist's work.

The other thing that I find interesting is that Frida was very dedicated. After she was partially recovered from the accident (could walk again) she didn't view her art as a crutch that was used in the past to help her cope. That is why she can paint and do art that revolves around her, yet it exemplifies what the culture was back in the 1900's. I know, too, that people have stated that Frida was trying to find herself more and more. The ironic thing is that if most people were put in Frida's shoes they wouldn't be able to look deeply into themselves. I would have guessed that she would be trying to escape her pain even more than she did. For example, she painted not for money or power but for the world; the world inside her. The way she drank alcohol was also eerily symbolic of the way she felt. She wasn't a partier or an angry drunk at all.

Wherever Rivera went he had to be careful of the work he did. He even had to learn to be careful about which people he associated with. Communism was trying to take hold in Mexico. It was risky business.

Which artist is the most interesting? That is who I would like the most. It is interesting to me that artists continue to get better and better as time goes on. For instance, Frida improved until the end of her life. But can each of her paintings be examined in the same fashion? Each one represents something unique, even though her message came from the same place or artist.

The pain of an artist is different than other people's pain. They have the desire to express their existence through art. One day they might have more pain that needs to be let out on the canvas. So they start another piece. Most of us don't know how to feel pain that way. Pain is just a message that we need to accept what is happening to us and not to fight it.

Many artists either go crazy, or die alone and miserable. Frida did not. Having as much willpower as she had seems unthinkable or impossible for any artist. If the chaos around her hadn't persisted would she have created the same art work? That is a question I don't want to have to answer. I think the stereotype that artists have of extravagant lifestyles and vice is inaccurate. The reason this stereotype came about is that there are fewer artists in the world, so any uncivilized behavior is magnified.

No one really knows how to define art. What is it? Sure, there are art classes, art majors, and tons of books on the subject; but what was the first piece of art ever made? One thing is for sure. Humans have always had a fascination with art whether it is nudes, nature, surrealism or other forms of art. Art needs to have a judging panel similar to that of professional ice skating. The rules are always improving, which uplifts the sport rather than stymie it. The collectivity of art can be found in things like math, video games, large skyscrapers, and even food preparation. Art can change the world. Frida was making a political statement with her art. Once more people become artists, the standard will be raised even higher; as if it isn't high enough already.

Finally, in this film I got to see a side of communism that I did not expect. It is not that communists are trying to take God out of society. They already say they know He doesn't exist. It is important to realize that as people strive to find their individual selves and their common ground they drift away from or eliminate cultural barriers. The world needs all types of people. It needs people who create art and people who observe, study, and enjoy art. There is much to be learned about life from religions or ideologies that don't align with Judeo-Christian values. Jesus said that even if we knew of the paradise that waits for the ones who love Him, that would not change enough people's hearts. People are limited by their earthly bodies for the duration of life. Thus, people may as well really know themselves like Frida did. There will always be problems that arise in every person's life. I wonder if Frida felt any better after she expressed herself through her paintings. If she did, I wonder if it was for the reasons we thought she did. It would have been great to discuss Frida's life with her as it was happening to her. People learn from each person that passes through their lives and into the next world that everyone is of value to at least someone. Therefore every person deserves respect.

SCIENCE/MEASUREMENT ESSAY: SICKO

Sicko compared and contrasted the medical insurance and payment for medical expenses in the United States and other countries. The film was loaded with statistics and other points about Michael Moore's observations, discoveries, and opinions. He calls his film a documentary, which tends to make people think that the information is completely unbiased. However, his personal point of view and agenda came through loud and clear throughout the film.

Governments pay for services with the money they raise in taxes. In the debate for government funded health care, the Democrats believe corporations and the wealthy do not pay enough taxes, and the government could provide health care if taxes were raised. Republicans, of course believe this would hurt the economy and increase unemployment. The increase in unemployment would reduce tax revenue because fewer people and businesses would be paying taxes. The countries that Michael Moore made out to be so lovely are in fact doing the opposite of what we do here. People are paying higher income tax rates in other countries. That is how some of these other countries can provide health insurance for its citizens. Their governments charge more in taxes and use this to provide health care programs. Lehr (2010) reported:

Pierre Lemieux, an economist at The University of Quebec, wrote in the April 23, 2004 issue of the *Wall Street Journal*, "The Canadian system is built around a compulsory public insurance regime that provides most medical and hospital services free." Lemieux adds that the system is not, of course, free for the Canadian taxpayer. Twenty-two percent of all taxes raised in Canada are spent on its health care system.

Moore doesn't mention that people could end up paying more in taxes than they do now in order to provide the government with the money to provide free health care.

The fact that there are citizens in other countries that have free health care isn't my point. Michael Moore held that up as the goal we should try to meet. After all socialism, if that is what the word for this is, might work if everyone is in favor of it. *Sicko* glorifies the healthcare system in Canada as well. However, the Canadian press reported that their citizens frequently come to the U.S. for medical treatment because of long waits for procedures or rationing of care in Canada. Pipes (2010) stated:

Danny Williams, the premier of the Canadian province of Newfoundland, traveled to the United States earlier this month to undergo heart valve surgery at Mount Sinai Medical Center in Miami. With his trip, Williams joined a long list of Canadians who have decided that they prefer American medicine to their own country's government-run health system when their lives are on the line. (p.1)

This isn't an isolated case. Pipes (2010) added "American hospitals are becoming popular vacation destinations for about 40,000 Canadians a year" (p. 1). Although Canadians do not have out-of-pocket costs when they obtain medical services, they pay for the insurance through their taxes. Pipes (2010) reported:

Canadian patients also face wait times for medical procedures. Nearly 700,000 Canadians are on a waiting list for surgery or other treatments. A Canadian patient has to wait roughly four months for the average surgical or other therapeutic treatment. Wait times were similar a decade ago – even though the government has substantially increased health care spending since then. (p.1)

This waiting list in Canada may mean there are fewer doctors in Canada because Canadians are healthier. Perhaps it is less of an issue to Canadians than to Americans.

This brings me to my next point. There is a sense of disconnectedness between the people who take care of their own health themselves and doctors in general. Thus, doctors end up with a skewed view of what keeps people healthy. There is an overemphasis on surgeries and prescriptions as opposed to a holistic approach to healthcare. Prevention is not emphasized enough.

It is important to analyze the statistics about the uninsured. The U.S. Census Bureau (2008) reported there are "45,657,000 (15%) uninsured people in the U.S. out of a population of 299,106,000. Of the uninsured: 20,548,000 (45%) are white; 2,234,000 (4.9%) are Asian; 7,372,000 (16.1%) are Black; 14,770,000 (32.3%) are Hispanic; and the rest are miscellaneous groups". The Census Bureau (2008) stipulated "of the 45,657,000 uninsured people, 9,737,000 people are foreign-born non-citizens". By subtracting the non-citizens from the total there are 35,920,000 (12%) uninsured citizens.

The Department of Health and Human Services (2005) reported that "59% of uninsured Hispanics are non-citizens. This means that approximately 59% of the 14,770,000 (or 8,714,300) uninsured Hispanics are non-citizens. The net number of uninsured Hispanics who are citizens, then, is 6,055,700".

Admittedly, these figures are for different years, so the comparison is not exact. Looking at the total Hispanic population of 46,026,000, subtracting the 8,714,300 uninsured non-citizens means there are 6,055,700 uninsured Hispanic citizens. This is 16 percent of the total Hispanic citizens. This removes a significant portion of the dramatic difference between the race groups regarding uninsured status, according to the statistics provided by the U.S. Census Bureau and the Department of Health and Human Services. These years were chosen to match the statistical years in the film as closely as possible.

How would people who favor healthcare reform feel about people who get sick when they normally use natural healing methods to prevent disease? Would they insist that those people have to pay for cheaper vitamins? But let's look at the free market. If you pay less for vitamins, you may get less quality.

Democrats and Republicans have disagreed for years about government provided healthcare insurance. Michael Moore pointed out that we need to focus on real problems and find real solutions. The purpose of his film is to convince people that the U.S. government should provide free health care to all, at no cost to them. Moore believes the best and only viable solution is for the government to handle all of it. He repeatedly points to Canada, France, Great Britain, and Cuba as models we should follow. Lehr (2004) reported "The Fraser Institute, a Canadian think tank, calculated in 2003 the average Canadian waited more than four months for treatment by a specialist once the referral was made by a general practitioner" (p.2). Part of the problem in comparing costs between the system in Canada and the U.S. involve the waiting time for care. Lehr stated:

Long waits for critical care are an uncalculated cost of the Canadian health care system. A price tag could easily be calculated by determining how much patients would be willing to pay to reduce or eliminate these waiting times. We do this calculation on a regular basis in the United States in determining the charges for all services provided. In the U.S., we choose to pay higher prices in order to get more immediate care; in Canada, patients have no choice but to wait. (p. 2)

Michael Moore leaves these rationing facts out of his film. Although it is admirable for him to try to help people to obtain affordable medical care, his film does not inform viewers that rationing exists in some of these countries. There was no investigation into the various hospitals in these other countries. This leaves the viewer with the false impression that all medical care and procedures are immediately available in pristine hospitals. People cannot make informed decisions about healthcare reform without all of the facts.

I believe that it is imperative to keep people from being bankrupted by medical bills. Moore's film added fuel to the health care debate of the past year and helped to pass President Obama's health care bill. This may bring much higher taxes and rationed health care to our country. If people are faced with much higher taxes to provide the government with the money so the government can provide free health care, I do not think they will view the government health care as free health care. They may discover they are worse off than they were before. *Sicko* was very persuasive but could be dangerous because of its partial truths. We are creatures of habit and Americans are used to immediate access to health care in many cases. America already has some rationing of health care. This is why some people's treatment is called experimental and is not covered by insurance. Both the insurance industry and the government run health care as a business. The two differ in history, location, and function. We don't like to move backward as a country but that is always defined as a matter of opinion. There are problems with the free market as well. The wide variety of choice does stifle prices in some areas and raises prices in others. I am sure that our country will fix this problem.

Having a mindset to care for the sick and hurt in our country is the best place to start. It might be unfair, but our political system is stubborn on both sides.

References

Department of Health and Human Services. (2005). *ASPE Issue Brief - Overview of the uninsured in the United States: An analysis of the 2005 current population survey* Retrieved from http://aspe.hhs.gov

Lehr, J. (2004). *Canadian health care is no model for U.S.* Retrieved from http://www.hearltland.org/policybot/results/15034

Pipes, S. (2010). *On health care reform: Why Canadian premier seeks health care in U.S.* Retrieved from http://articles.sfgate.com/2010-02-25/opinion/17955314 1

U.S. Census Bureau (2008). *Income, poverty, and health insurance coverage in the United States: 2007.* Retrieved from http://www.census.gov/prod/2008pubs

SOCIAL/CIVIC ESSAY: GRAN TORINO

The movie *Gran Torino* had a lot to say about social and civic duty. It addressed the age-old issue of "who is my neighbor and what is my duty to that neighbor"? We know that Clint Eastwood's character wouldn't have done his last courageous act if it wasn't for the good it would cause and the chance to get good with God, and see his wife again. It seems as if people reject things they are not familiar with. That is ironically why we learn so much, because we don't want to go around rejecting things unnecessarily. In any good drama about social change there is usually a desire for power or self rejection. People do not generally think that they can change things by their thoughts alone. But this is a false notion to believe that.

If one thinks that nobody else can or will help them, then they won't actually accept help when it is offered. We often tell ourselves that it is silly and hard to believe it when we accomplish something hard. It always seems easy when you understand the concept. While self criticism can be beneficial, it is my opinion that what matters most is the process in fulfilling our destinies, more than the outcome. Fundamentally, people are all the same in many ways. What gives us our uniqueness is how we live life with hope. Clint Eastwood's character, Walt Kowalski, had recently lost his wife. He first felt useless and then after accepting the gifts from his neighbors (of the Hmong religion) he was still in a state of unrest.

He interfered with his friend and son of the family next door. This caused a gang to do horrible things to that family who Walt Eastwood had recently bonded with more than his own family. The differences in the human person differ tremendously from one person to the next. Yet we need each other. This movie was about letting go of pride and failure. It was also about trying to find the good things in life. It was about becoming a man and protecting those you love and care about. This universal theme is the essence of the global world.

An actor once said that the only difference between a novel and real life is that the novel has to have a logical conclusion. This movie showed how if God didn't love us we wouldn't have a chance at all. Is it right to fight evil with evil? When do enemies stop reaching for a bigger weapon to destroy each other? Our old church says as a metaphor "At every moment do what love requires." Maybe that is why spirituality is so cut and dry. You can either serve God or not. You can't serve Him and not serve Him at the same time though. This is what Walt Kowalski realized when he calmed down and thought logically after the attack on his friend's house. Walt didn't listen to the priest at first.

The world will harden a man's heart and make him fearful. As soon as Walt faced his own fear he could then do his last courageous act for both his community in Detroit and for his friend. An economist once said that when people are financially well off that they are not active politically. Is the opposite true? Walt showed his initially timid friend next door how to be active in society; how to be a man. The question of which character learned the most in this movie is left unanswered and is open to the interpretation of the viewer. Walt initially refused charity, if that's the term to use here, from the priest and the family who helped him with his grief over his wife's death. He needed that help before he could find his way again. Walt ultimately did accept their help. For a man who hardly believed in God at first, to a man of outright selflessness, Walt Kowalski came a long way. One's life is not complete until it is complete. The dead teach us to be patient. Walt moved to a grace filled life with his final decisions.

VALUES/MEANING ESSAY: MALCOLM X

Malcolm X was a fascinating examination of Malcolm X's life and the growth of the Nation of Islam movement. Was there a relationship between what Malcolm's mother called swine and what the main members of the Islam nation called swine? Malcolm X was black and he even faced the ridicule of black men. Some thought he was using the Islam Nation to protect himself and his personal agenda. Elijah Muhammad considered himself to be the last prophet of the Islam Nation group. He is not to be confused with the Muhammad who started the original Muslim religion.

The concept of the skin color of Jesus was discussed in jail when Malcolm X was in jail for stealing, along with his group of friends. The concept of a totally black people existing before whites is not totally farfetched. Anthropologists now think that Eve, Adam's wife, was a black woman. Considering the part of the world that she, and later Jesus, lived, it makes sense that they may have been black.

Malcolm was confused as a young man because his father was killed by what was reported as a suicide but was actually a murder. After this Malcolm and his siblings were all taken away from their mother. Would the life of Malcolm have turned out differently if he became a Jew or Christian instead of turning to Islam? Even in his following of the Muslim religion, the Nation of Islam put their own slant on things. Similarly, there are offshoots from the Mormon religion that include polygamists. Although that group calls themselves Latter Day Saints as well, they are not really part of the true Mormon religion.

The movie did not do justice to the idea of how many people disliked or hated Malcolm X. There were blacks who didn't like him. There were whites who liked another civil rights leader named Martin Luther King Jr. Both had their followers. Malcolm X tried to apply the black suffering during the 400 years prior to the 1940s. Prohibition was going on during part of the film. Malcolm claimed that all vice was caused by the white man.

When blacks tried to be like white men, Malcolm told them that he used to try to chemically change his hair to be like white men's hair. He now renounced that behavior and criticized others who did that. He tried to inspire others not to participate in various vices. Malcolm was met by others claiming that his spiritualism was off base and that it really didn't affect change the way society needed to be changed. I don't know how I feel about Malcolm's attitude toward white people. He even refused to offer advice to a white woman who worked for and participated in his movement. Al Sharpton was even in the movie as a character.

Malcolm X agreed with other Muslims that women were property. He respected women but did indeed think they were property. Many women today probably don't like that idea but still accept this view from the men in their lives. I will point out that although some would criticize Malcolm just for this reason, he did have a change of heart.

The Nation of Islam shut Malcolm X out after Malcolm said in a way that he wasn't sorry or surprised by President Kennedy's assassination. A plot to blow Malcolm's car up was made but wasn't carried out. He was still marked as a dead man by many and eventually was assassinated. He said that people should know what a group's beliefs are before they join a group. He did not believe in forcing anyone into joining the organization.

The global implications of this film are vast. Malcolm X and the Nation of Islam did inspire the men in the film to forsake vice (smoking, drinking, pornography, prostitutes, and crime). He helped the black men to become strong and virtuous without resorting to violence. The key scene in the movie that drove this point home was when many of the men (including the leaders) calmly and forthrightly marched through the streets to the hospital to insist on medical treatment for their friend. This was a powerful scene, and the men all could see the power that came from their peaceful, insistent yet virtuous approach. People seeing this film and using this approach can effect change no matter which religion or group they belong to.

GLOBAL WARMING RESEARCH PAPER: MELDING OF SCIENCE AND POLITICS

Abstract

Worldwide attention and debate surrounds the issue of global warming. The difference between the global warming issue and other scientific issues is that politicians have become part of the team. Most notably, Al Gore has become a spokesman for the cause. As a result of his efforts, progress has been made. In addition, due to his leadership, the usual scientific debate about the issue has been squelched. This research study explores the impact of combining science with political strategy. While this helps the cause to catch fire and spread, it has also resulted in a completely dismissive and derisive attitude toward scientists that offer other explanations for global warming and climate change.

In *An Inconvenient Truth*, Gore spoke of an example of old science regarding continental drift. The answers to people's biggest questions don't just come from one angle or one point of view. Stephen Hawking tried to develop a theory for everything but he hasn't succeeded although he came close. Science and politics share much of the same reasoning. Scientists teach how global warming came about. Politicians teach what strategy can be used to address the problem. They both address the problem with different strategies in mind. This paper discusses the benefits and consequences of these strategic efforts regarding global warming and provides observations about the impact of them.

Introduction

What causes movements to take hold and gain strength? Fires begin with a spark and so do movements for change. They both need fuel in order to grow and spread. In the case of our country, the spark favoring independence was fed and strengthened by Thomas Paine's *Common Sense* and the Boston Tea Party. The abolitionist movement gained strength through the far-reaching impact of Harriet Beecher Stowe's *Uncle Tom's Cabin*. Martin Luther King's civil rights message spread fire because of the strength of his convictions and his personality. As a result of the fuel in these instances, the fires of independence, anti-slavery movements, and civil rights spread throughout our country and the world.

There are two people in the environmentalist movement who bookend the current debate about the environment. They provided the fuel which has helped environmentalism grow into a global fire. Marine biologist and author Rachel Carson, through her research and her book *Silent Spring* fed the early fires of environmentalism. She wrote about the effect pesticides (in particular DDT) had on wildlife, waterways, and humans. Al Gore, through his film *An Inconvenient Truth*, and his lectures and activism, has helped make global warming activism a worldwide phenomenon. His focus is on the dangers of carbon emissions. Both Carson and Gore have centered their work on a shared view; human activities are destroying the environment. Their passionate devotion to this view has shaped the global view of environmentalism and the actions that many people want our country to undertake. Rachel Carson approached the cause as a scientist and writer. By contrast, Al Gore approaches the cause as an attorney and politician. This caused a measurable shift in the global warming movement.

Global Warming and Carbon Emissions

Al Gore is so closely associated with the global warming movement that they have become one and the same. *An Inconvenient Truth* is without a doubt an effective film from the standpoint of dramatic tension and entertainment. But is it accurate, truthful, and scientifically reliable? Throughout the film he uses multiple charts, graphs, film clips, and photographs to drive home his points. Within the film of his lecture there was a major error. He stated that in the northern hemisphere, in the fall and winter the trees and plants exhale carbon dioxide and inhale oxygen. Nothing could be further from the truth, as any student of biology knows.

Global warming theory states that human caused carbon emissions are damaging the ozone layer and causing climate change that impacts humans, animals, and the environment. In his documentary, Gore shows two line graphs that show changes in CO_2 levels and the earth's temperatures. These lines do share the exact same pattern. Gore states that this proves cause and effect, since both lines move up and down at the same time. Actually, statistics theory states that what this shows is correlation. Correlation does not always prove cause and effect.

There is, of course cause for concern when it comes to the U.S. role in carbon emissions. McRae (2006) stated "the U.S. unsurprisingly is the world's largest user of energy (and hence accounts for 36 percent of carbon emissions of the industrialized countries" (p. 175). In the film, Gore stated the U.S. is responsible for about 30 percent of carbon emissions and Europe about 28 percent of carbon emissions. He did not break this down into per person figures to account for differences in population. Instead, to emphasize the differences in carbon emissions he pointedly stated that our carbon emissions are more than three of the other continents combined. One of the reasons for the differences between the U.S. and Europe in carbon emissions is our power sources. The U.S. is highly reliant on coal. Europe is much more reliant on nuclear energy than the U.S. This difference in electricity sources accounts for part of the difference between U.S and Europe. Regarding our carbon emissions, Holowka (2006) stated that "buildings are responsible for

39% of U.S. CO_2 emissions and 70% of U.S. electricity consumption" (p. 148). Not coincidentally, our increase in CO_2 emissions exactly coincides with the time period we stopped building new nuclear power plants, and increased coal burning plants instead. People in the world always try to point fingers at other peoples' errors. The U.S. could blame China more for their usage of dirty coal; but unfortunately the U.S. is heavily in debt to China. In that respect, politics and debt get in the way of the debate.

In the past if scientists disagreed with another scientist, that scientist could seek refuge in another country in order to conduct scientific research. Now the scientific efforts are far too coordinated to find any refuge. The Environmental News Service (2008) helps to coordinate these studies and publishes the results. The work has been done through the Intergovernmental Panel on Climate Change (IPCC) at the United Nations. Mooney (2008) stated that IPCC is "a global scientific body that would eventually pull together thousands of experts to evaluate the issue, becoming the gold standard of climate science" (p. 47). This group began in 1988. By 2001, Mooney (2008) reported that "IPCC consensus was notwithstanding (sic) some role for natural variability, human-created greenhouse gas emissions could, if left unchecked, ramp up global average temperatures by as much as 5.8 degrees Celsius (or 10.4 degrees Fahrenheit) by the year 2100" (p.47). Mooney (2008) further reported "that *Science* Editor-in-Chief Donald Kennedy agreed that consensus as strong as the one that has developed around this topic is rare in science" (p.47). Further explanation about IPCC's efforts is described by Brown (2008):

> The 2007 report by the Intergovernmental Panel on Climate Change found 'unequivocal' evidence of human-driven global warming. Written by 600 scientists and unanimously approved by 113 government-appointed delegates, the report found that the amount of CO_2 entering the atmosphere is 1.3 times more than just 20 years ago, the atmosphere is arming 0.13 C every decade, and the sea is rising about 3.1 cm each decade. (p.17)

Every step of the way Gore emphasized this IPCC consensus to strengthen his argument. History will have to be rewritten, stated Gore. No one thought there would be a hurricane in the south Atlantic. Regarding the oceans, he also discussed the impact carbon emissions have had on ocean life. The film lacked sufficient statistics or expert opinion to make this point stronger. Scientists and politicians each want to own the solution; but neither group really wants the other group to get all the credit. They are each willing to compromise, but not willing to be in the background.

Science and Politics Combine to Define the Movement

The difference Al Gore has made in the environmental movement is almost immeasurable. His commitment to his environmental cause goes back to his college days. His grass-roots methods are typical for people from his Baby Boomer generation and have been very successful in building consensus among many people world-wide. His passion about building consensus and action one person or family at a time is a classic heartfelt theme of Baby Boomers. How has politics and courtroom strategy entered science in a new way? When Gore and his team rolled out *An Inconvenient Truth* they used a very calculated strategy. Pooley explained (2009):

> They set up screenings for key audience segments: columnists, enviros (sic), clergymen, hunters, and anglers. The timing was right; the film was powerful; suddenly the same media that had been inclined to ridicule anything Gore did began treating him like a visionary. (109)

Those who disagreed with global warming theory had to increase their efforts when there was such a positive reaction to *An Inconvenient Truth*. Pooley stated (2010) "*An Inconvenient Truth* grossed 50 million dollars globally, making it one of the most successful documentaries ever, and sold more than 1.5 million DVD copies. Its viral effect was incalculable" (p. 110). This was the groundwork for the grassroots movement. Gore's movement has included recruiting and training people to deliver the same lecture and slide show that he delivers. He has recruited over 3,500 people thus far. His movie has been shown in schools, making it both educational and propaganda, since no contrasting side is presented. This is another way the movement has gone viral. He bypassed the parents by having the teachers show the movie and providing them with educational materials. Every aspect in the movie is designed to entice and draw the viewer in to make the viewer part of the message and buy into it all. It is all very subtly done so that it is impressive and convincing.

Although his movie is full of many photos and videos showing the effect of climate change, his critics state that they believe some of this work is doctored in order to make a point. It is hard to know whether photos or videos have been doctored. It should be considered, since there are also some misleading graphs and statements in the movie: cause and effect versus mere correlation in the data, as well as the glaringly incorrect statement that plants and trees exhale carbon dioxide in the winter in the northern hemisphere.

Dealing With the Other Side

Another flaw was in reference to the polar temperature differences causing more storms. Lindzen countered (2008) "If the models are correct, global warming reduces the temperature differences between the poles and the equator. When you have less difference in temperature, you have less excitation of extra tropical storms, not more" (p. 55). Although Gore insisted that these temperature differences will increase storm activity, Lindzen's research proved otherwise. Despite this evidence, the climate change crowd is unmovable on this argument.

Some scientists state that Gore's film created false impressions of timeframes for climate events. As Pooley (2010) stated "A valid criticism of *An Inconvenient Truth* was that it gave no hint as to how long it might take for the seas to rise that high; in the animation Manhattan was flooded in a second or two; in reality, it could take centuries" (p.112). Again, this is a visual imagery method that Gore used to create such a strong impression in viewers' minds that they will not listen to any evidence given to counteract the climate change scientists. Gore never really complained in order to make his points. He showed his struggle in his efforts, and how his personal losses made him determined to make a difference. He focused on his son's death, but not to gain sympathy. Instead he used it to show what loss is like and what a person can do as a result of loss. Visual, verbal, and emotional appeal persuades viewers. In dealing with dissenting scientists, Lindzen (2008) stated:

> In 1992, he (Senator Al Gore) ran two congressional hearings during which he tried to bully dissenting scientists, including myself, into changing our views and supporting his climate alarmism. Nor did the scientific community complain when Mr. Gore, as vice president, tried to enlist Ted Koppel in a witch hunt to discredit anti-alarmist scientists—a request that Mr. Koppel deemed publicly inappropriate. (p.55)

The anti-alarmist scientists appear to be intimidated either by Gore or the size of the movement. According to Solomon (2008) this intimidation of scientists who disagree has continued. In this, the age of electronics, millions of people have accepted his documentary as the gospel truth without exploring the subject in depth. Unfortunately, scientists who provide an alternative view or scientific data that disagrees with the global warming movement are now labeled as "deniers" by Al Gore and many others. This is an emotionally loaded term and purposely puts reputable scientists in the same category as Holocaust deniers. This is an effective way of discounting the opposition that is typical of defense lawyers and politicians. It is an essential strategy to winning a case or passing a bill. Obviously, in Al Gore's case he has used this same strategy in discounting the opposition. The only time that Al Gore and his colleagues give respectful consideration to scientists that disagree is when one of those scientists joins Al Gore's side. When deniers have changed and become climate change advocates, global warming scientists have used that scientist as an example of a denier that has finally seen the light.

Gore mentioned that some of the "denier" scientists are funded by ExxonMobil. Although it is true that some of them have been, many were not. He failed to mention that many of the scientists on his side have been funded by the solar energy industry and other similar industries! Anyone who has seen a legal drama will recognize this typical yet highly effective strategy of an excellent defense lawyer in action. He effectively built his case in his documentary and created in the viewer's mind an easy way to reject all evidence against the case for global warming.

In dealing with the implication that hurricanes are getting worse, Gore cited Hurricane Katrina statistics. Mooney (2010) countered that information "So far, data on damage from U.S. hurricanes that has been 'normalized' – i.e., adjusted for changes in population and wealth, as well as for inflation—does not show any trend over time. The 1926 Miami hurricane, if it happened today, would be expected to cause considerably more damage than 2005's Hurricane Katrina" (p.165). Statistics need to be normalized when comparing events so that the events are accurately compared. Thus, what Mooney and others are saying is that the storms themselves are not getting worse; the increase in damages is the result of more people and buildings in the path of those hurricanes. This is a far different argument. Beyond this, Christopher De Muth (2008) stated:

> Although it is fairly well-established that the Earth's atmosphere has warmed somewhat (one degree Fahrenheit) during the last century, it's not clear why this has happened. The warming may have been due to human impositions (the burning of fossil fuels and other incidents of industrial growth) or to climate variations, or to some of each. (p. 183)

The global warming/climate change crowd will not consider that it could be anything but entirely human-caused. This squelching of scientists has occurred before. Scientists belittled those scientists who disagreed with Stephen Hawking's black hole theories after initially belittling Hawking's theories. Now Hawking has disproved his own theories about black holes. It works best when scientists remain open to and include opposing views. This doesn't mean that scientists are closed to non-opposing views. To claim that science is completely unbiased ignores the fact that human beings (even scientists) are imperfect beings.

Conclusion

Obviously, Gore has been effective in his leadership and with his message even though he has not been 100 percent correct in his facts. By mixing his skill and experience in the Senate and as a lawyer, he has been able to put together a persuasive message that has spread throughout the world. This has been a far different method than solely having the scientists build scientific consensus through peer-reviewed journals and scientific conferences. As is always the case, peer-reviewed journals are run by professionals in the field. According to Solomon (2008) global warming opponents have been removed from the judging panels for these journals. As a result, conflicting articles are seldom published. When Gore and his colleagues say there are no significant scientific research articles that disagree with them, it is important to ask why that is the case. Similarly, it is rare that an environmentalist would disagree with Gore, but it happens.

Gore's goal has been to build consensus for his global warming and climate change cause. He has succeeded at that. This cause is a mission for him. He feels that it is crucial to act. Gore stated (2010):

> As Abraham Lincoln said during America's darkest hour, 'The occasion is piled high with difficulty, and we must rise with the occasion. As our case is new, so we must think anew, and act anew.' In our present case, thinking anew requires discarding an outdated and fatally flawed definition of the problem we face. (pp. 409-410)

Gore's goal was to have the film be so powerful that there would be no doubts left in the minds of viewers. I believe he accomplished that mission. The growth of the movement is proof of that. Global warming advocates are quick to point to the fact that in the past the world under-reacted to the dangers of smoking. Environmentalists urge the world that we cannot afford to delay or stall on this issue. Although there is a contradiction in how some politicians approach protecting life as seen in the fact they want to protect the environment but not protect unborn babies, their message to protect is still heartfelt. Gore doesn't insult the intelligence of the viewer. Obviously, most people avoid what they consider to be wrong or unethical. By definition, if people know it is completely wrong and unethical, and know the consequences, they would refrain from that action.

Lesser men would have stopped their efforts by now out of frustration or exhaustion. It is obvious that Gore believes in his cause. He has proven that he is trying to accomplish great good in the world. Even if people disagree with his message, they should admire his determination and dedication. When politicians criticize Gore for being too emotional about his cause, I have a problem with that. If a politician was to be re-elected by voters that vote their emotions, I strongly believe that politician would not have a problem with that. Perhaps in that case the politician would say that that wasn't emotion it was common sense. Sometimes those that are further removed from the issue, such as non-scientists, have the most to say about it. Maybe that was one of Gore's biggest contributions, to increase the conversation. What has driven him so relentlessly? He strives to influence those who are not onboard yet, but also to continue to inspire those who already agree with him. As he so eloquently said (2011):

> Of course, the best way—indeed the only way—to secure a global agreement to safeguard our future is by re-establishing the United States as the country with the moral and political authority to lead the world toward a solution. Looking ahead, I have great hope that we will have the courage to embrace the changes necessary to save our economy, our planet and ultimately ourselves. (p. 411)

Obviously, money, power, and fame do not drive him. Serving what he considers to be a higher purpose is what drives him. Through his messages, he seeks to have everyone join in to serve that higher purpose. I do not think that the global warming issue is just an emotional issue. However, our country could use some emotional issues to make more people realize how important their vote and participation in the process is. Our country takes awhile to jump on board with a cause sometimes, such as the Kyoto Treaty. Our economy is kind of in a jam right now, and this is part of our reason for delay. Perhaps our country will join the treaty and sign. The political gamesmanship in our country and around the world affects how this will all work out. If our focus remains on true, not just political solutions, any problem can be solved. Gore combining political strategies with scientific causes has reawakened people.

In looking to the future, more attention needs to be paid to other alternative sources of energy, such as nuclear and geothermal energies. Perhaps more people will come around if these options are considered. The environmentalist movement differs vastly from, for instance Malcolm X's movement. In Malcolm's case he wanted to know about the purity of motive that a person had when wanting to join his movement. This is definitely not how the global warming movement works. Although they wanted scientific consensus, they didn't care what the motives were of those who joined. If there is room for a variety of people in the movement, and purity of motive isn't the consideration, then the leaders of the global warming movement must be willing to bend and therefore accept nuclear and geothermal energy as proactive solutions. So much of what has occurred thus far in the global warming movement has been reactionary. Al Gore urged people to be proactive and think ahead. He wanted them to believe they can commit themselves to this cause without it lessening their commitments to other causes. It is essential to be truly proactive and open minded. All it takes is one miniscule fact said by the right person at the right time to persuade environmentalists so that they are just as likely to change their mind if a better or fresher way of thinking comes along. With enough facts, time, effort, and persuasion people join. That is what Al Gore believed: mission accomplished. After his efforts, they believe. Lighting a candle in the darkness always makes a difference.

References

Avery, D. (2006). Global warming benefits life on earth. In C. Bily (Ed.), *Opposing viewpoints: Global warming* (pp. 108 – 121). Detroit: Greenhaven Press.

Brown, A. (2008). Emerging energy consensus. *The Bent of Tau Beta Pi The Engineering Honor Society, 99 (4), 16-22.*

Bryant, L. (2008). Yes global warming is caused by human activities. In D. A. Miller (Ed.), *Current controversies: Global warming* (pp. 63-66). Detroit: Greenhaven Press.

De Muth, C. (2006). The Kyoto Protocol cannot address global warming. In C. Bily (Ed.), *Opposing viewpoints: Global warming* (pp. 182-101). Detroit: Greenhaven Press.

Doughton, S. (2008). Scientists have reached a consensus about global warming. In D. A. Miller (Ed.), *Current Controversies—global warming* (pp. 28 – 36). Detroit: Greenhaven Press.

Environmental News Service. (2008). The United Nations says the evidence on global warming is unequivocal. In D. A. Miller (Ed.), *Current controversies—global warming* (pp. 37 – 42). Detroit: Greenhaven Press.

Gore, A. (2011*)*. The climate for change. In G. H. Muller (Ed.), *The new world reader: Thinking and writing about the global community (3rd ed.)* (pp. 408 – 412). Boston: Wadsworth, Cenage Learning.

Holowka, T. (2006). The LEED rating system helps create greener buildings. In C. Fusniak (Ed.), *Opposing Viewpoints: Eco-architecture* (pp. 147-153). New York: Green Haven Press, Inc.

Lindzen, R. (2008). Claims about global warming are based on junk science. In D.A. Miller (Ed.), *Current controversies: Global warming* (pp. 54-58). Detroit: Greenhaven Press

McRae, H. (2006). The Kyoto protocol can help address global warming. In C. Bily (Ed.), *Opposing viewpoints: Global warming* (pp. 174-190). Detroit: Greenhaven Press

Mooney, C. (2007). *Storm world: Hurricanes, politics, and the battle over global warming.* Orlando, FL: Harcourt Inc.

Pooley, E. (2010). *The climate war: True believers, power brokers, and the flight to save the earth.* New York: Hyperion.

Solomon, L. (2008). *The deniers: The world-renowned scientists who stood up against global warming hysteria, political persecution, and fraud and those who are too fearful to do so.* USA: Richard Vigilante Books.

SELF ASSESSMENT ESSAY

Obtaining a bachelor's degree is very much like climbing a mountain. When the journey begins, the steep mountain looks almost insurmountable. I actually have climbed Heart Mountain in Cody, Wyoming; I do not use this analogy lightly. There are clear advantages to obtaining a bachelor's degree at Ottawa University because it includes the four breadth areas: arts/expression, science/description, social/civic and values/meaning.

Each of my courses has had a component that explored one or more of these breadth areas. In regards to the values/meaning breadth area, I have learned it is essential to consider the ethics behind decisions even in areas such as art, civics, communications, biology, computer science, and physics. Having solid, well-grounded values translates into ethical experiments and communications. Ethical actions are both truthful and take into account cultural differences when communicating with others. My values and ethics have become more finely tuned than when I began my education. My philosophy, Proseminar, and theology courses have encouraged me to define my ethics. I am rooted in God and my thoughts and actions are continually directed toward determining His will. I have worked hard to get to the point where I am free to make my own mistakes but now I make fewer of them. My government and constitution courses in particular have helped me to develop my social/civic learning. These courses have taught me the facts about laws and the views of our citizens. The readings and analyses that I have worked on in these courses, Proseminar, and Graduation Review have helped me to examine how I should lead as a citizen of my country and the world.

Arts/expression is a breadth area that is close to my heart. As a communications major the arts are very important to me. I have learned how to analyze commercials, film, art, and books so that I can see the overt and hidden messages in them. This has taught me how people affect each other both intentionally and unintentionally. Both books and film have a far-reaching impact on people and societies. I incorporated this knowledge into my communications capstone project and provided advice to a business regarding their website content and training programs. I showed them how to improve not only their image but also their performance. My courses have taught me that each person's action can be considered an expression of art, and must take into account values, social and civic considerations as well as the scientific side of things.

My education has led me through environmental biology, physics, computer science, and multiple math courses. These have led me to new, organized, and logical ways of thinking. I have learned about health, nutrition, and the physical, emotional, and mental effects of stress. The biggest impact of taking these courses was that it taught me that I can learn difficult things that are outside of my original interests. I have learned how to learn about anything and everything, and fell in love with learning.

My education has led me to the mountaintop. What does this mean for the future? My learning and dedication will continue throughout my life. I will continue to pursue knowledge through reading, courses, and visiting museums. I will continue my community involvement through volunteering through my church both at Friends of the Needy and the Knights of Columbus. I will keep in mind that it is important to stay connected to others. My career will help me to do this as I intend to help businesses with their advertising and website content, as well as help them fine-tune their training programs. People have much in common and I will use my talents to bring them together.

I am aware that it is important to have good role models to encourage my values. One of mine is Tom Peterson of Virtue Media. He has dedicated his life to creating commercials and ad campaigns that are wholesome and honest. I intend to emulate that in my own career. The scientific and mathematic skills that I have acquired will of course play a part in my work life, but the unique combination of that and the values/meaning lens and social/civic lens will help me to have my focus on the right thing for the right reason.

The world needs dreamers and the world needs doers. But most importantly, the world needs dreamers who do. That is me. My education has taught me to prioritize, work hard, and move towards my goals. Too often people debate who is supposed to offer a solution and who caused the problem. This is faulty thinking. I will keep in mind that not even knowing why you should listen to people is even worse than not listening at all. It is important to take care of each other, because we are connected beings, not islands. As a senior I am now aware that it is essential to jump in and help anyone when they need help. Bringing people together is important. I am not afraid to roll up my sleeves and get my hands dirty. I think life's purpose is to stay consistent. I have developed steady feet and a sharp mind, which is exactly what I will need as I head out with my bachelor's degree to climb my next mountain.

CPSIA information can be obtained
at www.ICGtesting.com
Printed in the USA
LVOW04s0128190717

541844LV00029B/782/P